In PURSUIT of
GODLINESS
and a LIVING JUDAISM

In PURSUIT of GODLINESS

and a LIVING JUDAISM

The Life and Thought of Rabbi Harold M. Schulweis

EDWARD M. FEINSTEIN

TURNER PUBLISHING COMPANY

Turner Publishing Company
Nashville, Tennessee
www.turnerpublishing.com

In Pursuit of Godliness and a Living Judaism: The Life and Thought of Rabbi Harold M. Schulweis

Cover design: Kerri Resnick
Book design: Tim Holtz

Otherless otherwise noted, all scripture translations are drawn from *JPS Hebrew-English Tanakh: The Traditional Hebrew and the New JPS Translation*, 2nd ed. (Philadelphia: Jewish Publication Society, 1985, 1999.)

Library of Congress Cataloging-in-Publication Data
Names: Feinstein, Edward, 1954- author.
Title: In pursuit of godliness : the life and thought of Rabbi Harold M. Schulweis / Edward M. Feinstein.
Description: Nashville : Turner Publishing Company, 2020. | Includes bibliographical references and index. | Summary: "The Life and Thought of Rabbi Harold M. Schulweis"– Provided by publisher.
Identifiers: LCCN 2019025063 (print) | LCCN 2019025064 (ebook) | ISBN 9781684424344 (paperback) | ISBN 9781684424351 (hardcover) | ISBN 9781684424368 (ebook)
Subjects: LCSH: Schulweis, Harold M. | Rabbis–United States–Biography.
Classification: LCC BM755.S32185 F45 2020 (print) | LCC BM755.S32185 (ebook) | DDC 296.8/342092 [B]–dc23
LC record available at https://lccn.loc.gov/2019025063
LC ebook record available at https://lccn.loc.gov/2019025064

CONTENTS

This commandment that I command you today is not beyond you;
It is not far away!
It is not in heaven—that you should say, "Who will go up to the
heavens and get it for us, and teach it to us, so we can do it?"
And it is not across the sea, that you should say, "Who will cross to
the other side and get it for us, and teach it to us, so we can do it?"
      No! It is very close to you.
It is in your mouth and in your heart to do it!

DEUTERONOMY 30:11–14 (translation my own)

INTRODUCTION

"The world makes many images of Israel," wrote the historian Simon Rawidowicz, "but Israel makes only one image of itself—that of being constantly on the verge of ceasing to be, of disappearing."[1] Every generation of Jews, beginning with Abraham, feared that it was the last. The Jews are, in Rawidowicz's memorable phrase, the "ever-dying people." Ironically, the ever-dying people is also the ever-living, ever-renewing people. The Jewish national talent for renewal is the greatest wonder of Judaism's long history.

The story of Judaism is conventionally told as a narrative of continuity. Jews typically vest authenticity and authority in the conviction that their religious culture has been passed faithfully from antiquity down to the present through an unbroken chain of generations. This narrative places upon each successive generation a solemn responsibility to transmit forward what has been received from the past—to "teach these words diligently to your children" (Deuteronomy 6:7). The anxiety that attends this responsibility is reflected in the pessimistic identification as the "ever-dying people."

Behind the conventional narrative of continuity there is another Jewish narrative—the story of Jewish discontinuity. At certain moments in history, conditions imposed from outside the Jewish community, or development from within, necessitated a radical rethinking of Jewish life. These moments demanded a reinterpretation of core values and truths, a revisioning of collective mission, a reinvention of central institutions and modes of expression. These moments of crisis required a departure from tradition. Had the community asserted faithfulness to established forms and beliefs at these moments, the Jewish people and its culture would likely have died. A special kind of bold, creative leadership is called for at these crisis moments. The miracle of Jewish history is that, again and again, at such moments of discontinuity, creative leaders emerged.

Jews revere tradition and continuity. But it was the moments of discontinuity that gave birth to Judaism's greatest intellectual accomplishments. The Torah emerged from the Exodus from Egypt and from Babylonian exile; the Talmud, from the destruction of the Temple; Saadia Gaon and Moses Maimonides, from the intellectual challenge of rational philosophy; the Zohar grew from the shifting fortunes of Spanish Jewry; Hasidism arrived in the wake of upheaval in Eastern Europe; and Zionism was the response to the failure of emancipation. The crises of discontinuity revealed the spiritual resilience and cultural creativity of the Jewish people. Over and over again, the Jewish people found the inner resources to reinvent, reinterpret, and renew Jewish life.

The twentieth century presented Jews with a unique set of crises. The greatest tragedy in all Jewish history was arguably the destruction of the Temple in 70 CE; the Holocaust of the twentieth century matches or exceeds it. The greatest moment of redemption in Jewish history was the Exodus from Egypt; the rebirth of the State of Israel in the twentieth century rivals it. The Exodus and the Temple's destruction took place 1,500 years apart. The Holocaust and the birth of Israel happened in the experience of one generation. How can a people make sense of such gyration?

These historical crises were complicated immeasurably by the fact that both took place against the background of an even greater unfolding cultural upheaval: the arrival of Jews into modernity. By the dawn of the twentieth century, modernity had already severely rocked the foundations of Jewish faith and Jewish identity. As a result, Jews faced the historical crises of the twentieth century without the spiritual tools available to previous generations. The intellectual structures that once accommodated, interpreted, and absorbed catastrophe had already been decimated by the cataclysmic arrival of modernity.

Historically, at a moment of crisis, the Jewish people approached their leaders with painful existential questions: What does this mean? Where is our God? What is the meaning of Judaism now? The Jews of the late twentieth century asked similarly acute questions. Many abandoned Judaism altogether, assimilating into the common culture—a new ten lost tribes. Others retreated from the world of modernity, embracing new forms of fundamentalism and isolation. For the majority, the moment of crisis inspired a resurgence of Jewish creativity and resilience. New ideologies, new institutions, and new energies emerged. The remarkable rebirth of Jewish life in the generation following World War II will one day be recorded among the greatest miracles of Jewish history. The ever-dying people proved once again to be an ever-renewing people.

Harold Schulweis was a dominant figure in the renewal of Jewish life in the postwar generation of American Jewry. Widely regarded as the most successful and influential pulpit rabbi of his generation, he shaped an extraordinary career as pulpit rabbi, theologian, public intellectual, and communal leader. His innovations in synagogue practice reshaped congregations across the continent, introducing synagogue-based *havurot*, launching "para-rabbinics" and paraprofessional counseling programs, initiating programs of outreach to alienated Jews and "unchurched" Christians, opening the traditional synagogue to gay and lesbian Jews and their families, and welcoming families of children with special needs. With Leonard Fein, Schulweis founded MAZON: A Jewish Response to Hunger, a national Jewish nonprofit dedicated to ending hunger in the US and Israel. He launched the Jewish Foundation for the Righteous, recognizing Christians who rescued Jews during the Holocaust—an effort chronicled on the CBS news program *60 Minutes*. In the closing years of his career, he initiated the Jewish World Watch, a communal response to the incidence of genocide worldwide.

In his voluminous writing, Schulweis reshaped the narratives of contemporary Jewish life in response to the pressing religious and moral questions of the twentieth century. He offered a way for contemporary Jews to return to a belief in God in the shadow of the Holocaust. He reconceived the synagogue for a generation that turned away from affiliation. He demanded that conscience be reintroduced to the heart of Jewish religious life, that Jewish law and practice be aligned with the deepest moral insights of the Jewish tradition, and that Judaism speak with prophetic moral passion to an indifferent, oblivious world.

As much a rebel as Schulweis was, he was also an extension of the history and culture of American Jewish life that preceded him. Part 1 explores his place in the story of the American Judaism experience: in chapter 1, his place in the history of the American rabbinate; in chapter 2, his place in the story of twentieth-century American Jewry; in chapter 3, his place in the development of postwar American and American Jewish culture.

Schulweis' rabbinate was expressed in three rabbinic voices that correspond to his teacher Mordecai Kaplan's observation that Judaism comprises "believing, behaving, and belonging." These voices are deeply interrelated but can be considered independently. Part 2 is devoted to these voices: in chapter 4, the theological voice; in chapter 5, the prophetic voice; in chapter 6, the voice of the community builder.

PART 1

SCHULWEIS and the AMERICAN JEWISH EXPERIENCE

CHAPTER 1

The American Rabbi, a Brief History

In a widely read article published in the January 1966 edition of the journal *Midstream*, Rabbi Arthur Hertzberg wondered, "Where have all the great rabbis gone?"

> A generation ago every major Jewish center in America had at least one rabbi whom people came to hear from all over the city. . . . But there is not a single pulpit in America today which leads opinion.[1]

Hertzberg's piece is more polemical than historical. In 1966, one could hear many great American rabbis—Robert Gordis in New York, Joachim Prinz in Newark, Arnold Jacob Wolf in Chicago, Morris Adler in Detroit (until his tragic death that year), Jacob B. Agus in Baltimore, Max Nussbaum in Los Angeles, and Harold Schulweis in Oakland, as well as Abraham Joshua Heschel, Mordecai Kaplan, Joseph B. Soloveitchik, and Eliezer Berkovits, and Eugene Borowitz. Hertzberg, never accused of excessive modesty, does not even count himself among the greats.

Because of his agenda, Hertzberg, both an extraordinary pulpit rabbi and a noted historian, missed the more important question: What makes a rabbi great? What Hertzberg observed was not the diminishment of the American rabbinate but its evolution. What counted as a "great rabbinate" in the 1960s and beyond was different from what counted as great in the 1920s, 1930s, and 1940s. Greatness in the rabbinate is not a static quality. Each generation embraces its own models of rabbinic leadership as it encounters new problems and opportunities. Each model carries its own standards of success. The role of rabbi in American Judaism has never been settled. The American rabbinate has been evolving, often changing radically, since the arrival of Jews on these shores. The American rabbinate has always evinced a strong element of experimentation, innovation, and improvisation. The greatest of America's rabbis did not fill a predetermined role but rather invented their own rabbinate. What constitutes greatness in the rabbinate can only be grasped by viewing the rabbinate through the perspective of this evolution, in the context of the evolution of American Judaism and the changing landscape of American religious life.

The First American Rabbis

In the first generations of American Jewish life, congregations were organized and led by lay leaders. The first paid professional spiritual leaders took the title of "hazzan." Most notable was Isaac Leeser (1806–1868). Hired by Philadelphia's Congregation Mikveh Israel in 1829, Leeser's contract called for him to "lead prayer in the original Hebrew according to the custom of the Portuguese Jews . . . attend all funerals and subsequent mourning services," and officiate at other life-cycle rituals.[2] Leeser took it upon himself to vastly expand this position. He preached—in English—sermons on selected Sabbath mornings, organized Jewish education for children and adults, and published an array of books and tracts defending Judaism, including the first Jewish translation of the Bible into English. Leeser reshaped the position of hazzan to resemble the American Protestant ministry. His tombstone memorializes him as "reverend, a minister . . . a preacher of the word of God."[3]

Leeser recognized that the environment of America would not sustain a Judaism reflexively transplanted from Europe. America presented unique cultural opportunities and challenges never before encountered by Judaism. The freedom of American Jews to enter and participate in the general society was historically unprecedented, as was the freedom to give up the vestiges of Jewish identification, to intermarry and disappear into the general culture. The American tradition of congregationalism changed the shape of the Jewish collective life. In Europe, the Jewish community was sanctioned by government and controlled all aspects of Jewish life—marriage, education, worship, charity, kosher food, and—most telling—religious burial. The community could compel conformity. To defy the community's authority was to be cast into a literal no-man's-land. In America, there was no communal authority that could coerce obedience. In America, religious life was entirely voluntary, separated from governmental authority and organized by congregation. If the style of worship, the personality of the rabbi, or the ambiance of the congregation were disagreeable, one could go and start a new congregation.

Adding urgency to Leeser's efforts were the activities of Christian missionaries who took full advantage of the spiritual paucity of early American Jewish life. The open invitation—indeed, the enticement—directed at young American Jews to participate in Christian life posed an immediate threat Leeser could not ignore.

Animated by a passion to create a new American Judaism that would engage America's Jews and bring vitality to Jewish life, Leeser took up these challenges with quintessential American pragmatism and a spirit of inventive creativity. Most significantly, he was prepared to draw lessons and borrow resources from the religious and cultural life around him to shape a new model of Jewish religious and communal leadership.

In contrast to Leeser, the first ordained rabbi to settle in America was Abraham Rice, who arrived from Bavaria in 1840. In his very first sermon, Rice set forth his intention "to establish pure Orthodox belief in this land."[4] Unwavering in his passion for true belief and practice, "Rice took pride in his *lack* of accommodation to America."[5] In 1849, he resigned his position in disgust at the intransigence and faithlessness of his congregants and took up life as a storekeeper.

The contrast between Leeser's vision of a revolutionary American Judaism and Rice's frustrated attempt to impose old-world European standards and traditions on America's Jews tells the story of the American rabbinate: Leeser's accommodation to America juxtaposed with Rice's dogged resistance; Leeser's pragmatic, inventive spirit and his willingness to draw on non-Jewish models of religious life and leadership juxtaposed with Rice's demand for ideological purity; Leeser's optimistic faith in the Jewish possibilities offered by America juxtaposed with Rice's despair that America was a wasteland of assimilation and spiritual indifference.

In the broadest historical perspective, Leeser's success and Rice's despair were rooted in the very institution of the rabbinate. Since its inception in the first century, rabbinic tradition defined the role of the rabbi as interpreter and transmitter of tradition for a particular generation. The rabbi mediates between the truths of the past and the conditions of the present. The rabbinic dictum *dor dor ve-dorshav* (Talmud, Sanhedrin 38b) assigns to each generation's rabbis the authority to shape the religious life of that generation. In each generation and locale, the role of the rabbi and the idiom of rabbinic authority were influenced by the cultural environment and the needs of the historical moment. In the communities of medieval Europe, where Jewish law governed daily life, the rabbi became the community's legal decisor and judge. In the Hasidic circles devoted to personal spiritual development, the rabbi became rebbe, a personal spiritual guide. In the Reform congregations of emancipated nineteenth-century Germany, the rabbi became *rabbiner*, mediator between the Jewish and non-Jewish world, between the essence of tradition and modern attitudes, values, and aesthetics. It is not surprising that America demanded its own kind of rabbi.

Like Leeser, Isaac Mayer Wise understood the uniqueness of America as a setting for Jewish life. In 1847, Wise created a new prayer book he titled *Minhag America*, literally, "the American custom." By his time, the Jewish community was divided between traditionalists, moderate reformers, and radical reformers. Wise's title testified to his conviction that American traditionalists and reformers were much closer to each other by virtue of their shared American experience than either was to European Orthodoxy or Reform. He mightily resisted the radical reforms of his contemporary David Einhorn as well as the rigid Orthodoxy of Morris Jacob Raphall and championed a unified American version of Jewish faith. He understood that Americans were much more pragmatic than ideological. They valued unity in their communal life above doctrinal purity and were prepared to reshape their religious life accordingly. The founding of Hebrew Union College, America's first successful rabbinical seminary, in 1875 under Wise's leadership represented a momentary triumph of his convictions. But the college soon became an expression of the dilemmas of American Jewish life.

On July 11, 1883, Hebrew Union College celebrated its first graduating class of ordained rabbis—the first rabbis ordained on American soil. One hundred lay and rabbinic leaders representing seventy-six congregations gathered at the Highland House for a celebratory dinner. The dinner menu, infamously known as the Treifa Banquet, violated every Jewish dietary law, save the prohibiton on eating pork. The menu of clams, crab, shrimp, frogs' legs, and the cheese course following the meat entrée caused the traditionalist to bolt the room and ended Wise's dreams of communal unity. To this day it is unknown if the menu was the work of an oblivious caterer or deliberate sabotage by Wise's ideological opponents. In the end, it was less the cause than the symbol of the disintegration of Wise's unified community. Henceforth, the true *Minhag America* would reflect a wide-ranging pluralism.

The American Jewish story is replete with exquisite ironies. The Treifa Banquet—at once the triumph and dissolution of Isaac Mayer Wise's dreams—was one such moment. A second came shortly afterward. To consolidate their power, the reformers, led by Kaufmann Kohler, gathered in Pittsburgh in 1885 to draft an ideological platform. Rarely in history have

Jews created a catechism; ideological purity was never a Jewish virtue. How ironic that at that very moment, more than two and a half million Eastern European Jewish immigrants were packing their bags for America—immigrants who would find Kohler's ideology and his Pittsburgh Platform incomprehensible and unrecognizable as a statement of authentic Jewish belief. The ideological debates that so captivated Kohler and his compatriots would be irrelevant to the newcomers who, by their very numbers, would soon come to dominate American Jewish life.

By the end of the nineteenth century, as this wave of immigration began, new leadership was sorely needed within the American Jewish community. Even the non-Jewish community noticed this. In an editorial printed on July 22, 1872, the *New York Herald* decried the lack of English-speaking rabbis in America:

> To maintain Judaism in America something more than a mere recitation of prayers in Hebrew and German is necessary. The people are much more intelligent than they were a century or half a century ago, and any religious system that keeps not up with the progressive spirit of the age must expect to meet just such crises as this in which the Jewish Church [*sic*] in America now finds itself. The rising generations demand a form of religion which their hearts can appreciate and hold fast to, though they ask for no change in the true spirit of religion at all; and it is the attempt to confine them to the iron bands of the system of bygone ages that has produced results which the Hebrew press so generally

and so frequently lament—namely, that the young Israelites do not manifest that love for the synagogue which
their fathers and forefathers showed. Rightly understood, this very religious indisposition is a sign of progress that calls loudly and earnestly on the Jewish Church
to furnish such spiritual food as young American souls
can digest.[6]

The Golden Age of the American Rabbinate, 1918–1950

The American Jewish community needed more than rabbis
who spoke English. The community needed rabbis who spoke
two languages with fluency—the language of tradition and
the language of American modernity. The community sorely
needed rabbis who would do for American Jews what rabbis of
every generation did—mediate between the Jewish tradition
and the conditions of contemporary life. The Eastern European newcomers needed rabbis to help them understand
America, to welcome them to modernity, to show their children how to be faithful to both Judaism and America, and
to guide them in shaping a Judaism appropriate to their new
American surroundings. The German Jewish establishment,
who had arrived in America half a century earlier, needed
rabbis to help them understand and communicate with the
Eastern European newcomers. The entire community needed
rabbis who would unify, mobilize, and speak for American
Jewry, gather and deploy its resources, and defend it from
material and spiritual threats.

It would take a generation for those rabbis to emerge. But
emerge they did. This was a generation of rabbis that can
rightly be called a golden age of the American rabbinate.[7]

The generation encompassed a unique collection of extraordinary rabbinic personalities—Stephen S. Wise, Abba Hillel Silver, Solomon Goldman, Israel Levinthal, Israel Goldstein, Simon Greenberg, and Milton Steinberg—who shaped American Judaism in its institutional and ideological life and deeply shaped the vision and career of Harold Schulweis.

As a group, the rabbis of this golden age shared a remarkably consistent biographical narrative. They were born in Europe in the last decade of the nineteenth century and arrived in America at an early age (except for Steinberg, born in Rochester, New York, in 1903 to immigrant parents). They were raised in traditional Jewish homes and received a traditional Jewish education. The fathers of Wise, Levinthal, and Silver were practicing rabbis; Steinberg's father was ordained at the Volozhin Yeshiva but never practiced; Goldman came from a long line of rabbis. They earned degrees from American universities and studied for ordination in American institutions (except for Stephen S. Wise, who was enrolled at Hebrew Union College but chose instead to travel to Vienna and study with the scholar Adolf Jellinek). They went on to complete doctoral degrees in fields of history and literature (Wise, Silver), philosophy (Goldman), and Jewish letters (Greenberg, Levinthal; Steinberg completed courses and exams under Professor Salo Baron at Columbia University but never completed his PhD). They served as rabbis of smaller congregations, usually outside of major Jewish urban areas, for some short time—Wise in Portland, Oregon, Silver in Wheeling, West Virginia, Greenberg in upstate New York, and Steinberg in Indianapolis—before arriving at the pulpits they would occupy for lengthy careers. The pulpit allowed them the opportunity to engage in outside pursuits. Wise and Silver held significant positions of leadership in the Zionist movement and in political causes. Steinberg lectured at the Jewish Theological Seminary, the 92nd Street Y, and across the nation. Goldman taught at the University of Chicago. All took great pride in remaining active in the pastoral care of the congregation. They authored popular as well as scholarly books. They married early, raised children, and maintained close family ties.

Like any golden age, this extraordinary moment of the American rabbinate was evident only in retrospect. Its chronology is inexact. A brief survey of its most outstanding figures establishes its parameters from roughly 1918 through 1950, with its heyday in the 1920s, 1930s, and 1940s. Stephen S. Wise was the elder and precursor of the group. Wise came to national prominence after World War I. He served in leadership positions until his death in 1949. Abba Hillel Silver became leader of the temple in Cleveland in 1917. In 1949, he was forced out of the leadership of the Zionist movement and retired to a career in scholarship. Solomon Goldman assumed leadership of the Cleveland Jewish Center (later called Park Synagogue) in 1922 and moved to Anshe Emet in Chicago in 1929. He died in 1953. Simon Greenberg became rabbi of Har Zion in Philadelphia in 1925. Greenberg left the congregational rabbinate to teach at the Jewish Theological Seminary in 1951. Milton Steinberg assumed the pulpit of Park Avenue Synagogue in 1933. He tragically died very young in 1950.

The golden age included Orthodox rabbis, most notably Zvi Hirsch Masliansky, Bernard Revel, Herbert Goldstein, David de Sola Pool, Leo Jung, and Joseph Lookstein. The Orthodox community struggled differently with issues of acculturation and resistance to America and established its own distinct pattern of synagogue life, education, and communal organization.

It is the genius of the Jewish people to raise leaders of vision and courage in moments of crisis to reimagine, reinvent, and renew Jewish life. At the end of the first century, following the destruction of the Temple of Jerusalem, a group of brilliant religious thinkers gathered around Rabbi Yohanan ben Zakkai in the academy of Yavneh to envision a new Judaism, a Judaism without a Temple, without priests or sacrifices, without its home in Jerusalem. This became the core of Rabbinic Judaism. In the sixteenth century, a group of religious visionaries, many of them recent refugees from Spain, found their way to the town of Safed in northern Israel. Theirs was the task to once again envision a new Judaism in the wake of the Spanish expulsion. This community gave birth to Lurianic Kabbalah. Again, in the seventeenth century, in response to the Khmelnitsky massacres and the unmasking of the popular false messiah Shabbetai Zvi, a group of religious insurgents gathered around Israel ben Eliezer, the Baal Shem Tov, to restore the spirits of the deflated Jewish communities of Eastern Europe through Hasidism.

This golden age of the American rabbinate is an expression of this same genius. The Eastern European Jews who immigrated to America at the end of the nineteenth century and the beginning of the twentieth century came from a world where they were spiritually secure but temporally—politically and materially—powerless. In America they found themselves in a world that was the other way around. In America they discovered political and material power but were plagued with spiritual anxiety. This paradox produced a generation of

uniquely creative, imaginative rabbis to reinterpret the truths
of the Jewish tradition, reinvent the institutions of Jewish life,
and renew the vitality of the Jewish people for the newcomers
and their American-born children.

The New Rabbinate, the New Synagogue, the New Judaism

Of all the problems that beset the American Rabbi of
today none is more complex and more difficult to solve
than that of how to bring the child closer to the Synagogue, how to arouse his interest in things Jewish and
how to secure his permanent attachment to the ideals
and faith of our people.

This problem which is of vital importance to the
future of Judaism in America was completely unknown
to our predecessors of a generation ago, particularly
in the more established communities of the old world,
where Jewish life was settled and well-ordered, and
where Jewish practice had been crystallized for centuries. . . . The child not only learned his religious duties
by precept but largely by example. The atmosphere in
which he moved, lived, developed, and grew was one
hundred percent Jewish. His environment was charged
with a sublime spirit that led him to adopt a wholesome
Jewish life. . . .

Here in America, however, where the Jew has lost his
firm grip on his ancient heritage, and where his loyalty
to the traditions of his fathers has weakened so much;
here, where the child moves from morning until night
in a non-Jewish atmosphere, the question of inspiring

14

his interest in the Synagogue becomes a difficult task indeed. We are confronted with the fact that neither the home nor the Synagogue, as they are constituted today, any longer exert that magnetic power over the child . . . [nor] generate any longer that spiritual force which in former generations influenced the child's life and made him conscious of his Jewish responsibilities. . . . Our American Synagogues are, with few exceptions, without traditions. Their foundations are not rooted in the firm rock of Israel's historic experiences, but are, spiritually speaking, flimsy and tottering structures, swayed by the slightest wind that threatens their collapse. . . . Their educational system, disorganized and faulty. Their religious services mechanical, lacking in decorum, in uniformity, in sincerity and in spiritual enthusiasm. . . . Is it a wonder, then, that under conditions such as these the Jewish child is crushed between the upper and nether stones of indifference and neglect, and that his Jewish consciousness is nipped in the bud beyond resurrection ere it has had a chance to blossom forth and bear fruit?[8]

These are the words of Rabbi Israel Goldfarb of the Kane Street Synagogue in Brooklyn in 1925. Goldfarb, who doubled as an instructor of Jewish music at the Jewish Theological Seminary, is best known as the composer of the popular melody for the Sabbath hymn "Shalom Aleikhem" and for officiating at composer Aaron Copland's bar mitzvah. His anxiety is palpable. Whatever physical dangers they faced in Eastern Europe, Jews were spiritually secure. They knew who they were, and they knew that their children—albeit threatened by poverty and violence—would follow the pathways of tradition, adopting their values and lifestyle. America presented a topsy-turvy world that offered abundant freedom, prosperity, and physical security but raised serious doubts that Judaism would be embraced by the next generation. More frustrating, there were no mechanisms for this transmission—neither home nor synagogue nor school, nor any of the institutions carried from the old world, were capable of engaging the young. Worse, there were no leaders. Nothing in Goldfarb's training prepared him to teach children—American children—to embrace Judaism. Never before was that the rabbi's principal role.

Goldfarb, however, was pragmatic and resourceful. In response to this crisis of identity, he experimented and molded a Jewish experience to the needs of his generation. Goldfarb elevated the experience of bar mitzvah into a major life-cycle event and established a rigorous program of bar mitzvah preparation. He invented a post–bar mitzvah boys' club, Bnai Zion, and later a parallel girls' club, both with strict admissions requirements, and he instituted a special, exclusive Sabbath afternoon program for these clubs. He concludes with a call for a new kind of rabbinic professional preparation. No longer would advanced learning in Talmud be sufficient; rabbis needed to understand the lives of children.

> I have mentioned only some of the activities . . . with which I have experimented and which I found to a great degree to be successful. I wish only to add that the future of Judaism in America lies in a proper, intelligent and sympathetic understanding of the child. We may preach inspiring sermons, we may organize fine musical

services, we may create a fine aesthetic atmosphere in our Synagogues and Temples, but unless we study the child's mind and heart and seek to develop in him a sense of Jewish responsibility our fine superstructure is doomed to collapse.[9]

Goldfarb's talk, "The Child and the Synagogue," was delivered to a unique audience. In 1925 and 1926, the monthly meetings of the New York Board of Jewish Ministers were devoted to an ongoing symposium on the challenges of the rabbinate. Yes, "Jewish Ministers." The organization was formed in 1881 by six rabbis of differing affiliations, including Gustav Gottheil, Kaufmann Kohler, Frederick de Sola Mendes, and Henry Pereira Mendes. At the 1925–26 meetings, papers and responses were presented to this symposium by the luminaries of the New York rabbinate and were vigorously debated. Subsequently, the symposium transcript was edited by the board's president, Rabbi Israel Goldstein, and published in a slim volume entitled *Problems of the Jewish Ministry*. The board represented a membership of nearly one hundred rabbis—Orthodox, Conservative, and Reform—forming the most comprehensive organization of rabbis in the United States. Goldstein introduced the volume, noting, "The American Rabbi of the present generation is called upon to cope with many phases of Congregational and communal activity which do not seem to belong to the traditional sphere of the Rabbinate."[10] The anxiety expressed by Rabbi Goldfarb is echoed by each rabbi in every chapter. They were not prepared for the community they found themselves leading. Their very role as rabbis was uncertain. They were improvising, making it up as they went along. The papers presented at the symposium displayed their worry and frustration but, at the same time, a spirit of experimentation, pragmatism, and invention. Taken collectively, these papers document how these rabbis shaped the institution of the American rabbinate.

The chapters of the book set out the principal elements of the rabbinic role, as they were understood in 1925:

The Sermon

Pastoral Duties

The Religious School

The Child and the Synagogue

The Synagogue Center

Administrative Duties

The Rabbi as Scholar and Teacher

The Community at Large

The Problem of Chaplaincy

And a special addendum, The Wife of the Rabbi

Nowhere in these chapters is the traditional role of rabbi as halachic decisor and judge even mentioned. Instead, the emphasis is entirely on the challenge of attracting a new generation into Jewish life. There is an implied recognition that in America the rabbi has no temporal power as rabbis did in Europe. The rabbi possesses only the power of moral authority. American rabbis cannot command; they can only persuade. The culture of American individualism and religious freedom supplanted traditional structures of rabbinic authority. Cultural values that once invested the rabbi with divine authority were abandoned along with so many other Jewish artifacts brought from the old country. In response to this loss of authority, the rabbis fashioned a new rabbinic role centered on religious education and moral inspiration.

The book's opening essay is entitled "What Is a Jewish Sermon?" In traditional Eastern European communities, a rabbi spoke from the pulpit twice a year: in preparation for Passover on Shabbat Hagadol and in preparation for Yom Kippur on Shabbat Shuva. It was Isaac Leeser who introduced a more regular Sabbath sermon. The early Reform rabbis adopted the American Protestant custom of building Sabbath worship around the weekly sermon.[11] Stephen S. Wise held meetings of the Free Synagogue on Sunday morning and normally preached for more than an hour. Israel Levinthal is credited with introducing the late Friday night service, inviting families to worship together after Sabbath dinner and allowing the rabbi an opportunity to speak to entire families.[12] By 1925, American rabbis typically maintained a schedule of speaking three times each weekend: on Friday night and Saturday morning and again at a Sunday morning lecture. In an age before television, when even radio was rudimentary, oratory was a central cultural expression. The great rabbis of the golden age were all great orators. Wise held his Sunday morning meetings at Carnegie Hall and filled it week to week for thirty years. Levinthal preached to a thousand people every Friday night.[13] Through the medium of oratory the rabbis would shape the new age. According to Levinthal,

> Not only is preaching an art, but it stands today as the great means to attract our people to the Synagogue and to win their loyalty to our Faith and our People. . . . To

the preacher is granted the opportunity to bring the
Jew to the Synagogue and to win him to the ideals which
the Synagogue represents. . . . If that is his opportunity,
it follows that the preacher must consider the Congregation, must take into account who and what his Congregation is.[14]

As they refashioned the rabbinate, the rabbis of the
golden age reimagined the synagogue. The concept of the
"synagogue-center," originally conceived by Mordecai Kaplan
in 1916, was brought to reality by Israel Levinthal in Brooklyn
and Solomon Goldman in Chicago. On the first anniversary of
his Brooklyn Jewish Center in 1925, Levinthal preached,

The very tragedy in our Jewish life, especially here in
America, lies in the fact that we have turned our Synagogues into Houses of Prayer alone, and that we have
divorced the life in the Synagogue from the life outside
of its walls.[15]

The synagogue-center opened the synagogue to the totality of life, offering a wide range of cultural, recreational,
educational, and religious activities. Of the Anshe Emet congregation, Goldman's biographer notes, "Nothing human was
alien to its program."[16] The synagogue-center replicated on
American soil the sense of belonging to a total, organic community life that Jews experienced in the old country. For children, there was a playground; for youngsters, a scout troop; for
adults, dance lessons, cooking classes, and a gymnasium, all at
the synagogue and all among their Jewish neighbors. And the

synagogue-center offered programs of quality. In the 1920s, the social and drama director at Levinthal's Brooklyn Jewish Center was the playwright and theater director Moss Hart, until he departed for Broadway and Hollywood; its art director was the abstract expressionist painter Mark Rothko (née Markus Rothkowitz). The great operatic tenor Richard Tucker served as cantor from 1943 through 1946, before turning to the Metropolitan Opera.[17]

Against critics who doubted the relevance of the synagogue-center's activities to the sacred tasks of the synagogue, Levinthal boasted of his center's gym: "The perfection of our physique is also part of religion."[18] He asserted his full pride in the center's social gatherings: "We feel that if dancing is today an essential part of the life of so many people, we should encourage them to dance before the Lord rather than to dance before the devil."[19] Proud that his center was a "seven-day Synagogue, not a one-day Synagogue," filled with the young and the old, day and night, he summarized the philosophy of the synagogue-center:

> The Synagogue must be "*Shaul K'neged Shomayim Vo'aretz.*"
> It must aim at uniting Heaven and Earth—the highest
> ideals of our religious life with the needs of our everyday
> worldly life—so that through "*Aretz*," earthly activities, we
> may reach out into "*Shomayim*" and touch the very dome
> of Heaven, and through the inspiration of our Heavenly
> ideals mold a better, nobler existence here.[20]

The synagogue-center model included a dazzling array of educational opportunities. Lectures on literature, history, culture, and current politics, delivered in English and Yiddish, were featured every night, including Friday nights. For children, there were classes four afternoons a week, junior congregation on Saturday, and Sunday school.[21] Milton Steinberg, who possessed none of the organizational genius of Levinthal or Goldman, nevertheless organized dozens of small study cells meeting in congregants' homes all over the city so that "night after night the new rabbi made his way up and down Park and Fifth Avenues and over to the West Side leading discussions on current Jewish problems and aspects of Jewish history and religion."[22] Although he was a close disciple of Kaplan, Steinberg never endeavored to turn his Park Avenue Synagogue into a synagogue-center. Instead, he worked with the leadership of the nearby 92nd Street Y to bring Jewish learning and spirit to its program. He served as the chair of the Cultural Arts Committee at the Y and taught in its Adult School of Jewish Studies.[23]

Out of this model of the comprehensive, educating synagogue came the concept of the synagogue-based day school. In 1927, Levinthal opened the Center Academy with a curriculum that integrated secular and religious teaching, Jewish culture, and spoken Hebrew.[24] Goldman opened the Anshe Emet Day School in 1945 with much the same emphases.[25]

Some rabbis doubted the synagogue-center model. Rabbi Samuel M. Cohen, executive director of United Synagogue of America, delivered the paper on "The Synagogue Center" to the 1925 symposium. He worried that the institution would become more social center than synagogue and neglect its primary role "as an institution that educates Jews to live a Jewish life," effectively relegating the rabbi's role to an activities director.[26] Many joined Cohen in this worry. In 1920, Abba

Hillel Silver's temple erected a magnificent new building that housed worship, educational, and recreational venues, including a gymnasium. But in 1929, the temple's leadership decided to suspend the recreational and social programs, turning the gym into an assembly hall. Silver explained the change at the congregational meeting: "Activities of a purely social and recreational nature aimed at entertaining people . . . contribute little or nothing to spiritual life."[27] Stephen S. Wise, characteristically, was even more direct. In a speech to the students of the Jewish Institute of Religion on "The Present Task of the Minister" in 1923, he excoriated the whole idea of the synagogue-center:

> If you have something to say to these people that fills you as with living fire, it will not be necessary to have any music or any cooking classes or any bowling alleys or any gymnastics in order to bring men to the source of things for which they must long. If you feel this, you can preach in such seething syllables as to make them feel it; and unless you preach in that wise I advise you to go into some more honest occupation.[28]

While Wise's Free Synagogue eschewed the program of recreational activities, it offered a uniquely ambitious program of social services. The first employee engaged by the Free Synagogue after Rabbi Wise himself was Sidney Goldstein, its director of social services. Goldstein, an ordained rabbi with a degree in social work, had been assistant superintendent of Mount Sinai Hospital. He recognized that the hospital staff had little awareness of the social and economic circumstances of their patients. This became his cause. In 1906, he published a paper entitled "The Social Function of the Hospital," which caught the eye of Stephen S. Wise, who invited him to become a partner in building his new synagogue. At the Free Synagogue, Goldstein gathered an army of volunteers who provided assistance and support to the poor, to new immigrants, and to the infirmed. Goldstein discovered that Bellevue Hospital, New York's preeminent public health center, handled six thousand Jewish admissions a year. He organized a program that visited every Jewish patient within twenty-four hours of admission and remained in contact with the patient during the hospitalization and even after discharge.[29] Wise may have scoffed at the notion of the synagogue-center, but the Free Synagogue was far from his father's traditional shul.

Implicit in the concept of the synagogue-center are the revolutionary ideas that would later form the core of Mordecai Kaplan's *Judaism as a Civilization* in 1934. In the synagogue-center, the totality of Jewish culture—indeed, all expressions of life embraced by Jews—became sanctified. Judaism was much more than religion. A robust concept of Jewish identity as peoplehood was the ideological core of the synagogue-center. For those newly arrived in America and newly arrived into modernity, peoplehood remained a compelling connection to Judaism even as ties to faith and tradition waned. Kaplan articulated the idea most fully. He was anticipated by the rabbis of the golden age. According to his biographer, Stephen S. Wise paid little attention to matters of theology, "but if one wanted to identify a lodestar in his religious thought, it would have to be the unity of the Jewish people."[30] Solomon Goldman, invited by Wise to address the 1932 commencement of the Jewish Institute of Religion, articulated this Judaism of peoplehood:

> Judaism . . . is rooted in the soil, blood, life-experience
> and memory of a particular folk—the Jewish people. It
> is inseparable from people, land, language and Torah.
> Its emphasis is conduct; its institutions are the fam-
> ily, the schul, the synagogue, and primarily society; its
> major problems are national continuity and perfection,
> social justice and world peace. Its signal promise is a
> better world order.[31]

The rabbis of the golden age indelibly changed the American rabbinate, the American synagogue, and the Judaism embraced by American Jews. They met the spiritual anxiety of the immigrant generation and their children with remarkable creativity, resourcefulness, pragmatism, and courage. That spiritual anxiety was one side of the generation's experience. The other side was the discovery of new power, a power expressed in passionate Zionism and political activism.

Zionism and Power

Stephen S. Wise would become the most powerful advocate of Zionism of his generation. But he was a most unlikely Zionist. He was raised in the community of uptown New York German Jews for whom Zionism was considered lunacy, if not treason. He was trained as a Reform rabbi at a time when Reform Judaism defined itself as an expression of universal, rational faith, firmly rejecting nationality. His biographer attributes his connection to Zionism to his association with Richard

Gottheil, his friend and teacher, twelve years his senior, and son of Gustav Gottheil, the rabbi of Temple Emanu-El.[32] Richard Gottheil, a young professor at Columbia University, was the leading Zionist in America. Gottheil recruited Wise to help him organize the factionalized Zionist clubs of the Lower East Side into a Federation of American Zionists. The two friends appointed themselves delegates to the Second Zionist Congress. There, Wise had an epiphany:

> For the first time in my youthful life I got a glimpse of world Jewry. There I sought and met for the first time with great men who were great Jews, with great Jews who were great men. . . . Suddenly as if by magic I came upon a company of Jews who were not victims or refugees or beggars, but proud and educated men, dreaming, planning, toiling for their people. Veritably I suffered a rebirth, for I came to know my people at their best. Thrilled and gratified, I caught a glimpse of the power and pride and the nobleness of the Jewish people, which my American upbringing and even service to New York Jewry had not in any degree given me. I was a Jew by faith up to the day of the Congress in Basle and little more. At Basle I became a Jew in every sense of that term. Judaism ceased to be a type of religious worship. The Jewish people became my own.[33]

Wise worked with Louis Brandeis to formulate the text of the Balfour Declaration in 1917, the landmark statement articulating the support of the British government for the establishment of a Jewish homeland in Palestine, and supported

Brandeis in his struggle to focus the nascent Zionist movement on settlement in Palestine above all other priorities.

American Zionism is something of an oxymoron. Wise visited Israel but never contemplated immigrating there. Nor did he ever urge others to do so. Wise's Zionism reflected his personal devotion to Theodor Herzl, the founder of modern Zionism, and his dedication to the plight of his people. Jews faced danger in so many corners of the world. A Jewish homeland was desperately needed. Zionism needed the support of America's Jews. Wise would marshal his formidable powers of oratory and persuasion to convince them.

More than a political movement, Zionism was an expression of a new kind of Judaism for Wise. In Basel, he declared, "I caught a glimpse of the power and pride and the nobleness of the Jewish people."[34] While the process of achieving a Jewish homeland was wrought with frustration, Wise never ceased to share the sense of wonderment at a people, once so powerless and pitiful, now liberated and rising up to take responsibility for its own destiny. Zionism was a revelation of newly found Jewish power, and Wise would be its prophet.

The quintessential uptown German Jew, Wise became a champion of the downtown *yidin*, the Eastern European newcomers, and a foe of his uptown German kin. "The Jews are not a nation," fumed *New York Times* publisher Adolph Ochs, the uber–uptown Jew. "They only share a religion." Terrified of accusations of dual loyalty, Ochs worried openly about what would happen to him and his circle of "100 percent Americans" if a Jewish nation came into being.[35]

Wise perceived the need to wrest control of the Jewish community, and especially its voice, from the entrenched German establishment and share it with the newcomers. He proposed a new organization, an American Jewish Congress:

> The real difficulty lies in the circumstances that the German Jewish millionaires in this country, led by [Jacob] Schiff, persist in treating the Jewish masses as if they were forever to be in a state of tutelage and incapable of having anything to say with respect to the management of their own affairs.[36]

The American Jewish Committee, the organized expression of the German establishment, assumed provenance over matters of Jewish communal policy. Its chair, the venerable Louis Marshall, declared, "The problems with which we have to deal are of so delicate a nature that the mob cannot grapple with them."[37] Wise took on Marshall and the German leadership of the committee and was victorious. In March 1916, the American Jewish Congress was convened with Nathan Straus, another German Jew with strong Zionist convictions (the city of Netanya in Israel is named for him), as its elected chair. Wise served as president, honorary president, or vice president of the congress from 1920 until his death in 1949.

Abba Hillel Silver came to Zionism much earlier in life. Upon the untimely death of Theodor Herzl, Silver's father, a staunch Zionist, urged his sons, Abba (then "Abe"), only eleven years old, and Maxwell, thirteen, to establish a Dr. Herzl Zion Club among the boys of their Lower East Side neighborhood. By the time of his bar mitzvah, Abe ascended to the club's presidency. A year later, the club was chartered by the Federation of American Zionists, and Abe, at age fourteen, found himself addressing the national convention.[38] The Dr. Herzl Zion Club would eventually become the Young Judaea youth movement, and Abe, soon Rabbi Abba Hillel Silver, would become one of America's greatest Zionist leaders.

Silver joined Brandeis and Wise in their efforts to mobilize American Jewry on behalf of the Zionist cause, though he clashed frequently with Wise over internal matters of Zionist policy. Renowned as a riveting public speaker—Wise once called him "the finest orator I have ever heard"[39]—Silver raised millions of dollars for the reclamation and building of Palestine and served as national chair of the United Palestine Appeal and the United Jewish Appeal, founding chair of the American Zionist Emergency Council, and chair of the American section of the Jewish Agency. On May 8, 1947, he presented the case for an independent Jewish state to the United Nations General Assembly. It was Silver who organized and directed the strategy to secure American support for the Partition Plan passed by the United Nations on November 29, 1947. So relentless were his lobbying efforts that President Harry Truman swore "it would help if, figuratively, both the Mufti and Rabbi Silver where thrown into the Red Sea."[40]

According to his biographer, Marc Lee Raphael, following World War I, Silver, like so many in America, felt a deep disillusionment with the nineteenth-century faith in the inevitability of social progress and the triumph of ethical universalism. In place of these ideals, so central to the classical Reform tradition in which he had been trained, Silver developed a "dramatic, powerful, intense, even passionate, assertion of Jewish national particularism . . . [that] made him no longer able to subordinate Jewish national particularism to anything," even social justice, his other driving commitment.[41] Silver embraced the philosopher Ahad Ha'am's vision of Zionism's cultural program together with Herzl's political program:

> For only in Palestine, he asserted, with their own state could the Jews hope to be fully free (the Herzl influence) while only in Zion could a Jewish community hope to evolve a vibrant, contemporary Hebrew culture (following Ahad Ha'am) and radiate that cultural center to world Jewry.[42]

Silver's authority, like Wise, derived from the power of his oratory and the force of his personality. Like Wise, Silver possessed the ability to capture and express the collective exhilaration of a people discovering its own power to resurrect its national existence and its culture. Through Zionism, Jews found power. Wise, Silver, Goldman, and Levinthal—all Zionist leaders—symbolized and articulated the revelry of that discovery.

Political Power

In 1905, the pulpit of the venerable Temple Emanu-El opened in New York City, and Stephen S. Wise, then a rabbi in Portland, Oregon, was the obvious candidate. With a reputation as a fiery speaker, he seemed the perfect match for America's "Cathedral Synagogue." After he delivered a series of sermons at the invitation of the temple's leadership, Wise met with a committee of the trustees, who extended to him an offer to become their next rabbi. In response, he set three conditions:

that he have a part in the religious service of the temple; that he be provided a personal secretary; and most importantly, that the pulpit be free. Thereupon, Louis Marshall, the most powerful attorney in America and secretary to the temple trustees, responded testily, "Dr. Wise, I must say to you at once that such a condition cannot be complied with; the pulpit of Temple Emanu-El has always been and is subject to and under the control of the board of trustees."

Wise responded, "If that be true, gentlemen, there is nothing more to say."

One committee member, startled by Marshall's finality, asked Wise, "What do you mean by a free pulpit?"

Wise responded,

> I have in Oregon been among the leaders of a civic-reform movement in my community. [Addressing a member of the committee,] Mr. Moses, if it be true, as I have heard it rumored, that your nephew, Mr. Herman, is to be a Tammany Hall candidate for a Supreme Court judgeship, I would if I were Emanu-El's rabbi oppose his candidacy in and out of my pulpit. Mr. Guggenheim, as a member of the Child Labor Commission of the State of Oregon, I must say to you that, if it ever came to be known that children were employed in your mines, I would cry out against such wrong. Mr. Marshall, the press stated that you and your firm are to be counsel for Mr. Hyde of the Equitable Life Assurance Society. That may or may not be true, but, knowing that Charles Evans Hughes's investigation of insurance companies in New York has been a very great service, I would in and

out of my pulpit speak in condemnation of the crime committed by the insurance thieves."[43]

At this, one of the trustees stammered, "But politics is never discussed in the pulpit of Temple Emanu-El!"

Wise retorted, praising the decency of New York's crusading district attorney, William Travers Jerome:

> The Hebrew prophets were politicians in the sense in which Mr. Jerome is, furtherers of civic and national righteousness. As a Jewish minister I claim the right to follow the example of the Hebrew prophets and stand and battle in New York as I have stood and battled in Portland for civic righteousness.[44]

Ignoring the contretemps, the committee sent Wise a written invitation to assume its pulpit with an addendum reaffirming Marshall's condition. Wise responded, "I beg to say that no self-respecting minister of religion, in my opinion, could consider a call to a pulpit which, in the language of your communication, shall always be subject to, and under the control of, the board of trustees."[45] To this, he appended an open letter to the members of Temple Emanu-El, which he published on the editorial page of the *New York Times*, arguing the principle of the free pulpit: "The chief office of the minister, as I take it, is not to represent the views of the congregation, but to proclaim the truth as he sees it."[46]

In this bold young rabbi, Louis Marshall and his generation faced something they had never before encountered. Wise was outspoken, unafraid, and highly political. The world was his sanctuary; the subject of his preaching would be the real lives of his congregants. No one would muzzle him. Wise returned to New York a year later, but on his own terms. With the notoriety the incident generated—after all, what kind of man turns down the pulpit of Temple Emanu-El!—he founded the Free Synagogue. Years later, after a cool reconciliation, Wise welcomed Marshall to the pulpit of the Free Synagogue, humorously introducing him as "the author and founder of the Free Synagogue."[47]

At the beginning of the twentieth century, American politics, particularly in New York, were a battleground between the political machines fed by graft, violence, and ethnic ties, and the Progressives who insisted on clean government and civic-minded righteousness. Nationally, rapid industrialization yielded a host of disturbing social problems. Labor unions, government regulation, and muckraking journalism arose as counterforces, representing the interests of the worker and the citizen against the power of corporations. In the Christian world, a social gospel was preached by pastors who took as their calling the task of saving souls in this world.

The rabbis of the golden age joined the fight. Wise wrote,

> To me, neither religion nor politics was remote or sequestered from life. Religion is a vision or ideal of life. Politics is a method. To say that the minister should not go into politics is to imply that ideal and reality are twain and alien. Politics is what it is because religion keeps out of it.[48]

Using the visibility of his pulpit, his powerful voice, and a newly found political power now that a third of New York City was Jewish, Wise raised and toppled candidates, condemned corruption, and demanded better government. According to his biographer,

> He once commented that the world's greatest sin was indifference, and of that sin he could not be accused. Judaism, especially the teachings of the prophets, would not allow him to stand by passively as long as injustice and bigotry oppressed people.[49]

Wise was fearless. Where other clergy condemned evil but refrained from naming the evildoers, Wise had no compunctions. Where other clergy worried about losing congregants and support because of their political action, Wise served only one master—his moral truth. In response to the tragic Triangle Shirtwaist Factory fire in 1911 and the muted response of the owners and political officials, Wise stood at the public rally and proclaimed:

> If the church and the synagogue were forces of righteousness in the world instead of being the farces of respectability and convention, this thing need not have happened. If it be the shame and humiliation of the whole community, it is doubly the humiliation of the synagogue and the church which have suffered it to come to pass. We may not be ready to prescribe a legislative program nor devise an industrial panacea, but we must demand and demand unceasingly an ever-increasing measure of social equity and social justice. . . . The hour has come for industrial peace.[50]

Wise was a cofounder of the NAACP and of the American Civil Liberties Union. His most passionate cause was labor. In 1919, steel workers, having waited patiently for the end of World War I to organize, were violently blocked by the brutal power of Judge Elbert H. Gary, chairman of the United States Steel Corporation. Wise knew that speaking out against Judge Gary would cost him the valuable support of his wealthiest members, many of whom were stockholders in US Steel. But once again he was drawn by the prophetic call. With a certain quality of glee, he recounts in his memoirs,

> Before going to Carnegie Hall that Sunday morning, I said to my wife, "My sermon of this morning will light a million-dollar blaze." As she smiled incredulously, I explained that the synagogue building, for which we had gathered large sums and which was to cost more than a million dollars, would not be built because of the cancellation of large gifts sure to follow upon my sermon. It all happened as I predicted—only more so![51]

And so he proceeded to thunder that Sunday morning,

> The men in the iron and steel industry are striving for a fundamental right of industry—the right to organize and deal organizedly with their employers. . . . I charge the United States Steel Corporation with resorting to every manner of coercion and even of violence. . . . I charge Judge Gary and the men associated with him with resorting to every manner of coercion, intimidation, violence . . . in order to avoid the organization of the workers.[52]

Indeed, Wise's prediction came to pass. His donors withdrew their gifts, and the Free Synagogue did not complete its building until 1949.

In Cleveland, Abba Hillel Silver stood for similar principles. There were 237 strikes in 1919 in Ohio, and Silver stood firmly and spoke frequently for the rights of workers to organize and bargain. In 1920, he resigned from the Chamber of Commerce and fought the National Association of Manufacturers over the issue of the open shop. The president of his own synagogue was a major clothing manufacturer who strongly opposed the organizing of his workers. Silver confronted him publicly:

> No religious leader dare shirk these problems if justice and truth and democracy are part of his doctrine and part of his theology. . . . Any man who sets about fighting trade-unionism without first finding an equally effective and beneficial substitute to protect the interests of the workingman, and to ensure his further progress and development—that man is an enemy of society, and I care not who he is.[53]

The plight of the unemployed industrial worker dominated Silver's attention. Ohio was one of only two states in the 1920s to consider the adoption of unemployment insurance. Silver took up this cause. On March 28, 1928, he preached on "Our National Debt to the Unemployed," arguing, "Above all, a law should be passed establishing compulsory unemployment insurance for all working men."[54] A bill was readied for the legislature, written largely in Silver's office by a group of state senators and liberal manufacturers that he gathered. Silver testified before the state senate committee considering the bill. His advocacy attracted vicious reaction. One legislator argued that unemployment insurance was the "most menacing and revolutionary piece of legislation ever proposed in the history of Ohio [and] a threat to Christian charity, family, love, neighborly kindness and human brotherhood."[55] Another questioned,

> Is it reasonable to suppose that men cradled in Old Russia can have absorbed our American traditions and ideals sufficiently to make them trustworthy guides for the descendants of the men and women who came over the mountains in covered wagons in social and political problems of major importance and revolutionary character?[56]

It took eight years and the Great Depression, but Silver's bill finally passed the Ohio legislature in 1936 and became a model for unemployment insurance in every state.

The sanctuary of Anshe Emet congregation in Chicago is decorated with beautiful stained glass windows. On one side of the sanctuary, they depict the biblical patriarchs; on the other side, the biblical prophets. Bridging the two sides and above the congregation are windows depicting Washington, Jefferson, and Lincoln. Solomon Goldman, the rabbi who commissioned the windows, believed that the American patriarchs deserved that exalted place amid the biblical heroes. The rabbis of the golden age held that the ideals of Judaism and the ideals of American democracy were fully congruent, and more, they needed one another.

Judaism needed a dose of American pragmatism and democracy. What was "free" in Wise's Free Synagogue was more than the pulpit and the policy that no dues were charged and no seats reserved. "Free" meant a place for the free exchange of all ideas. As much, America needed to hear the voice of the prophets' righteous indignation. This proposition was surely astonishing to the masses of new immigrants and their children. With political speech and activism, the rabbis of the golden age declared their place not at the periphery but at the center of the American conversation. America, they held, needs the moral ideals and passions of the Jewish tradition. Jews need not be silent in this land. Jews must raise their voices, demanding justice, and when they do, America will respond with favor. Jews can stand together with like-minded Christians, with social activists, with the best of Americans as equals in the democratic process and fight for their ideals. And this fight is sacred. It is sanctioned by the sacred symbols of the synagogue.

Near the end of his life, Simon Greenberg remarked that his greatest fear in the rabbinate was seeing Judaism turned into Chinatown, a place filled with curious cultural artifacts, attracting tourists and sightseers, but without a word to say to contemporary life.[57] The assertion of political power by the rabbis of the golden age restored vitality to Judaism in America by sharing a Judaism that speaks in the present tense.

The Dynamic Rabbinate

The first ordained rabbi to arrive in America, Abraham Rice, brought from Europe a fixed idea of what a rabbi is and does. He insisted upon this role. In short order, he resigned his pulpit in despair. The rabbinate in America has always been dynamic, improvisational, and experimental. Where have all the great rabbis gone? Wherever their communities needed them to go. *Dor dor ve-dorshav*, every generation calls for its own unique rabbinate.

The greatest of American rabbis embraced the opportunity to interpret their role and shape their rabbinate in response to the community's needs and challenges. The rabbis of the golden age reveled in this freedom. Using the power of oratory, political action, and community organization, they shaped a distinctly American Judaism and reinvented the synagogue and the institutions of American Jewish life. They established a sense of Jewish mission in America, launching American Zionism and setting the American Jewish community at the center of the American political conversation.

The beginning of Harold Schulweis' career coincided with the end of the golden age. He was ordained in 1950, the year Steinberg died and a year after the death of Stephen S. Wise and the retirement of Abba Hillel Silver. The contours of Schulweis' rabbinate correspond much more closely to the rabbis of this golden age than to the rabbis of his own generation. His ability to exploit the power of oratory as a source of rabbinic authority, his insistence on speaking to the adult community in an adult idiom, his commitment to scholarship, his devotion to Jewish community and Jewish peoplehood, his vision of social responsibility as the mission of Judaism, his expansive vision of the synagogue, and his bold inventiveness in remaking Jewish life are all vestiges of the generation of the golden age. Schulweis might properly be seen as the last of that generation. Most significantly, like the rabbis of that age, Schulweis fully embraced the freedom to author his own rabbinate, to shape the roles and tasks he would fulfill as rabbi in answer to the demands of his historical moment. That is what allows him to be counted among them as great.

CHAPTER 2

Three Languages, Three Voices

Identity: Speaking Three Languages

On the day of his bar mitzvah, in the spring of 1938, young Harold Schulweis ascended the bimah of a small *shtiebel* in the Bronx as Tzvi Hersch ben Moshe v'Shaina Henya and proceeded to deliver his bar mitzvah speech three times: once in English, at his mother's insistence; a second time in Yiddish, for his father; and for his maternal grandfather, he gave it again in Hebrew.[1]

English was the language of America, "the *goldene medina*," the land of refuge and dreams. English was the gateway to acceptance and success in America. Young Harold's fluency in its language and culture meant everything to his mother, Helen (née Shaina Henya Rezack), who worried, like so many immigrant mothers, that her son would find a place in this bewildering and alluring new world. She named him Harold, as Anglo a name as she could imagine, and sent him to the neighborhood public school so that he might become fully and fluently American.

Maurice (née Moshe) Schulweis, Harold's father, had been an actor and a socialist in Warsaw before immigrating to New York, where he sold tea and coffee and occasionally wrote for the *Forverts* (*The Forward*), the leading Yiddish daily. Moshe

Schulweis was a disciple of the Yiddish nationalist Chaim Zhitlovsky and an advocate for Zhitlovsky's vision of a Yiddish cultural renaissance in the diaspora.

For his grandfather, Abraham Rezack, a pious traditional Jew who spent his days and nights immersed in Talmud study, the speech had to be given in Hebrew, the language of traditional learning, the language of the Jewish past, the idiom of Jewish authenticity.

Harold Schulweis was born April 14, 1925, in the Bronx, an only child to immigrant parents. He was born into three worlds at once: twentieth-century America, a rich nationalist Yiddish culture, and the world of traditional Jewish learning. He would spend the rest of his life reconciling and unifying these worlds. All three of these worlds found their locus in the Bronx of Harold Schulweis' childhood.

Between the wars, the Bronx was the most intensely Jewish neighborhood in America. In 1905, the same year the brutal Kishinev pogrom sent masses of Jews toward America, the New York subway was extended into the Bronx. New immigrants and first-generation Jews moved up along the Grand Concourse. It was in the Bronx that revered Yiddish writer Sholem Aleichem had lived his last days and was buried. It was in the Bronx that Bess Myerson, the first Jewish woman chosen Miss America, was raised. By the time of young Harold's bar mitzvah, the Bronx was home to 592,000 Jews, 42 percent of the borough's population.[2] By one estimate, there were 260 registered synagogues and twice that many unregistered in the South Bronx alone.[3]

The Schulweis home was a refuge for Yiddish writers, poets, musicians, artists, thinkers, and cultural vagabonds who shared visions of the coming Jewish renaissance. Young Harold grew up surrounded by iconic images of Jewish dreamers and revolutionaries, Yiddish authors and poets, Yiddish actors and creative spirits.

Chaim Zhitlovsky, Moshe Schulweis' inspiration, presaged the major intellectual themes that would eventually preoccupy Harold's rabbinate. Zhitlovsky clearly perceived the crisis of Jewish modernity. The sacred Jewish narratives sustaining the Jewish people and their culture for centuries had been overturned by modern science and liberalism. Offered the promise of emancipation, the Jews of Western Europe gave up their identity as a Jewish people and turned to sterile philosophies of religious rationalism. Jews everywhere faced vicious anti-Semitism. In response, they turned either toward dogmatic religion or assimilationist ideologies. Neither strategy offered any promise for a Jewish future. Without religion as its bond, Zhitlovsky maintained, the collective of the Jewish people could only be held together by a resurgent secular Jewish culture. And that culture was in Yiddish:

> What is Jewish secular culture? Jewish secular culture in its modern form is Yiddish. It is not the first form of secular Jewish culture in our history. But it has brought a new feature into Jewish life. Previously, belonging to the Jewish people was associated with belonging to the Jewish faith. Leaving the Jewish faith meant leaving the Jewish people. Today, any Jew who lives with his people in the Yiddish language sphere, whether he believes in the Jewish religion or whether he is an atheist, belongs to the Jewish people. When a Jew satisfies

his spiritual-cultural needs in Yiddish—when he reads a Yiddish newspaper, or attends a Yiddish lecture, or sends his children to a Yiddish secular school, when he holds a conversation in Yiddish, he is without a doubt a Jew, a member of the Jewish people.[4]

"The national poetic rebirth of the Jewish people" envisioned by Zhitlovsky would push back assimilation and impart a new Jewish identity based on a synthesis of historical Jewish symbols and values, socialism, Yiddish language, and literary culture.[5]

Zhitlovsky separated Jewish nationalism from religion but maintained a deep respect for the power of Jewish religious symbols as nationalist insignia and treasured cultural artifacts:

Now, every religious yearning—for God, for holiness, for "something outside ourselves," for something transcendent—is a kind of poetry. But this is not the kind of rebirth of the Jewish religion that I have in mind. I am talking about conscious poetic expression, where religious images, myths, and ceremonies become precious to us not because we believe in their divine origin, but because our spirit is moved by their human beauty. They evoke in us such poetic feelings and thoughts that we consider them humanistic sanctities. Only this kind of rebirth can remain free of any metaphysical and theological traces. With the appearance of modern Jewish nationalism and its acceptance by the masses of our people, the possibility of a world-view is created that neither rejects its own people nor spits in the face of its religious parents.[6]

In his 1930 essay "Oifn Sheidveg" ("At the Crossroads"), Zhitlovsky insisted that his nationalism was secular but not anti-religious. The practice of religion, he maintained, belonged in the private sphere. Most especially, supernaturalism and coercive religious authority must be banished from Jewish discourse:

> With many of our people, secularism has become a synonym for anti-religion. It is nothing of the sort. In general, public life, secularism simply means that religion is a private matter. . . . In the educational and cultural sphere secularism means that we exclude anything which comes in the name of supernatural revelation, of Divine Authority, and which requires man that he follow the will of that authority.[7]

Moshe Schulweis lacked Zhitlovsky's sensitivity for the poetry of religious expression. As a young man in Poland, the elder Schulweis was subjected to cruelty at the hands of rabbis and religious teachers. He once witnessed his own father upturn the pushcart of a poor woman selling apples late on a Friday afternoon, too close to the onset of the Sabbath. Moshe held a lifelong bitterness toward religious Judaism, the faith practiced by those he called "fanatics." He would treat his son's achievements as a religious leader with ambivalence. His son, Harold, however, would one day articulate a philosophy of religious life that closely echoed Zhitlovsky's deep humanism, reverence for the poetry of ritual, and rejection of supernaturalism.

As a result of his father's fierce opposition to religion, young Harold grew up in an environment rich with Yiddish poetry and music but no prayer or ritual. Every afternoon after elementary school, he attended the *Yiddish schule,* the Yiddish culture supplementary school, but never learned Hebrew. Moshe took his son to the Yiddish theater and mingled socially with its stars, but until his twelfth year, young Harold had never stepped foot into a synagogue.

In a story reminiscent of a classic Hasidic tale, an eleven-year-old Harold Schulweis was wandering his Bronx neighborhood on the morning of Rosh Hashanah, his public school having declared a holiday. He saw crowds of people from the neighborhood dressed in their finest clothes and followed them into one of the buildings. Harold had accidentally found his way into a neighborhood synagogue. Because he was of small stature and because he was alone, the synagogue ushers assumed he was a younger child looking for his family and sent him up to the women's section. From the vantage of the balcony, Harold was overwhelmed by the synagogue worship service. Seventy-five years later, he could still recall the rabbi's stirring appeal for support: "Anyone can send a letter to God," explained the rabbi, "but if you want your letter to arrive, you need to affix a stamp."[8] Harold ran home and reported this astonishing experience to his mother. Ashamed that her son had grown so estranged from the Jewish religious life she knew from childhood, his mother brought him to her father.

Abraham Rezack, Harold's grandfather, his "Zeyde," was a relic of Eastern European traditional Jewry. A difficult and stubborn man, he sent his wife and children to work so he could spend his days in sacred study. He looked upon the young Harold as his immortality, and so Harold became his pupil each afternoon after school, studying for his bar mitzvah and sharing the books of Jewish sacred tradition. Every holiday through his teenage years was spent with his grandparents. It was at his Zeyde's insistence that Harold left public school and enrolled in the Israel Salanter Yeshiva in the seventh grade and continued his high school education at Yeshiva University's Teachers Academy. His Zeyde opened Harold's eyes to the sacred Jewish tradition of learning. Zeyde represented the life of the book:

> I remember once staying at my Zeyde's apartment for a holiday. I got up in the middle of the night, maybe three o'clock in the morning, and came into the kitchen for a glass of water, and there was my Zeyde, sitting with a Gemara, learning. He was not a rabbi. He was not learning for any other purpose but to learn, as a Jew should learn. I realized that he really lived that life.[9]

Raised in three languages, in three worlds, Harold Schulweis' upbringing captures the experience of first-generation American-born Jews at the beginning of the twentieth century—a community searching for its identity in America and its way of Jewish life. Schulweis' mother, father, and grandfather personify the forces grappling for priority in this American Jewish experience. They embody the questions he would spend a lifetime addressing: Can Jews speak the language of America, participate in its culture, contribute to its civilization, and still remain Jewish? Can they acclimate to this new environment without giving up what is authentic to their tradition? What kind of Jews would America make them? What can be preserved from the Jewish past, and what must be discarded? What must be reinvented, and what must be renewed?

In his thought and career, Harold Schulweis would come to speak all three languages. He assimilated his Zeyde's love of learning and ideas and became a lover of Jewish texts. In his articles and addresses, Jewish authenticity is consistently substantiated by textual citations. His writing is marbled with quotations from the Bible, the Talmud, medieval Jewish authorities, and Hasidic stories. Jewish truth, he demonstrates, begins and ends in the text. At the same time, he internalized the love for the Jewish people and Jewish culture from his father's Yiddish circle, as well as his father's rebellion against established forms of Jewish life. While eschewing the socialism of the *Forverts*, he assumed the insistent demand for social and economic justice, and his concern for the disenfranchised was expressed by the best of Yiddish culture. From his mother, Schulweis grasped that life must be lived in the present tense. Jews are not in America—or for that matter, in modernity—either tentatively or temporarily. Judaism must live in the here and now. Jews must see themselves as citizens of this civilization and embrace the moment.

Fluent in all three languages, Schulweis devoted his life to the project of reconciling and harmonizing them. In his religious thought and social activism, he attempted to persuade his fiercely antireligious father that traditional religious Judaism need not be cruel and authoritarian. At its heart, traditional Judaism shines with all the poetry and beauty celebrated by Zhitlovsky. The practice of religion is not antithetical to the pursuit of social justice. At its best, religion does not overturn the applecarts of the poor and the powerless. On the contrary, Torah does not permit the Jew to stand idly by the humiliation of the poor and the weak but is devoted to the cultivation of

Jewish conscience, the development of *hesed, rachmanut, tze-dek*—kindness, mercy, and justice. Authentic Judaism recognizes the presence of God in the drive to heal a broken world.

Schulweis tried to prove to his grandfather the insufficiency of a piety celebrated for its own sake, a piety isolated from the world of real people. God is not detached from human affairs. Jewish religiosity is no sanctuary from the world. He frequently reminded his congregations that according to tradition, a synagogue must have a window so that holiness may interact with social reality. The most authentic expression of worship, Schulweis argued, is the activist life of conscience, the constant quest for justice. The Jew is not permitted to spend life in a holy cave of meditation when the vision of *tikkun olam*—healing a broken world—is yet so acutely unfulfilled.

For his mother, Schulweis embraced America, not as an escape from Jewish identity but as an opportunity to build a new edifice of Jewish life upon the wisdom of the Jewish past. He enthusiastically accepted the invitation of America to add his voice, an authentically Jewish voice, to the chorus of American culture—to become a creator of America, reshaping and reinventing America to reflect the ethics of Jewish tradition.

In an ironic way, Schulweis' upbringing taught him the value of community, a driving theme of his rabbinate. Moshe Schulweis was a harsh, controlling man. Young Harold never forgot the emotional abuse meted out on his helpless mother and her loneliness in a difficult marriage. An only child with very little extended family, Harold knew his own moments of loneliness. The sanctity of human relationship, its value as an essential part of human being, was impressed upon Schulweis from a very young age and as a very painful lesson.[10] The very deep need to live in community ultimately explains why Schulweis declined numerous invitations to enter academia, despite his prodigious scholarly productivity, and remained in the active pulpit rabbinate through the last weeks of his life. His congregation became his extended family, and he cherished his connections with them.

Formation

In sharp contrast to his father's experience of authoritarian tradition, Harold discovered the gentle, ethical face of religious Judaism. He found a Judaism that was intellectually alive and open. The yeshiva culture he encountered at Israel Salanter was accepting and nurturing. When his family went to the Catskills for a summer retreat, his Hebrew teacher, Rabbi Solomon Wind, sent him a postcard every day, written in Hebrew, so that he would continue his learning over the vacation. Enrolling in the *Beit Midrash L'Morim* (Teachers Academy) at Yeshiva University, he encountered an environment that welcomed his intellectual drive. Under the leadership of Rabbi Samuel Belkin, Yeshiva University in the 1940s prided itself on its intellectual openness and its ability to prompt creative conversations between Torah and secular knowledge. Schulweis attached himself to Alexander Litman, Yeshiva University's sole professor of philosophy. Under Litman he met the masters of Western philosophy. Litman's influence followed Schulweis for the rest of his life:

> [Litman] taught with earnestness, ardor, and I followed him in every class he taught. His philosophical *weltanschauung* was so magnificent that it played an important

role in my rabbinate. Because of Litman, I was able to see the "forest" of Judaism without it being blocked by the "trees."[11]

Litman was a maverick who was often at loggerheads with the administration of Yeshiva University for publicly questioning the tenets of Orthodox faith. He took full advantage of Belkin's offer of intellectual freedom at the university. His independence was celebrated in the tribute offered him in the 1956 edition of the Yeshiva University student yearbook, the *Masmid*. Honoring Litman's twenty-five years of "service to the students of Yeshiva College," the student editor misquotes Thomas Carlyle: "No iron-clad chain, or outward force of any kind, could ever compel the soul of man to believe or disbelieve; he will reign and believe by his own indefeasible light—that judgment of his."[12] Perhaps as a reflection of Litman's singular independence of mind and defiance of ideological convention, the Yeshiva College yearbook editor chose to omit the closing phrase of Carlyle's quotation: "He will reign and believe there by the Grace of God alone." A curious omission for a senior faculty member of Yeshiva University!

Schulweis found an enriching environment at the university. He participated in drama and debate societies, and he starred in the year-ending show of 1944. In a letter to an interviewer, he recalled his years there fondly:

I graduated from Yeshiva College in June 1945 with an illustrious class. Some of my classmates continued at Yeshiva, some went to the Jewish Theological Seminary, some to Hebrew Union College, some to secular schools;

but all were raised in a Yeshiva ambience that was inclusive, compassionate, and loving. Yeshiva remains with me a God-intoxicated institution with a love of our people extended to all denominations and all schools of thought.[13]

Among the sixty-four men in the graduating class, eleven were asked to write brief essays in the class yearbook; Schulweis was among them. This was his first published work. His four-page essay, "Freedom and the Religion of the State," foreshadowed the themes of religion and morality that would come to dominate his mature years. Can religion be immoral? Or does that violate the very definition of religion? Must a religion be tolerated if it teaches behaviors that violate the collective sense of the common good?[14]

The very definition of religion, the young Schulweis argued, involves "the general improvement of man, economically, socially, spiritually." Religion in its truest form "cries out for the welfare of Man, not men; it strives to make him a better man; it asserts his G-d-given rights to economic, political and social justice; it re-affirms man's dignity and innate goodness."[15]

Any religion that violates basic morality is no religion at all and is therefore unworthy of tolerance. Religion, he insisted, is the moral heart of civil society and can never be separated from the politics. Rendering unto Caesar what is Caesar's and unto God what is God's deprives both religion and society. "This false cleavage has separated the soul from the body, leaving the body unclean, uninspired, doomed to eternal evil and hopelessness. This religious schism from politics makes of religion a dormant, static metaphysics, a theory motionless in the void."[16] The essay concludes with a statement of ideology that would become the centerpiece of Schulweis' religious thought. As its function is to advance morality, "Religion can be tested on empirical grounds. The sincerity of religious theory is to be manifested in human behavior, in the relationship between man and his neighbor."[17]

Upon his graduation in 1945, Harold was still undecided about his future. Several classmates stayed on at Yeshiva University's rabbinical training program. Others went on to graduate training elsewhere. It took a newspaper article to set him on his future course.

On June 12, 1945, the leaders of the Union of Orthodox Rabbis of the United States and Canada gathered in New York's Hotel McAlpin to formally excommunicate Rabbi Mordecai Kaplan for "atheism, heresy, and disbelief in the basic tenets of Judaism" and to publicly burn his *Sabbath Prayer Book*. The event disheartened Kaplan, who in his journal condemned "rabbinical gangsters who resort to Nazi methods in order to regain their authority."[18] It shocked the New York Jewish community, still reeling from the images of Nazi book burnings during the Holocaust. The event was reported in the *New York Times* on June 15, 1945, causing further consternation in the Jewish community.[19]

The report was read by the newly graduated Harold Schulweis. Having been taught by intellectual maverick Alexander Litman, Schulweis was intrigued by a rabbi who could earn such bitter condemnation from the Orthodox establishment. More, he was taken with the description of Kaplan's project as described by the *New York Times*: "The preparation of the book,

Dr. Kaplan explained, was motivated by a desire to develop a religious service that would give 'modern-minded Jews a form of worship in which they could participate with devotion and sanctity.'"[20]

This project fired Schulweis' imagination.[21] It ultimately inspired him to enroll in the Rabbinical School of the Jewish Theological Seminary and initiated a lifelong relationship with Kaplan. Schulweis was drawn to Kaplan by their shared conviction that Judaism cannot be shielded from the revolution of modernity. Modernity was a new moment in Jewish history. The future of Judaism depended upon the arrival of a new interpretation of Jewish beliefs, a reinvention of institutions, and a rethinking of Jewish practice. The opening note of Kaplan's magnum opus, *Judaism as a Civilization*, sounds this alarm: "Before the beginning of the 19th century all Jews regarded Judaism as a privilege; since then most Jews have come to regard it as a burden."[22]

The young Schulweis resonated with Kaplan's boldness in addressing the Jewish community's failure to address contemporary questions. In a 1980 lecture on Kaplan's theology, he confessed,

> When I look over the history of the Jewish community, I am embarrassed by the fact that we had a very difficult time intelligently debating issues of religion, of ethics, of theology. When I was a young man, the first time I came across the excommunication of Baruch Spinoza I wanted to deny it. That's not like us. . . .
>
> There is no debate, no conversation going on in Jewish life today. . . . There is only one way of dealing with

dissent and that's to regard it as heresy. Sociologically, I can understand it very, very easily: We are a very frightened people.[23]

Schulweis cherished Kaplan's boldness in confronting the challenge. Kaplan's relentless pursuit of truth, his ferocious rejection of religious mediocrity, and his dauntless openness to new thinking were irresistible to the young Schulweis. In Kaplan Schulweis found a resolution of his childhood dilemma. Rejected by the Orthodox establishment, Kaplan was a rebel in the style of Harold's father, but he was also a *talmid hacham*, an accomplished rabbinic scholar, in the manner of his Zeyde.

Years later, Schulweis would celebrate Kaplan as a philosopher, a theologian, and, most significantly, as a "statesman," profoundly devoted to the task of defending his people from internal decay and degeneration. In contrast to the obsequious and destructive reverence for the Jewish past—what he called "quotational Judaism"—so prevalent at the Jewish Theological Seminary and in the rabbis it trained, Kaplan demanded that Judaism speak to the needs of contemporary Jewry. Kaplan, wrote Schulweis, "restored the present tense to Judaism."[24] Unlike so many of his colleagues and contemporaries, Kaplan was unafraid of the new. That earned him Schulweis' reverence and loyalty.

Outside of his relationship with Kaplan, Schulweis found the atmosphere at the Jewish Theological Seminary intellectually stagnant. The 1941 publication of Kaplan's radical *New Haggadah* made Kaplan an anathema, a loner in the seminary community. Faculty colleagues refused to sit next to him in meetings or ride the elevator with him. Schulweis found this atmosphere intolerable. In search of a more congenial intellectual environment, he retreated downtown and began coursework in philosophy at New York University under the philosopher Sidney Hook. Having attended a yeshiva high school, Yeshiva College, and the Jewish Theological Seminary, Schulweis' exposure to Sidney Hook and New York University was his first intellectual encounter outside the Jewish world. But Sidney Hook was not entirely outside the Jewish world.

Hook was born Jewish but was an avowed secularist, democratic socialist, and universalist. In an autobiographical note offered much later in his life, Hook reflected regret for his obliviousness to Jewish concerns:

[One thing] we were wrong about was the Jewish question. None of us were Zionists. We were sensitive to the national aspirations of all other persecuted people, were positively empathetic with them. Yet when it came to our kinfolk, we lapsed into proud universalism. We did not for a moment deny our Jewish origins, but we disapproved of what we thought was an excess of chauvinism. We were among the first to organize protests against anti-Semitism in Poland, in Germany, at the first sign of it in the Soviet Union, or in any corner of the world. But we were indifferent—when not overtly hostile—to Zionism, which we regarded as merely another variety of nationalism. Things changed, of course, after the U.N. established the state of Israel and the grim facts of the Holocaust were revealed.[25]

Hook was intrigued at the brilliant young rabbinical student who had come to study with him. He tried constantly to dissuade Schulweis from pursuing the rabbinate and persistently challenged him to defend his Judaism in a modern, intellectually sophisticated, and socially conscious idiom. Hook was not overtly antireligious. He maintained an "open-minded atheism" and possessed a deep respect for the psychological benefits of religious faith, so long as faith did not intrude into the political arena:

> It was from Feuerbach that Marx derived the view that "religion is the opium of the people" at a time when opium was not considered a degrading drug but an anodyne for suffering beyond the relief of medical treatment. Feuerbach recognized that in this world there will always be inconsolable suffering, resulting from death, tragedy, heart-breaking failure, whose pangs might be stilled by the illusions of immortality and other psychologically sustaining myths. Not everyone has the courage to face a precarious world in which nothing is guaranteed except ultimate extinction. It is needlessly cruel to mock or jeer at such private beliefs—the assumption being of course that they are private and not institutionalized, requiring no public recognition or support.[26]

In Kaplan and Hook, Schulweis once again found himself drawn between two powerful personalities, a struggle that mirrored the tension between his pious grandfather and his socialist, Yiddishist father. Both Kaplan and Hook had studied under John Dewey at Columbia University and were deeply influenced by Dewey's pragmatism. Kaplan, turning inward, brought Dewey's philosophical program to bear on the problems of Judaism in modernity. The very name of his movement, Reconstructionism, echoed the title of Dewey's seminal work, *Reconstruction in Philosophy*. Hook, who also did his doctorate under Dewey, turned outward and devoted his career to synthesizing Dewey's pragmatism with Marxism as a method for addressing contemporary social issues.

Mordecai Kaplan would become Schulweis' intellectual godfather. He bequeathed to Schulweis his intellectual boldness, his genius for turning grand ideas into tangible programs and initiatives, and his faith that a reimagined Judaism could fruitfully coexist with modernity. Sidney Hook would forever be Schulweis' imagined audience. He was the skeptical, alienated Jewish intellectual. Schulweis' principal theological statement, his 1994 book *For Those Who Can't Believe*, is addressed to an imaginary character, David, who has Jewish background but no Jewish connection. David is a younger expression of Sidney Hook's skepticism and alienation from Jewish life.

Reconciling his two masters, Schulweis sought to demonstrate to Kaplan that Jewish peoplehood must not be self-absorbed but face outward, taking responsibility for the world. The Jewish tradition required not just reconstruction but expansion. At the same time, he argued to Hook that the only sound basis for a committed universalism is a strong sense of particularism. He sought to prove that religion, properly understood, could become a powerful impetus for social change, even more than Hook's Marxism.

When it came time to prepare a thesis for his master's degree, Schulweis confounded both his teachers and chose to write on Martin Buber. Hook tried to dissuade him from the topic, rejecting Buber's mysticism and existentialism as contrary to the empiricism and rationality he demanded of philosophy. But Schulweis persisted and completed what was, in 1952, the first English-language thesis written on Buber's thought. In the thesis Schulweis was very critical of Buber's mysticism. He noted Buber's failure to come to grips with the problem of evil, presented most radically in the Holocaust. Nevertheless, he appreciated Buber's emphasis on the centrality of relationship in human life and its implications for theology. Human beings, maintained Buber, do not meet God in lonely solitude, as Kierkegaard put forward, but in social solidarity and mutual responsibility.[27] This insight became a core theme of Schulweis' entire career.

Schulweis completed his rabbinical studies and was ordained a rabbi in May 1950. With the outbreak of the Korean War, newly ordained rabbis were required to stay in the New York area to be ready for service as military chaplains. Schulweis took a part-time rabbinical job as assistant to Rabbi Nathan Lubin at Temple Emanuel in Parkchester, New York. Rabbi Lubin offered the young rabbi very few opportunities to share his genius.

Schulweis' real love was philosophy. With a strong recommendation from Sidney Hook, Schulweis obtained a teaching position in the Philosophy Department at New York's City College, teaching a course on the philosophy of religion. Unsatisfied with the available textbooks, Schulweis assembled his own. His department chair, Daniel J. Bronstein, arranged for the publication of the book and assumed primary authorship credit. *Approaches to the Philosophy of Religion* was published in 1954 and remains a standard in the field.

Hook tried to persuade Schulweis to work toward his doctorate in philosophy and a tenured teaching position at City College. But that was not the direction of his ambition. When the military chaplaincy released him, Schulweis was determined to begin his career in the rabbinate. He was drawn to the West Coast, where the atmosphere was ripe for his creativity and vision.[28] Schulweis was a rebellious spirit in the confining community of the Jewish Theological Seminary, and the seminary leadership was only too glad to send him to the other side of the continent. On the recommendation of the seminary's vice chancellor, Simon Greenberg, Schulweis was offered the pulpit of Temple Beth Abraham in Oakland, California. In the summer of 1952, Schulweis went west to begin his career and a new life.

Family

At a Purim dance held at the Jewish Theological Seminary in 1945, Schulweis met Malkah (née Muriel) Savod, still just a senior in high school. He was immediately smitten. Mustering the courage and the cash to ask her out, he took her to the Automat for their first date. By the third date, young Harold proposed marriage. She responded, "But I don't even know you!" He retorted, "You will!" Six months later, she accepted his proposal. Malkah and Harold were married by Rabbi Morris N. Kertzer on June 22, 1947, at the Park Avenue Synagogue, where Malkah taught Sunday school. When Rabbi Kertzer stumbled over a few of the words in the ketubah during the ceremony, Harold's grandfather assertively corrected his reading.

Malkah studied literature at Hunter College while Harold completed his studies. By the time Harold accepted the pulpit in Oakland, Malkah was pregnant with their first child. Their son Seth was born in January 1953, followed by Ethan in 1954, and then his daughter, Alyssa, in 1956.

Malkah and Harold shared an unusually affectionate and close marriage. She was not only a life companion but also his *hevrutah*, his intellectual partner, critic, and muse. Malkah was the only one Harold relied upon and trusted to preview, edit, and critique his writing and speaking. Her review of his sermons was the one that mattered most.

In Oakland, their first pulpit, Malkah took up life as homemaker, mother of small children, and hostess. She frequently entertained congregants and community leaders in their home. As the children grew older, Malkah returned to school with Harold's encouragement and completed a master's degree in literature at University of California, Berkeley. When they moved to Encino, she continued to be the gracious hostess, frequently welcoming congregational and community leaders into their home. Once her children were independent, Malkah took a position as an instructor in English literature at the San Fernando Valley State College (later known as California State University, Northridge). In the late 1980s she completed training in family and personal counseling and established a private practice as a psychotherapist. As Harold consciously shaped his rabbinic role, Malkah established a firmly defined role within the synagogue. She was the rabbi's wife and a professional with her own life—never a "rebbetzin." She was visible in the synagogue, attending synagogue services regularly, particularly when Harold was speaking, and participated in important synagogue and community events. Each year, she presented a lecture on Jewish literature to the Sisterhood learning program, a program that was highly anticipated and celebrated. Within the congregation, she elicited deep respect as a humble and gracious personality, supportive of her husband and the community, but she was always a professional and recognized as a formidable intellectual in her right. As she set boundaries for herself, she also protected her children from the "fishbowl" syndrome of clergy kids. She and Harold never allowed their children to be judged by the congregation. When his sons demanded to come to synagogue services in jeans, work shirts, and boots—the uniform of 1960s rebels—Harold announced that all youngsters so attired would be welcome. To members who objected, he retorted, "At least they come to shul!" When Ethan left college to make aliyah to Israel, Harold and Malkah shook off the whispers of gossip and expressed pride in their son's commitment. Malkah Schulweis shared the independence of mind that characterized Harold's rabbinate and carried it over into their family life.

Oakland, California, 1952–1970

The American writer Gertrude Stein once derided Oakland with the quip, "There's no *there* there!" But, in fact, Oakland had been a significant city since the California gold rush of 1849. In 1869, Oakland became the terminus of the transcontinental railroad, and the city grew rapidly thereafter. Jews played an important role in the city's history from its beginnings. The first Jewish cemetery was dedicated there in 1865, and First Hebrew Congregation was founded in 1875. In 1893, the congregation affiliated with the Union of American

Hebrew Congregations and identified as a Reform temple. As Eastern European Jews began arriving in the 1880s, a community of observant Polish immigrants formed Beth Jacob Congregation in 1893.[29]

In 1907, a group of Hungarian and Lithuanian immigrants split from Beth Jacob to form the Hungarische, or Hungarian, shul. The shul met in a former Chinese temple in far West Oakland until its leaders located a building at the foot of Oakland's prominent Harrison Street. A wealthy widow, Mrs. Bertha Bercovich, offered the money to buy the building on the condition that the synagogue would be named for her late husband, Abraham. Thus, Temple Beth Abraham found its first home. In 1925, the State of California seized the temple through eminent domain and razed the building to construct the Posey tube tunnel to Alameda. For four years, the temple congregation wandered from place to place, holding religious services in storefronts, churches, and other borrowed facilities. In 1928, Temple Beth Abraham hired its first rabbi, Rabbi Moses Goldberg, who set out immediately to build a permanent home for the congregation. Rabbi Goldberg was tragically killed when a train hit his car on his way home from an errand to collect a sizable check for the temple's building campaign. In 1929, the temple constructed a majestic building on Perry Street, later renamed MacArthur Boulevard. At the time, it was one of the largest Jewish sanctuaries west of Chicago. In order to attract a younger generation of members, the new sanctuary was built with "family pews," allowing men and women to sit together as families. With this architectural decision, Beth Abraham declared its allegiance to the new Conservative movement of American Judaism.[30]

Following World War II, Oakland experienced a population boom. The war brought workers from across the country for jobs in its shipyards, war industries, canning factories, and rail yards. The young Rabbi Harold Schulweis arrived in Oakland to find a temple ready to grow, with a younger generation eager to begin Jewish family life. Schulweis set to work organizing a religious school to accommodate the rapidly expanding population of young families with young children and began a campaign to raise funds for a school building.[31] The school building was completed in 1955. By 1964, the temple membership approached six hundred families, the largest it had ever been—and has ever been since.

Having grown up with no synagogue experience and without a personal family rabbi, Schulweis' sole model for his rabbinate was his mentor, Mordecai Kaplan. Like Kaplan, he believed modernity demanded a new, reconstructed Judaism. He saw Temple Beth Abraham as his laboratory for shaping that new Judaism and set out on this quest with all the bravado of a young revolutionary, unafraid to overturn set traditions and unabashed by controversy.

Schulweis began by upending the synagogue's ritual practices. He fired the long-serving cantor and sought a prayer leader who would engage the congregation in collective prayer.[32] In place of the traditional Sabbath morning sermon, he introduced an interactive Sabbath morning Torah discussion and distributed a weekly reading list so that congregants might come prepared for the discussion. Most significantly, he changed the role of women in the congregation's ritual life. Kaplan had introduced the bat mitzvah ceremony for girls in 1922. The women at Temple Beth Abraham of the 1950s had no role in synagogue ritual life or congregational leadership. Women were not permitted on the bimah and the congregation did not celebrate girls' *b'not mitzvah*. Schulweis began a conversation within the congregation that soon led to a more egalitarian stance, inviting girls to celebrate bat mitzvah, counting women in the minyan, and allowing women *aliyot* to the Torah.[33]

At Temple Beth Abraham in Oakland, Schulweis found the three rabbinic voices that would characterize his rabbinic career—his theological voice, his prophetic voice, and his community voice. Schulweis never abandoned Kaplan's core convictions that modernity demanded a new Judaism, but in developing the voices of his rabbinate he surpassed his mentor in significant ways, shaping a rabbinate beyond Kaplan's conception and beyond the imagination of his contemporaries.

The Theological Voice

As Schulweis stepped into his new pulpit, he brought with him the conviction that the principal obstacle to modern Jews' participation in Jewish life was theology. A significant task of the modern rabbinate is to shape a new understanding of Jewish beliefs. Mordecai Kaplan opened his magisterial work *The Meaning of God in Modern Jewish Religion* with a simple statement of the dilemma of Jewish belief in modernity: "Traditional Jewish religion belongs to an altogether different universe of discourse from that of the modern man."[34]

Like Kaplan, Schulweis began with the opinion that the obstacle to belief was a problem of knowledge. Modern Jews could not accept the truths of their tradition because they knew the world in ways that differed from their ancestors. Tradition placed God in the realm of the supernatural. Tradition believed in miracles, revelation, and prayer as transactions between the natural and the supernatural worlds. Modern science demolished this worldview. The foundational premise of modern science is that nature is ubiquitous and that the patterns of phenomena elevated as "laws of nature" hold sway in all places under all circumstances without exception. There is no realm of the supernatural. Science separated modern Jews from the cognitive foundations of traditional faith. Modern Jews, Kaplan posited, required a new conceptual groundwork for their religious life.

Schulweis never completely departed from this line of thinking. But the daily routine of a congregational rabbi demonstrated to him that science was not the principal challenge to faith for modern Jews. Modern Jews, by and large, did not reject traditional faith because they found it hard to reconcile with their science worldview but rather because it had so little to say at moments of personal and collective tragedy. It was the problem of evil—when bad things happened to good people—that overturned faith:

> In the cavern of darkness, the cry "Why me?" cuts across all generations and all ages. Murmured or shouted, it is for many the straw that breaks the back of faith. "Why me?" "Why us?" Asked in different situations and in different stages of life, it clings to religion's Achilles' heal.[35]

The rabbi meets the problem of evil not as a theoretical issue of the study or the classroom but as an acute existential challenge on a daily basis. Schulweis reflected on this in a 1957 article entitled "The Problem of Evil and the Pastoral Situation":

The testing ground of any theology is the arena of our prosaic lives. Our theology must be rooted in our daily existence and respond to the challenges posed by the problems of man. For the rabbi, this challenge takes place within the pastoral situation. Here, the rabbi functions as a *pastoral theologian*, not as speculative metaphysician or clinical psychologist. The pastoral situation is his laboratory, in which he can test the value of his theological commitments. For, beside the hospital bed, or seated close to the mourner on a low stool, one must counsel an individual whose crisis has called forth an urge to ask and listen with deadly earnestness.[36]

Shortly after his arrival at Temple Beth Abraham, the child of a prominent member of the synagogue died. The young rabbi came to do the funeral and found himself stammering the traditional formulae in the face of grieving parents.[37] Day in and day out, the rabbi confronts tragedy and the eternal question, Why me? Schulweis could find no solace in traditional theologies. The tradition's belief in an omnipotent, omniscient, and perfectly good divinity offered no explanation for evil, and little comfort to those who suffered. In many traditional sources, evil is interpreted as punishment for human transgression. The graveside benediction *Baruch Dayan Emet* grew out of the Talmudic idea that death comes as a judgment, a punishment for transgression (cf. Talmud Shabbat 55a). In his daily pastoral work comforting parishioners through experiences of loss and grief, Schulweis found this intolerable. Having internalized Kaplan's ethic of theological candor, he refused to mumble the words, or recite them quickly without translation, as so many rabbis are wont to do.

Ironically, evil is the one issue Kaplan's theology is particularly unsuited to address. Rooted in the sunny optimism of the nineteenth century's faith in progress, Kaplan's faith in God as the "power that makes for salvation"[38] leaves little room for the tragic dimension of human existence.

In addition to the daily barrage of human suffering absorbed by the congregational rabbi, two additional factors exacerbated Schulweis' dilemma—one micro, one macro.

Schulweis' youngest child, Alyssa, was born in 1956 with a severe heart defect. She was hospitalized frequently during the first years of her life. The young rabbi and his wife spent days and nights sitting vigil over their gravely ill child. Watching his young daughter struggle for life amid a hospital ward filled with families experiencing the tragedy of desperately ill children removed the problem of evil from the realm of abstraction and made it excruciatingly personal and vivid.

At the same time, the evil depths of the Holocaust were being revealed. In 1961, Adolf Eichmann was tried in Jerusalem. In 1966, Schulweis' rabbinical school classmate, Richard Rubenstein, published *After Auschwitz*, a radical theology declaring that all traditional theologies are obsolete in the face of the radical evil of the Shoah. Schulweis was as unsettled by the Holocaust as Rubenstein, but he rejected the radical steps of Rubenstein's thought because he worried about the effect such a theology of despair would have on future generations of Jews:

> To know me, to know us, is necessarily to understand the Holocaust. The Holocaust remains the dominant psychic reality of our lives. . . .

It is clear that the children must know it all. And yet I wonder whether in transmitting the memory of the Holocaust I lay a stone upon their hearts. Do I plant in them the seeds of cynicism? . . . Do I inadvertently rob them of the possibility of a normal and healthy relationship with a non-Jewish world?[39]

Schulweis' confrontation with the problem of evil—his own personal experience, his experience as a community's pastor, and the radical evil of the Holocaust—would push him to seek a new interpretation of core Jewish beliefs. Schulweis concurred with Abraham Joshua Heschel's observation that the problem of Jewish modernity is not the corroding influence of science or secular philosophy but the irrelevance of Judaism, as it was then taught, to the real problems of life.[40] In his search for a new narrative, Schulweis stepped beyond his teacher Kaplan's theological solutions. Kaplan was correct that a new Jewish theology was desperately needed. But Kaplan misunderstood the problem. For Kaplan, the core question of modern Judaism was one of reconciling modern ways of knowing with traditional beliefs about God. Schulweis discovered that the problem is not epistemological but moral—not reconciling science and faith but finding the presence of God in a world of real and radical evil.

Searching for new ways to frame a solution, Schulweis enrolled at the Pacific School of Religion, the largest nondenominational school in the Graduate Theological Union in Berkeley, to begin research for his doctorate in theology. His conversations with Christian thinkers opened new possibilities. In 1971, Schulweis completed his dissertation, entitled

"The Idea of Perfection and the Moral Failure of Traditional Theodicies: Towards a Predicate Theology." The dissertation was published as *Evil and the Morality of God* in 1984. Schulweis offered the bold argument that all theodicies fail. Theology cannot reconcile God's morality with the reality of human suffering. In response to the problem of evil, all classical and modern theologies either compromise God's goodness or denigrate human moral sensibility. They demand that the believer split morality between heaven and earth, asserting that what is moral for God is not moral for humanity. This split, Schulweis argues, is an anathema, pushing morality out of religion. In response, Schulweis offered a proposal for a predicate theology, a theistic humanism celebrating human moral responsibility. These ideas had animated Schulweis since the early 1960s[41] but found their most academic and thorough treatment in his dissertation.

The Prophetic Voice

When Schulweis was a boy, his father took him to Madison Square Garden to hear Stephen S. Wise and Abba Hillel Silver. These rabbis became heroes to him. Their prophetic voices and the image of the rabbi as activist never left him.[42] These boyhood impressions shaped Schulweis' rabbinate.

Like the heroic rabbis who preceded him, Schulweis built his rabbinate upon oratory. He found his natural oratorical gifts in the drama club and debate society of Yeshiva College and developed them under Kaplan's tutelage. He discovered the power to change minds and hearts with the spoken word. Schulweis' sermons and classes were meticulously researched and carefully constructed with a poetic sensitivity for language and turns of phrase. His talks were always written out, revised through numerous drafts, and conscientiously rehearsed.

At Temple Beth Abraham, Schulweis spoke to the congregation three times each weekend—at a late Friday night service, at the Sabbath morning discussion, and at a Sunday morning "Coffee and Conversations" program. Where so many of his contemporaries focused exclusively on welcoming children into synagogue life, Schulweis rejected this "juvenile Judaism" and aimed his oratory squarely at adults and adult Jewish life. He consciously spoke in the intellectual idiom he had used in his classes at City College and expected his congregants to rise to his intellectual level. It was his intention to demonstrate through his idiom that Judaism in particular, and religion in general, could be intellectually mature, politically challenging, and morally contemporary. His vocabulary on the pulpit often reached such heights of obscurity, congregants quipped that membership to Beth Abraham came with a free gift—a dictionary of philosophical terms.[43]

Schulweis convinced the temple leadership to open the synagogue balcony during High Holiday services to students and faculty from the nearby campuses of the University of California, Mills College, and San Francisco State University. Because of the rhetorical power, intellectual sophistication, and political timeliness of his talks, a large contingent of collegians and professors filled the Beth Abraham sanctuary, which further raised the intellectual temperature of the synagogue.[44]

Kaplan had focused narrowly on the particularist dilemmas of Jews and Judaism in modernity. Speaking week after week to his congregation, Schulweis discovered that the Judaism of his congregants was projected on a much broader canvas of community, national, and world events. He discovered that Judaism could be a tool for examining and engaging a broad spectrum of contemporary social issues, in the same way his philosophy professor Sidney Hook had used philosophy. Judaism could not be taught in isolation from the world around him. The momentous events of the day required a Jewish understanding. And more, the historical moment demanded a response not solely in scholarship but in action and activism. In his Oakland pulpit, Schulweis discovered his prophetic voice. The most important word in the Jewish prayer book, he taught, was *therefore*, the word that bridges the inner world of conscience and reflection with the empirical world of acts and consequences. Every sermon led to a "therefore," a call to action, a plan, a new initiative.

History is filled with irony. The leadership of the Jewish Theological Seminary knew that Schulweis was a maverick. They were only too glad to send him to the far reaches of the West Coast where he could not harm the core of American Jewish life. They could not foresee that Schulweis' Oakland neighborhood and its environs would become the epicenter of so many cultural upheavals that rocked American life in the middle of the twentieth century—the Berkeley free speech movement, the rise of the 1960s counterculture, the "hippies," the sexual revolution, the drug culture, the escalation of the Vietnam War and the anti-war protest movement, the civil rights movement, the advent of Black Power, the beginnings of feminism, and the birth of countercultural Judaism. Schulweis found himself at the center of it all.

Schulweis' rabbinate turned from Kaplan's focus on the inner life of Jews to a politically conscious social activism. He turned from the task of reconstructing Jewish life to the challenge of healing the world. The political and cultural revolutions erupting around him forced Schulweis to develop a new Jewish moral and religious idiom—a language of Jewish conscience. Two examples:

The summer of 1967 was known as the "Summer of Love" in San Francisco, marking the flowering of the San Francisco counterculture. Schulweis met that counterculture at Passover in 1967. In Temple Beth Abraham's centennial journal, Schulweis recalled the moment:

> When I went to Haight-Ashbury, I realized that there were many Jewish young men and women who were on the streets. I asked for help from the [Jewish] Federation, and they assured me that there were no Jews among the hippies. I knew they were wrong. . . . I recall vividly asking my Christian counterpart in the Haight-Ashbury church to allow us to use the church's basement for a second Seder. It was an unlikely event spread by word of mouth. When we entered the church basement, there were over 200 Jewish youngsters ready for the Seder. I remain indebted to the Sisterhood of Beth Abraham for providing the meals for the second Seder, from the matzo to the maror and charoseth. . . . I needed readers for the Passover Seder, and at random called on one young man and asked him whether he knew the Chad Gadya. He was wearing a beard, bangles, beads, and bongo drums, and he answered me, "You bet Rabbi! I know Chad Gadya. You want it with drums or without drums?"[45]

More than simply seeking to reconnect alienated young people with their religious traditions, Schulweis recognized and celebrated all that was deeply Jewish and deeply moral in their countercultural rebellion. With or without drums, the young of Haight-Ashbury pointed out to Schulweis what was missing from the life of his Jewish "establishment." In their bangles and beads, Schulweis discovered that the rebels of Haight-Ashbury had left behind the superficiality of their parents' values and the moral emptiness of the conventional Judaism of their upbringing for reasons that were profoundly Jewish. These were far from rebels "without a cause."

> That evening and for many months, we recognized the vacuity of bourgeois life that many of these entitled kids were seeking to escape. That Seder for many was freedom from mindless materialism to Jewish moral idealism.[46]

Schulweis participated actively in the civil rights movement in Oakland, serving as the only white member of the board of the Oakland NAACP. He witnessed the rise of the Black Power movement and the growing alienation of the African American community from the Jewish community. He recalled that when his eldest son, Seth, celebrated his bar mitzvah at Temple Beth Abraham in 1966, the entire NAACP board attended the service. But when Ethan, his second child, had his bar mitzvah just two years later, none of the black leaders attended.[47]

The alienation of the African American community from the Jewish community and the growth of black anti-Semitism disturbed Schulweis, as it did his community. It was seen as a betrayal of the close alliance between Jews and blacks in the fight for civil rights, an alliance cemented by the 1964 martyrdom of three young civil rights workers in Mississippi, two of whom, Andrew Goodman and Michael Schwerner, were Jewish. The growing alienation was evident in the violent riots that erupted in American cities in the mid-1960s. Some two-thirds of the businesses destroyed in the 1965 Watts riots in Southern California were owned by Jews.

Schulweis endeavored to understand how the communities had grown apart. An African American community leader took him for a personal tour of the Oakland black ghetto and pointed out the pawnshops and ghetto slums owned and operated by Jews, particularly by members of Temple Beth Abraham. Suddenly Schulweis saw the anti-Semitism of the African American community in a new light.

At the High Holidays of 1965, Schulweis delivered the sermon that would eventually change his relationship with his Beth Abraham congregation. He began by describing the tragedy of black anti-Semitism and decried the broken alliance between the Jewish and black communities. The congregation found this agreeable. But then Schulweis turned to the deeper question: What were the causes of black anti-Semitism? Citing a recent study by University of Chicago professor David Caplovitz on the exploitive practices of low-income marketing, and noting that in most cases the merchants were Jews and their victims black, Schulweis presented an unsettling question: In what way are Jews complicit in the exploitation of African Americans? In the published version of the sermon, entitled "The Voice of Esau," he explains,

> James Baldwin in *Notes of a Native Son* spelled it out
> clearly. "Jews in Harlem are small tradesmen, rent

collectors, real estate agents and pawn brokers; they operate in accordance with the American business tradition of exploiting Negroes, and they are therefore identified with oppression and are hated for it. I remember meeting no Negro in the years of growing up who would really trust a Jew, and few who did not, indeed, exhibit for them the blackest contempt."[48]

The prophetic conscience of the rabbi was unwilling to let the problem remain impersonal and abstract. Schulweis turned his attention toward his own community at Beth Abraham, to those he knew owned the pawnshops, the slums, and the businesses well known for their exploitive practices in the black underclass:

That cry is hurled against those who call themselves Jews and who rob the blind, setting a stumbling block before them. Those who exploit them do more damage to you and me, to your children and mine, to the name Jew, than a thousand Jewish freedom riders may ever hope to repair. Those who practice "*Genevat da'at*" (stealth of mind), and "*Onaat d'varim*" (practicing oppression by words), desecrate the name of the God of Israel and the image of the Jew. That Negro trapped in the ghetto does not care what the rabbi preaches or what the Jewish organizations declare in formal resolution. That Negro knows us through those most visible to him: the salesman, merchant, creditor, landlord, with whom he deals daily in his quest for life. It is no small irony to contemplate that the very same men who violate the ethics of our tradition and create such resentment and hate may be making generous contributions to Jewish defense agencies which seek to battle anti-Semitism.[49]

Undaunted by the consternation of his congregation, the rabbi called for community-wide *kaparah*, moral cleansing. He demanded that the community expose and confront those responsible:

There is always an alternative to complicity with evil. The alternative for the Jew is to get out. GET OUT. [*sic*] This is no way for a Jew to make a living. Exploitation of the weak and ignorant is no way for a Jew to make his profit. It may truly be that you and I cannot clean up the slums, or eliminate the ghetto—but we can at least say, "Our hands have not shed this blood." If we cannot demand of ourselves surrender of this kind of parasitic existence, what does Judaism amount to? . . .

I ask of the respectable members of the Jewish community who verbally support the cause of the Negro community, what are we doing with those discriminators and exploiters who deceive, who tax and take advantage of such people and frustrate them? I ask whether we are guilty of duplicity, of a conspiracy not so much of silence but of passivity. I ask whether there is in the synagogue an "Ethical Actions" Committee? Whether the Jewish Welfare Federation and Jewish Community Relations Committee and the Synagogue Council can organize itself so that, with evidence, it can confront those who desecrate the name of God in business practices and say to them: "We come to you in the name of the Jewish people, and in the name of the God of Israel we demand that you cease this exploitation."[50]

The sermon changed Schulweis' relationship with his congregation. It made him a hero in the eyes of the young Jews who came to hear him from the Berkeley campus and a problem for the leadership of the congregation struggling to balance their annual budget. Ironically, his call to "get out" would lead soon to his own departure. For Schulweis, it marked the transition of his rabbinate from the cerebral role prescribed by Kaplan to the prophetic, activist stance initiated by Stephen S. Wise a generation earlier.

The Voice of Community

Schulweis wrote the first English-language thesis on the philosophy of Martin Buber. In 1952, he received word that Buber was coming through New York on his way to a lectureship in Los Angeles. He cabled Buber and requested an interview, identifying himself as a writer for the *Reconstructionist* magazine. When the interview was complete, Schulweis mentioned the thesis. Buber asked to read it and promised to return it a month later on his return trip through New York. When they met again, Buber presented Schulweis with a page of handwritten notes. He asked Schulweis, "Why did you reject me before you even read me?" Years later, Schulweis acknowledged that Buber was right.[51] Trained in Kaplan's rationalism and Hook's pragmatism, Schulweis had little patience for Buber's approach to philosophy, his mysticism, and his elusive style of his writing.

In the late 1960s, Schulweis was invited to teach a class on contemporary Jewish thought at the University of Judaism (now American Jewish University) in Los Angeles. In preparation for the class, he went back and reread Buber. His fifteen years in the pulpit opened his eyes to elements of Buber's thought he had never considered before, particularly the concept of relationship and its role in religious life. The 1960s saw the arrival of a literature sharply critical of the loneliness inherent in American individualism. Schulweis experienced this firsthand. Jewish life assumes a community of Jews sharing life together. After a decade in Oakland, Schulweis discovered that for many in his congregation, real community did not exist. Jews appropriated religious life, as they did all other parts of life, as individuals. The task of rebuilding the connections of Jewish community, Schulweis concluded, came prior to the task of teaching belief or observance.

To resolve the dilemma of loneliness, Schulweis adopted a notion made popular in the Jewish counterculture—the *havurah*. The *havurah* was a lay-led fellowship of learning, worship, and mutual support. In the late 1960s, notable *havurot* formed in Boston, New York, and Washington, DC, as alternatives to mainstream communal institutions. Schulweis brought the idea to the synagogue and introduced the idea of the in-synagogue *havurah*—a circle of families who would meet regularly to learn together, celebrate together, share life-cycle moments, and support one another through crises.

Schulweis experimented with the idea in Oakland, but he met with difficulty. Temple Beth Abraham's leaders did not feel the need for the additional layer of institutional life in the synagogue.[52] *Havurot* never took hold in Oakland the way they would in Encino and elsewhere. But Schulweis did not abandon the idea. The failure of *havurot* was an indication that the time had arrived to begin looking for a new community, a new laboratory, for his vision of the new synagogue.

New Narratives

At Oakland's Beth Abraham, Harold Schulweis found the three voices of his rabbinate—a theological voice, a prophetic voice, and a voice of community. Each voice emerged from his rejection of the prevailing narratives shaping Jewish life and his formulation of a new narrative. These new narratives, in turn, served as the foundation for an agenda of innovative programs and projects to revitalize Jewish life.

By all measures, Schulweis was an extraordinarily successful rabbi in Oakland. Forty years later, his tenure is still celebrated as the synagogue's highest point.[53] This does not mean he was without his critics and flaws. No rabbi can do everything and satisfy everyone. By temperament, Schulweis was relentlessly cerebral and was highly effective in roles that reflected his intellectual disposition and academic training. He cherished the opportunity to teach adults and engage with college students, but he took no role in the education of children. He waxed eloquent about the value of Jewish education but never set foot in the religious school. He actually forbade children from entering the sanctuary during the High Holidays. And woe to the mother whose baby dared to cry during his sermon! He would speak about the value of community and shake every hand at the end of services, but he maintained his distance in social settings. It would take many decades and personal crises before Schulweis would appreciate the importance and power of the emotions that matched his love of the intellect.

Transition

By the end of the 1960s, Schulweis felt the need to step onto a larger stage. He traveled widely and spoke frequently to major Jewish organizations. Twice monthly, he flew to Los Angeles to teach in the rabbinical programs at the University of Judaism and Hebrew Union College.

Once he announced his intention to move on from Temple Beth Abraham, Schulweis was invited to pulpits at Beth Shalom in Kansas City and at Shearith Israel in Dallas. At the urging of University of Judaism president Dr. David Lieber, the leaders of Valley Beth Shalom in Encino, California, a rapidly growing suburb of Los Angeles, invited Schulweis to interview for their pulpit. He immediately recognized the possibilities of this congregation. Unlike the other placements in older, more established congregations, Valley Beth Shalom had little institutional culture of its own. Valley Beth Shalom was still a relatively new institution, having been founded in 1950. A notoriously underperforming congregation in an affluent suburb, Schulweis perceived that Valley Beth Shalom was ripe for development. It had few entrenched stakeholders and would offer little resistance to his vision for remaking synagogue life. But as a flagship congregation in a major Jewish community, it would also offer him the national platform he desired.

CHAPTER 3

Encino, 1970

On the evening of September 26, 1970, Harold Schulweis stepped to the bimah of Valley Beth Shalom in Encino for his debut in his new congregation. It was Selichot, the traditional midnight service conducted on the Saturday night prior to Rosh Hashanah. The atmosphere in the synagogue was electric.[1] The moment brought together a unique religious personality with a community at a propitious moment in its history. A crowd of more than one thousand worshippers came to hear the new rabbi speak about the kabbalistic concept of *tzimtzum*, divine contraction, as a model for human creativity. Before diffusing energies into the universe, God drew inward, taught the kabbalists, concentrating all the divine creative energies into one intensive point of focus. It was a poignant introduction to his vision—his intention to marshal the community's intellectual and spiritual resources toward the project of reinventing modern Judaism and reimagining Jewish life.

Who did Harold Schulweis face on that Selichot evening? Who was his audience as he launched this episode of his rabbinate? Who were these Encino Jews?

Mrs. Chandler Courts the Jews

The story of Los Angeles Jewry is best represented by the tale of Buffy Chandler. Mrs. Dorothy Buffum Chandler, known to intimates as Buffy, was the wife of *Los Angeles Times* publisher Norman Chandler and the grand matron of the downtown elite society of Los Angeles from the late 1940s through her death in 1997. It was Mrs. Chandler's great dream to see a cultural center constructed downtown, giving Los Angeles the cultural gravity it had never possessed. To finance the center, the county floated three bond issues in the late 1950s, but each was turned down by voters. Mrs. Chandler took it upon herself to raise the construction funds privately. She exploited every social contact in her vast network, squeezing friends and acquaintances alike. She formed a Blue Ribbon 400 Committee to solicit one thousand gifts of $1,000 each. She held a benefit showing of the film *Cleopatra* for $250 a seat and a gala evening at the Ambassador Hotel featuring Dinah Shore, Jack Benny, and Danny Kaye. But she was still short. Her downtown social circle could not raise the necessary funds. So, she did the unthinkable. In 1961, she took a trip to the Hillcrest Country Club to lunch with Mark Taper. That's the *Jewish* Mark Taper at the *Jewish* Hillcrest Country Club.[2]

Taper of American Savings and Loan had made his fortune in suburban development during the 1950s. Facing the fierce vocal opposition of her downtown circle, Mrs. Chandler knew that she needed his support to build her center. So she crossed the invisible boundary that divided Los Angeles society, and she got her music center. Taper contributed $1 million. His gift forced his rival, Howard Ahmanson of Home Savings, to match the gift. And to the horror of elite, downtown Protestant society, the three buildings of Los Angeles Music Center today are called the Dorothy Chandler Pavilion, the Mark Taper Forum, and the Ahmanson Theater.

Mrs. Chandler did not go to Hillcrest just for the money or to build the center. Had she wanted nothing more than an opera house, she could eventually have found the support within her own circle. She wanted something much more important. She wanted to bring the city together. By 1960, Los Angeles had grown into a metropolis of over four million that spread out across some sixty miles of coastline. In Mrs. Chandler's vision, the city desperately needed a center, a meeting place. Mrs. Chandler wanted to build an acropolis and to begin a new era in Los Angeles. To do so, it was necessary to bring the Jewish community into the civic conversation. Mrs. Chandler needed the Jews because she knew that for most of its history, Jews had been decisive in shaping the life of Los Angeles. And she recognized that by the 1960s, the Los Angeles Jewish community had grown into a significant cultural presence in the city.

Founded in 1781, Los Angeles was incorporated as an American city on April 4, 1850. A census that year showed a population of 8,624, including eight Jews. One of those eight, M. L. Goodman, was elected to Los Angeles's very first city council in 1850, and another, Arnold Jacobi, was elected in 1853. From 1850 through 1880, there was hardly a year without one or two Jews on the city council and the county board of supervisors. As the gold rush hit Northern California, Jews drifted southward to Los Angeles from the Gold Country, and by the mid-1850s most of the town's merchants were Jews. A traveler to Los Angeles in the early 1860s described Los Angeles as a "city of 4000 inhabitants, a mixture of old Spanish, Indian, American and German Jews."[3]

In 1859, Isaias Hellman arrived in Los Angeles from Bavaria. He found a job in his cousin's general mercantile business until he had saved enough to buy his own clothing store. Because he owned a safe and had a reputation for honesty, miners would deposit their gold dust with Hellman when they went out on the town. From this practice, Hellman began Los Angeles's first bank. In 1871, he partnered with former governor John Downey to found the Farmers and Merchants Bank of Los Angeles. In 1890, Hellman left Los Angeles to become the president of Wells Fargo in San Francisco. Until the Depression, Hellman's family controlled Los Angeles's most powerful financial institutions.[4]

The first minyan held in Los Angeles took place in 1851. Its first rabbi, Joseph Newmark, arrived in 1854, and that same year it saw the formation of the first Jewish institution, a Hebrew Benevolent Society organized for the purpose of maintaining a Jewish cemetery. In 1861, Los Angeles's first synagogue, Beth El, held High Holiday services. Seats could be reserved for three dollars. In 1862, the B'nai B'rith Congregation was founded. An Orthodox synagogue, it would later change its affiliation to the American Reform movement, change its location to Wilshire Boulevard, and change its name to the Wilshire Boulevard Temple. In 1914, the temple engaged a young assistant rabbi, Edgar Magnin. Rabbi Magnin remained in that pulpit for sixty-nine years.[5]

The coming of the Southern Pacific Railroad in 1883 and the Santa Fe Railway in 1886 brought a boom that changed Los Angeles from frontier town to metropolis. The population of Los Angeles in 1880 was 11,183; by 1900 it soared to 102,500, by 1920 to 577,000, and by 1940 to 1,500,000. Who came to Los Angeles? During those years, East Coast cities received massive immigration from Europe—Italians, Irish, Poles, and

Jews. These cities turned from Protestant to Catholic, and their power structures turned from Anglo to ethnic. In Los Angeles, it was the opposite. Los Angeles attracted white, Protestant midwesterners. The city turned from Catholic to Protestant, and from a rich ethnic mixture to a dominant Anglo majority. By the 1920s Jews were pushed out of the center of political and economic power and were excluded from the circles of powerful downtown elite society. Neighborhoods, schools, clubs, and industries were openly restricted. The Cedars of Lebanon Hospital was founded in 1910, for example, because Jewish doctors were not permitted to practice elsewhere.

The joke was that Groucho Marx was once invited to visit the Los Angeles Country Club. While his children were splashing in the pool, the president of the club quietly informed him that the club was restricted and his children would have to leave the pool. "They're only half Jewish," he replied, "let them go in up to their waist."[6]

Excluded from the centers of power, Jews found other ways to exert influence on Los Angeles. In the 1920s and 1930s, Jews brought the movies to the city. The great studios—MGM, Twentieth Century Fox, Universal, Warner Bros, Paramount, and Columbia—were founded and run by Jews: Louis B. Mayer, Samuel Goldwyn, William Fox, Carl Laemmle, Jack and Harry Warner, Adolph Zukor, and Harry Cohn.[7] All were born within a hundred miles of one another in Poland, all immigrated to the United States within ten years of one another, and all failed at a first career before finding their way into motion pictures. It was considered an unseemly business in the beginning. Movies were shown in the back of seedy nickelodeons and were not considered socially acceptable. Restricted from so many industries—banking, insurance, oil, mining—a class of Jewish entrepreneurs found in movies an open field and realized the potential of this new medium. Defeating Thomas Edison's monopoly in 1915, they proceeded to build empires integrating production, distribution, and presentation of motion pictures. Thus was Hollywood born of Jewish hands.[8]

In the 1950s and 1960s, Jews again changed the shape of the city. Excluded by the Protestant elite, Jewish developers and bankers turned away from downtown and created an alternative city center on the city's west side. Flying into Los Angeles, one sees what amounts to two downtowns: the skyscrapers of the central city core and the development along Wilshire Boulevard culminating in Century City and Westwood. This is the geographic reflection of the social history of Los Angeles—the social bifurcation of power in Los Angeles.[9] Turning their backs on the downtown that excluded them, Jewish developers advanced a plan to decentralize the city's expansion. Shopping would be located in each suburban neighborhood, eliminating the need to go downtown, essentially choking off its economic life. Some 40 percent of the housing constructed in Los Angeles since the end of the World War II—including the vast majority of the San Fernando Valley—was financed and built by Jewish developers and bankers.[10]

The congregation Harold Schulweis faced from the bimah of Valley Beth Shalom in 1970 reflected the resurgence—in numbers, power, and spirit—of Los Angeles Jewry that Mrs. Chandler recognized. It was an optimistic community, a growing community, a community of open possibilities. It was a community finding its voice in the 1960s and rising to become a major cultural force in Los Angeles. It was a community ready to assert its own identity, independent of its East Coast antecedents, and to create its own forms of Jewish life, led by visionary, entrepreneurial leaders.

Los Angeles featured two major Jewish colleges, the Conservative, University of Judaism (later known as the American Jewish University), and the Reform, Hebrew Union College, where students for the rabbinate could begin their studies before moving on to New York or Cincinnati. At Hebrew Union College, Professor Gerald Bubis launched the first program of Jewish professional communal service. The Los Angeles community was home to the Brandeis Institute (later known as Brandeis-Bardin Institute), a unique experiment in adult Jewish learning, led by the pioneering educator Dr. Shlomo Bardin. Los Angeles spawned the very first campus-based Chabad House at UCLA, led by the energetic Rabbi Shlomo Cunin; the Simon Wiesenthal Center, led by Rabbi Marvin Hier; and the Skirball Cultural Center, founded by Rabbi Uri Herscher. This was a community of visionaries, innovators, and social and spiritual entrepreneurs—an ideal setting for an ambitious young rabbi with a plan to remake contemporary Judaism.

A Congregation of Newcomers

Following the end of World War II, Americans were in a mood to begin again. The war had brought austerity and self-sacrifice. The country was ready to enjoy its life. The postwar economic boom, together with the benefits of the GI Bill, the Full Employment Act, and the Housing Act, offered Americans a chance to join the middle class and reinvent themselves. The most visible sign of this was the mass movement out of central cities and into the suburbs. In 1954, 18.6 percent of Americans changed their place of residence; in 1955, the figure was 20 percent. Between 1948 and 1958, twelve million Americans moved to the suburbs.[11]

This postwar movement brought a population boom to Southern California, most particularly among Jews. Returning veterans who had been stationed or trained on the West Coast quickly retrieved their families and moved into the sunshine and optimism that was California. Between 1940 and 1950 more than 168,000 Jews came to Los Angeles—more Jews than lived in Detroit, Boston, Cleveland, or Baltimore.[12] The scale of postwar Jewish migration to Los Angeles is revealed in its Jewish population numbers, assembled by Vorspan and Gartner from various Jewish community studies:

1900	2,500	1946	168,000
1917	20,000	1948	260,000
1923	43,000	1951	315,000
1927	65,000	1959	391,000
1941	130,000	1965	509,000

[13]

By 1965, Los Angeles was the second-largest Jewish community in the world. Significantly, only 8 percent of adult Jews living in the city in 1950 were native Angelinos, and only 16 percent had settled there before World War II.[14]

The San Fernando Valley, site of Schulweis' Encino synagogue, was everything Los Angeles—only more so. The major suburb of a city of suburbs, the Valley sits just north of Los Angeles, separated by the Santa Monica Mountains. Yearly cycles of drought and flood rendered the Valley underpopulated through the 1930s. In 1913, the first Los Angeles aqueduct brought water from the Owens Valley in the Eastern Sierras to the city of Los Angeles. The aqueduct's engineers planned to store the water in the aquifer that lies beneath the Valley floor. A group of prominent investors bribed the project's chief engineer and gained insider information about his plan, then bought up large tracts of Valley land at bargain prices and moved to have them incorporated into the city limits of Los Angeles. This scandal was retold in the movie *Chinatown*. With the arrival of the aqueduct, the Valley had a steady supply of water.

Floods devastated the Valley every ten years. In 1938, 144 people were killed when a flood overflowed the banks of the Los Angeles River. After numerous local efforts to stem the flooding failed, the US Army Corps of Engineers constructed the Sepulveda Dam in 1941, together with the adjacent floodplain, ending the threat of floods and inviting the postwar boom in development.

As Los Angeles's population exploded after the war, the San Fernando Valley became the fastest-growing area in the United States. Ranches, orchards, and dairy farms gave way to sprawling tracts of new homes, shopping centers, and freeways. The Valley population grew from 112,000 in 1940 to 400,000 in 1950, and doubled to 800,000 in 1960.[15] Jewish migrants quickly found their way to the Valley, drawn by inexpensive housing and abundant opportunities. In 1953, Valley Jews constituted just 9 percent of the Jewish population of Los Angeles. The Valley Jewish population grew to 19 percent of Los Angeles Jewry in 1958, 26 percent by 1965, 42 percent by 1979, and 46 percent by 1996. By 1996, the areas of Encino and the adjacent neighborhood of Tarzana, the principal residence of Schulweis' congregants, were the most densely Jewish areas in Los Angeles, with Jews constituting 48 percent of the resident population.[16]

Valley Beth Shalom was founded in Encino in 1950 by a small circle of families. The synagogue met in a school building that had been relocated to a site on Sepulveda Boulevard. In 1952, the synagogue purchased a motel on Ventura Boulevard and developed the site into the synagogue. The impressive sanctuary building was dedicated in 1966. The synagogue grew slowly as the surrounding neighborhood was developed, changing from farmland to movie lots, then ultimately to suburban housing. The classic *It's a Wonderful Life* was filmed only a mile away on the RKO Ranch set.

The synagogue was governed by a small group of very strong, self-made businessmen. Before Schulweis' arrival, Valley Beth Shalom had experienced a parade of rabbis, not one of whom remained more than five years.

Mobility was the chief characteristic of the synagogue community Harold Schulweis addressed on Selichot in 1970. Up to 90 percent of the community were born outside Los Angeles. They had come to California in the decades preceding his arrival and had settled in Encino only years before. It was all new. The streets, homes, businesses, indeed the synagogue itself, had all been established and constructed in the very recent past. There was no history, no legacy, and no established patterns of life. The synagogue had gone through a dozen rabbis in as many years. It was a community geographically, ideologically, and existentially unsettled, unfixed, and unresolved; it was the ideal setting for a rabbi who had spent two decades formulating and refining a distinctly revolutionary vision of

Jewish life and Jewish identity. In that first sermon on the theme of *tzimtzum*, Schulweis urged his community to gather their diffuse energies and focus upon the task of constructing a new Jewish identity and a new synagogue community.

The Suburban Paradise

It was the promise of the good life that brought Jews to Los Angeles and then out to the Valley. What made Los Angeles so attractive was its contrast with the cities most American Jews called home. In place of the grit and grind of East Coast and Midwest urban centers, Los Angeles offered year-round sunshine and a casual lifestyle.[17] Instead of crowded neighborhoods of densely occupied rented apartments, Los Angeles offered easily affordable single-family homes. The billboards along the highways leading to Los Angeles promised it all: Here you can have your own space—your own yard, your own pool, in a shiny, new suburban development. Instead of a long daily commute by crowded bus or train, you will speed in the comfort of your own car along one of Los Angeles's ultramodern freeways.

The move to Los Angeles was unlike the migration of Jews to eastern and midwestern suburbs. In trying to explain Los Angeles to New York Jews in 1959, sociologist Nathan Glazer pointed to its inherent freedom: the suburbs of Brooklyn and Queens were communities of necessity; "here [in Los Angeles], everyone has chosen his way of life."[18] Los Angeles offered a unique opportunity to reinvent oneself. The city was even different from Florida. In her study of postwar migration, historian Deborah Dash Moore notes that Los Angeles "promised a life of leisure that blurred distinctions between work and play. . . . [Migrants] saw an open city and a chance to make themselves over in their own image."[19]

But this freedom came at a cost: "Like their immigrant parents, Jews migrating to Los Angeles sought personal success and risked losing the nurturing ties of family and friends in the hope of finding prosperity. Their daring set them apart from their peers."[20] Moore draws a very important distinction: Jews moving from eastern and midwestern central cities out to the surrounding suburbs remained connected to their home cities and consequently to traditional family structures, networks of friendship, and patterns of culture. On weekends, they trekked back to the city to see family and friends, to shop or partake of cultural institutions. Many commuted daily to work in the city from the suburbs. Suburban Jews maintained their membership in the city's congregations or brought rabbis and teachers from the city out to the suburbs.[21] Migration to Los Angeles was different:

> Suburbanization did not disrupt the family network, as migration [to Los Angeles] did by cutting individuals off from their roots. . . . Migration to Los Angeles . . . transformed a Jew's relationship to his or her hometown . . . severed structures of collective continuity. Jews thought about themselves and their Jewish institutions differently after they settled in . . . LA. . . . [Migration] allowed Jews not only to change their residence but to change their identity.[22]

The move to Los Angeles meant separation from family, established networks of relationship, familiar cultural patterns,

and supporting institutions. It meant raising children without grandparents or extended family. It meant meeting life
changes and challenges without childhood friends to share
them. It placed all the pressures of life onto the nuclear family. Sociologist Samuel Heilman describes the dilemma:

> Although putatively built for the sake of the children,
> this new suburban culture actually placed intense pres-
> sures on the nuclear family. In the suburbs, this family,
> left pretty much on its own in the splendid isolation of
> the one-family home, was commonly separated from
> the support structures of relatives and the plethora of
> institutions that remained in the old neighborhoods of
> the city . . . [with] life in the new suburbs . . . came deep
> feelings of loss and even vulnerability.[23]

Suburbia could be a very lonely place. And if this was true
generally, it was more so for those newly arrived in Los Angeles.
Unlike their eastern and midwestern cities, Los Angeles had few
public spaces and very little sense of neighborhood. Children
played in backyards, not parks. Commuters took their cars to
work, not the bus or train. Los Angeles sidewalks were famously
empty; people would even drive to the corner mailbox. There was
rarely a reason to leave the house. Homes came equipped with
built-in laundry, backyard swing sets, and in-ground swimming
pools. The Adohr Dairy milkman delivered milk and dairy products directly to front doors, and the friendly Helms bakery truck
made neighborhood rounds bringing fresh bread and cakes.

The move to the Valley represented a double dose of alienation for migrants: first, leaving behind cities of origin, and

second, abandoning the family and friendship networks and cultural institutions of the older neighborhoods of Los Angeles. Every Valley child came to understand that Bubby and Zeyde lived far away—if not still in New York or Chicago then in the Fairfax neighborhood, near the iconic Canter's Deli, Diamond Bakery, and Solomon's Book Store, all of which could be reached only by a long, exhausting drive over winding, treacherous Laurel Canyon.

When homebuilder William Levitt developed the Levittown suburbs in New York and New Jersey, deeds to Levitt's homes specified that no fences were to be built between houses.[24] By contrast, homes in the San Fernando Valley were set on large lots, set back from the street, and separated by high block walls, ensuring privacy and keeping neighbors apart. In February 1964, Topanga Plaza opened. California's first indoor shopping mall was a sensation with its air-conditioned comfort, spectacular rain forest fountain, and Ice Capades skating rink. The mall offered the Valley its very first shared public space—a social gathering place. The felt need for human connection made the mall a faux community, as neighbors gathered around the artificial rain forest and the refrigerated ice rink. Everyone met at the mall.

In the Valley, there were virtually no trees; no one had roots. Schulweis' congregation fervently sought connection, community, and patterns of authentic living. The Valley was a youthful community. Schulweis' congregation sought wisdom older than themselves. The Valley epitomized California's offer of endless new possibilities. Schulweis' congregations sought purpose—a sense of personal meaning that would guide them through the confusing panorama of endless choices.

Hear Me Roar

Television arrived in American homes in the 1950s, and among its first and most enduring images was the blissful housewife and mother. June Cleaver, mother to Wally and the Beaver; Harriet Nelson, mom to Ricky and Dave; and Margaret Anderson of *Father Knows Best* doted cheerfully on their husbands and children, doled out life wisdom with home-baked cookies, and never appeared anyway but fresh and energetic, and never in anything but high heels and pearls. This was the culture's feminine ideal. Women of the 1950s were expected to marry early, begin families, and find bliss in domesticity. The average age of marriage dropped to 20.1 for women in 1950, the lowest of the entire century. Meanwhile, fertility rates rose sharply. American women in 1941 bore an average of 2.2 children. By 1950, the rate increased to 3.65 and peaked in 1957 at 3.77 children per family.[25] Women were expected to define themselves as wife, mother, and homemaker, an image reinforced relentlessly in popular culture. But this definition coupled with the isolation of the suburban neighborhood left many bereft:

> During the day suburbanites were all off early on their separate tracks. The children went to school and the commuter husband/father left for work in town. . . . Women left behind in the house were expected to obtain all their satisfaction from a primary career as wife and mother. . . . For many, it became harder and harder to find meaning in a life that left them with more time but less to do. . . . Women often felt "kind of isolated

and lonely." . . . The suburban wife and mother of the
fifties was expected to devalue most social roles outside
the family.[26]

Novelist Nora Johnson reflected on the disparity between
the 1950s romantic ideal of marriage and motherhood and
the dreary reality of a life spent with dirty diapers and runny
noses. The "Captivity of Marriage" appeared in the pages of
the *Atlantic* in 1961:

> Wives are lonelier now than they ever used to be . . .
> [when] people moved less, and families stuck closer
> together. The young college-educated mother with a
> medium amount of money is the one who reflects all
> the problems at once. In spite of her hopes for fulfill-
> ment through her children and contentment with a
> woman's great career, she vaguely feels that she is frit-
> tering away her days and that a half-defined but import-
> ant part of her ability is lying about unused; she is guilty
> about her feeling of futility because of her belief in the
> magic medicine of love. This is the housewife's syn-
> drome, the vicious circle, the feeling of emptiness in
> the gap between what she thought marriage was going
> to be like and what it is really like.
>
> The old illusions of what life was supposed to hold, the
> restless remnants, the undefined dreams do not die as
> they were supposed to. Probably every educated wife has
> found herself staring at a mountain of dirty diapers and
> asking herself desperately, "Is this all there is?" And at
> the same time she is embarrassed by her dissatisfaction.[27]

This strong sense of dissatisfaction contributed to the birth of the women's movement of the 1960s and 1970s. In 1963, Betty Friedan launched the movement with her groundbreaking book *The Feminine Mystique.* The Supreme Court's Griswold decision in 1965 made birth control widely available. The National Organization for Women (NOW) was founded in 1966. In the 1971 Reed decision, the Supreme Court applied the Fourteenth Amendment's equal protection clause to discrimination by sex. The plaintiff's case was argued by Ruth Bader Ginsburg, later appointed to the Supreme Court. Helen Reddy sang, "I am woman, hear me roar," in 1972. And in 1973, Billie Jean King defeated Bobby Riggs in the "Battle of the Sexes" tennis match. At the same time, Jewish women experienced the beginnings of Jewish feminism. Ezrat Nashim, a coalition of young Conservative women, staged a protest at the 1972 Rabbinical Assembly, demanding a greater role in synagogue life. In 1972, Sally Priesand was ordained the Reform movement's first female rabbi. The magazine *Lilith* was launched in 1976.

By the 1970s, the women's movement was actively redefining what it meant to be a woman in America. Along with this revolution came changes in American family life. Two major demographic shifts changed American families during the 1970s: By 1971, the fertility rate dropped to 1.8 children per family, half of its 1957 peak. At the same time, more women began working outside the home. According to the Bureau of Labor Statistics, the percentage of married mothers with children under the age of eighteen who worked outside the home rose from 18.4 percent in 1950, to 27.6 percent in 1960, to 39.7 percent in 1970, and up to 54.1 percent in 1980. By

1980, the percentage of married mothers with children ages six through eighteen working outside the home reached 61.7 percent.[28]

Concurrent with the changing family came the rising prevalence of divorce. Between 1962 and 1973, the divorce rate in the United States doubled. The rate continued to rise rapidly through the 1970s. In 1962, the divorce rate was 2.2 per 1,000 population. In 1975, the United States recorded more than a million divorces for the first time in its history, a rate of 4.9 per 1,000 population.[29] Demographer Bruce Phillips notes the same doubling of divorce rates within the Los Angeles Jewish community from the '60s through the '70s. The purported Jewish immunity to divorce had worn off as Jews assimilated into California culture. Phillips reports that in 1979 the percentage of Jews ages thirty through thirty-nine who had been divorced was three times as high as in 1967 (12.6 versus 3.9 percent), while the percentage of those ages forty through forty-nine was twice as high (13.6 versus 6.8 percent).[30]

The congregation Harold Schulweis addressed on Selichot in 1970 was composed of predominantly married couples with children living a "traditional" 1950s pattern of family life—father working outside the home, mother staying at home with the children. But that pattern was already changing rapidly. Mothers found the isolation and narrowing of their lives unsatisfying, and they were moving out of the home and their traditional roles and into the workforce and roles they found more fulfilling. Falling fertility rates meant that women now had time for other pursuits. Feminism pushed them to redefine themselves. The women of Schulweis' congregation were less and less likely to accept subordinate roles as the supporting

cast of a male-dominated society and a male-dominated synagogue. Families were changing. Divorce was becoming more
common. What was once the norm became less normal. There
was a growing number of single-parent families, blended families, multigenerational households, mixed-faith households,
households without children, and single adults. They came
that Selichot evening to meet the rabbi who would show them
how to live their tradition in untraditional settings.

Is That All There Is?

In the early morning of February 9, 1971, the San Fernando
Valley shook from an earthquake that measured 6.5 on the
Richter scale. The Olive View Hospital in the north Valley col-
lapsed. Numerous freeway overpasses were rendered impass-
able, multiple school buildings were unusable, and everyone's
nerves were set on edge. The earthquake was a palpable symbol
of a decade that saw the core values of American life shaken.
Following the upheavals of the 1960s, with the Vietnam War
continuing unabated and the counterculture in full bloom,
there was widespread disillusionment with established institutions and leaders. Many doubted the capacity of a democratic
society to shape its future. A strong sense of insecurity with
the very capacity of human rationality characterized the 1970s,
which in turn brought a retreat into the irrational. Political
pundit David Frum notes, "They were strange feverish years,
the 1970s. They were a time of unease and despair, punctuated
by disaster."[31] Frum ticks off the events that colored the decade:

> The murder of athletes at the 1972 Olympic Games. Des-
> ert emirates cutting off America's oil. Military humiliation

in Indochina. Criminals taking control of America's streets. The dollar plunging in value. Marriages collapsing. Drugs for sale in every high school. A president toppled from office. The worst economic slump since the Great Depression, followed four years later by the second-worst economic slump since the Depression. The U.S. government baffled as its diplomats are taken hostage. And in the background loomed still wilder and stranger alarms and panics. The ice age was returning. Killer bees were swarming up across the Rio Grande. The world was running out of natural resources. Kahoutek's comet was hurtling toward the planet. Epidemic swine flu would carry off millions of elderly people. Karen Silkwood had been murdered for trying to warn us that nuclear reactors were poisoning the earth. General Motors was suppressing the patent on a hyper-efficient engine. Food shortages would soon force Americans to subsist on algae. There were, wrote a columnist for the *New York Times*, "fleeting moments when the public scene recalls the Weimar Republic of 1932–33."[32]

The corollary to the disillusionment with traditional values and institutions was a new and virulent preoccupation with the self. American culture turned inward. In the 1960s, notes social analyst Daniel Yankelovich, the search for self-fulfillment was confined to the young. Their elders were still loyal to the ethics of the "Greatest Generation"—duty, service, responsibility, hard work, and deferring life's rewards to the next generation. By the 1970s, the culture changed. Yankelovich's surveys showed that 72 percent "spent a great deal of time thinking about themselves and their inner lives."[33] Looking back from the end of the decade, Yankelovich describes a world turned upside down by a new quest for self-fulfillment:

> The self-fulfillment search is a more complex, fateful, and irreversible phenomenon than simply the by-product of affluence or a shift in the national character toward narcissism. It is nothing less than the search for a new American philosophy of life.[34]

This attitude carried into the workplace, politics, personal and family life, popular culture, and religion.

Bookstores stocked a new genre of literature—self-help books. Thomas A. Harris's *I'm OK—You're OK*, published in 1971, was on the *New York Times* best-seller list for two years. A new emphasis on the body prevailed. Jogging became popular. Dr. Kenneth Cooper's *Aerobics*, published in 1969, sold twelve million copies and introduced an entirely new vocabulary of physical culture. The 1970s brought a new openness to sexuality. *Midnight Cowboy*, released in 1969, won the Academy Award for best picture in 1970—the first and only X-rated film to win the award. In 1972, the pornographic film *Deep Throat* premiered and became chic among middle-class Americans. *The Sensuous Woman*, a frank instruction manual for sexual pleasure published in 1969, became the fastest-selling paperback book in history, selling 6.2 million copies in three months.

In search of self-fulfillment, Americans turned to new religious expressions. In the decade 1955–1965, mainstream American religious denominations grew substantially. Americans flocked to church and synagogue in conformity with President

Eisenhower's quip, "Our form of government has no sense unless it is founded in a deeply felt religious faith—I don't care what it is." Religion was the American thing to do. "The family that prays together, stays together," announced a familiar billboard. But during the following decade, 1965–1975, the mainstream denominations gave up their gains. Methodists lost 10 percent of their members, Presbyterians 12 percent, Episcopalians 16.7 percent. Seventy-five percent of Catholics reported attending weekly mass in 1957. The number dropped to 54 percent by 1975.[35] In contrast, the Southern Baptist Convention grew by 18 percent, and the Pentecostal Assemblies of God grew 37 percent in the same period.[36]

Frum proposes four characteristics that distinguished the growing churches: (1) Thriving churches were evangelical rather than sacramental. More performance space than sacred sanctuary, churches were expressive and emotional, engaging the congregation in shared ritual. (2) They emphasized forgiveness over rectitude—the readiness of divine love and acceptance over the imminence of divine punishment—and held out the opportunity to every sinner to be "born again." (3) They were eschatological, proffering vivid pictures of an imminent, apocalyptic redemption. The most-read religious book of the 1950s was Norman Vincent Peale's *The Power of Positive Thinking*, a guide to navigating the difficulties of daily life with faith. By contrast, the most popular religious book of the 1970s was Hal Lindsey's *The Late Great Planet Earth*, which sold ten million copies between 1970 and 1977, and which depicted the end-time in graphic, often gruesome images. (4) The growing churches were politically conservative. While mainstream Protestantism drifted toward the left, focusing on societal issues and professing faith in collective political action against social ills, the growing churches focused on healing individual sin.[37] In sum, Frum notes:

> American faith was more emotional, more forgiving, more individualistic, more variegated, and often more bizarre. It was less obedient, less ritualistic, less intellectual. It concerned itself more with self-fulfillment and less with social reform. Americans yearned as fervently as ever for a direct encounter with the transcendental, but they chafed against the authority that had once guided them toward that encounter. They hungered for religion's sweets, but rejected religion's discipline; wanted its help in trouble, but not the strictures that might have kept them out of trouble; expected its ecstasy, but rejected its ethics; demanded salvation, but rejected the harsh, antique dichotomy of right and wrong.[38]

The search for self-fulfillment led many in the 1970s beyond established forms of religion into cults—what have since come to be known as "new religious movements." These groups typically demanded absolute loyalty and obedience to authority. Their ideologies were self-contained, often secretive and isolated, blocking out outside influences and impeding the critical faculties of adherents. In return, they promised bliss, certainty, community, acceptance, and redemption. They offered access to transcendent truth, an answer to the search for self-fulfillment.

In 1966, the International Society for Krishna Consciousness—the Hare Krishna movement—was founded in the United States and flowered into the 1970s, sending adherents,

in familiar orange robes, to airports and public places to pros-
elytize new recruits.

The Unification Church of Sun Myung Moon arrived in the
United States from South Korea in 1965. In 1971, it boasted
some five hundred members. By the end of the decade, the
membership was over five thousand.[39]

There is no data that cult membership was more prevalent
among Jewish young people than within the general population, but the stories of Jewish youngsters taken in by cults
abounded within the community. Secular cults thrived as well.
In Los Angeles, the Santa Monica–based drug rehabilitation
center Synanon was reorganized in the 1970s into an alternative community centered around the personality of its founder,
Charles "Chuck" Dederich. The community practiced radical
forms of therapy, seen widely as brainwashing.

In a television commercial that ran frequently in the early
1970s, a weary man stares into the bathroom mirror early in
the morning. Suddenly, a hand slaps him hard across the face.
"Thanks," he replies, "I needed that!" The search for a more
intensive experience of the inner life moved some toward even
more radical pathways. Primal therapy, pioneered by Arthur
Janov and presented in his 1970 book *The Primal Scream*, promised relief from neuroses by reexperiencing and confronting
the pain of infantile and childhood trauma. Rolfing, a form
of intense, often painful bodywork, spread across the country
following the founding of the Rolf Institute of Structural Inte-
gration in 1971. Erhard Seminars Training (EST), also founded
in 1971, offered participants an experience that would liberate
them from the expectations and roles that denied their personal
freedom and demanded they take responsibility for their lives.

In 1969, singer Peggy Lee scored a hit with a recording of a song written by Jerry Leiber and Mike Stoller, "Is That All There Is?" The song was inspired by the 1896 short story "Disillusionment" by Thomas Mann. In each verse, the singer describes powerful life experiences—witnessing the family house burning down; visiting the circus, "The Greatest Show on Earth"; falling in love for the first time—but follows each with a plaintive sense of disappointment:

> Is that all there is?
> Is that all there is?
> If that's all there is, my friends, then let's keep dancing
> Let's break out the booze and have a ball
> If that's all there is.[40]

At the song's end, even the prospect of death leaves the singer weary with anticipated disappointment that can be drowned only by "breaking out the booze and having a ball." The 1970s expressed this yearning for something more from life. Having achieved unprecedented affluence, middle-class Americans of the 1970s tried to shake off their growing disillusionment and boredom and answer the gnawing question, "Is that all there is?" The congregation Harold Schulweis addressed in 1970 came to hear their new rabbi to find an answer to that gnawing question.

Encino Jews

Jewish Los Angeles came of age on Sunday afternoon, June 11, 1967. That Sunday, immediately following the Six-Day

War, more than twenty-five thousand people crowded the Hollywood Bowl for a "Rally for Israel," organized by the Jewish Federation Council and the organs of the Jewish community.[41] Frank Sinatra and Barbra Streisand sang the national anthem and Hatikva. Ross Martin, star of the TV series *The Wild Wild West*, was master of ceremonies. Governor Ronald Reagan, Senator George Murphy, and Mayor Samuel Yorty spoke. A cavalcade of Hollywood stars came to the stage to pledge allegiance to Israel: Edward G. Robinson, Danny Kaye, Joey Bishop, Peter Sellers, Kathryn Grayson, Carl Reiner, Dinah Shore, Robert Vaughn, Eva Marie Saint, Ernest Borgnine, Nehemiah Persoff, Agnes Moorehead, and the New Christy Minstrels.

For the first time, Los Angeles Jewry found its collective voice. It was the first time the community made itself visible, declared its presence, and exerted its influence. The Hollywood Bowl event changed the tenor of Jewish life in Los Angeles, just as the Six-Day War changed American Judaism in general. The prospect of the imminent demise of Israel followed by the miraculous redemption of a stunning military victory awakened American Jews to their Jewishness. Sociologist Neil Sandberg, in his study of Los Angeles Jewry, testified,

> What we are witnessing is a differential Jewish renaissance in all generations that can be described as a "second law of return." This rejuvenation was especially true for the second generation, the children of the immigrants, who had earlier sought to divest themselves of their Jewish characteristics. . . . As ethnic identity became more and more fashionable, the second-generation rejection of ethnicity . . . gave way to a resurgence of

group awareness and pride greater than that of the third generation.[42]

The moment was ripe for the flowering of Jewish ethnic identification and pride. The 1960s "black is beautiful" movement opened the door to expressions of ethnic pride in America. The 1965 Delano grape strike by the United Farm Workers raised up Mexican-American Chicano identity into mainstream visibility. It was no longer un-American to be ethnic. On the contrary, real Americans celebrated their ethnic roots. The 1960s saw the stirring of Jewish ethnicity. *Fiddler on the Roof* opened on Broadway in 1964. In 1966, Harry Belafonte sang "Hava Nagila" on national television. Second-generation American Jews, the children of immigrants, typically deeply ambivalent about ethnic identity, reasserted their Jewishness. Third-generation Jews turned toward Jewishness for an expression of identity comparable to their "Afro-American" and Chicano friends. Colorful *kippot* were seen for the first time on Los Angeles streets, often balanced precariously atop "he-'fro" hairdos.

The Hollywood Bowl event was not without its ironies. The greatest communal ritual of identity in the Los Angeles Jewish community's history took place not in any synagogue or Jewish setting but in the most iconic Hollywood venue. For a generation, Hollywood strove to hide its Jewishness. The fact that the seven leading studios were launched and led by Jews, and the fact that so many of the producers, writers, directors, and actors were Jews, was hidden behind a veneer of authentic Americanism. Hollywood put forward the images of Gary Cooper and Jimmy Stewart deliberately to hide the Jewishness of

Louis B. Mayer, Harry Cohn, and Irving Thalberg. Stars were routinely forced to change their names. Edward G. Robinson and Joey Bishop were born Emanuel Goldenberg and Joseph Abraham Gottlieb, respectively. But that afternoon in June 1967, they all came out of the closet to stand with Israel, saying "we" when referring to the Jewish community. The community's ultimate validation was not the participation of so many stars, or even Reagan, Murphy, and Yorty. The ultimate validation came from the presence of Frank Sinatra: if the quintessential American, Frank Sinatra, "the chairman of the board," proudly associated with Jews and supported Israel, there was no longer a need to conceal one's Jewishness.

The Six-Day War catalyzed a redefinition of Jewish identity in Los Angeles as elsewhere in America. At the center of this new identity was an acute awareness of Jewish vulnerability, the real prospect that the Jewish people could indeed vanish. Survival became the community's priority. For the first time, attachment to the State of Israel, as the most visible symbol of the Jewish will to survive, became the very heart of American Jewish identity. As well, a new attunement to the memory of the Holocaust, the most powerful symbol of all that threatened Jewish life, became a vital part of the core narrative of American Jews. Together, loyalty to Israel and reverence for the Holocaust became the emotional engines of American Jewish life. A new resolution to rescue Jews trapped in the Soviet Union, the most threatened extant Jewish population, became a core commitment of the Jewish community.[43]

This new identity was itself fraught with irony. The Six-Day War was a moment of redemption. A great tragedy was averted. In the euphoria of the days following the war, the American

Jewish community celebrated the plucky resilience of Israel. No longer were Jews the limp, passive yeshiva scholars of Chaim Nachman Bialik's poems. Jews were now Moshe Dayan, the cocky, tough, self-reliant Israeli. Rabbis, including Abraham Joshua Heschel and Zvi Yehuda Kook, suggested the war was a revelation of a new divine providence at work in Israel's experience. The Jewish community could have made the war a new Purim. Instead, American Jews turned the moment into a new T'sha B'av, obsessing on their collective vulnerability. The Holocaust came to dominate the contemporary Jewish narrative. In 1970, the philosopher Emil Fackenheim cemented these tropes of memory and survival together and invested them with religious sanctity in his pronouncement that out of Auschwitz came a new, 614th commandment: "You shall not hand Hitler a posthumous victory." This dictum became the operant ideology of post-1967 American Jewish life.

Though passionately expressed, the survival imperative had no settled content. It became the obligation of American Jews to "support Israel." Not to live there or even to visit. Not to learn Israel's language or to participate firsthand in its culture. Similarly, it was the obligation of American Jews to remember the Holocaust. Museums and monuments of the Holocaust sprang up across the continent. "Never Again" became the community's watchword. But no code of ethical or political behavior grew from the memory because there was no consensus on what lessons were to be learned from the Holocaust. Communal survival became a sacred imperative. That imperative was translated neither into an obligation to live a Jewish life nor to practice its rites or embrace its symbols—not even to gain mastery of Jewish culture—but solely to transmit Jewishness to the next generation. Having averted annihilation, the sacred obligation extended only to ensuring that one's children identified. Intermarriage, not illiteracy or indifference, became the community's definition of apostasy.

The ironies and paradoxes of the Hollywood Bowl rally reflect the complex identity of American Jews in the 1970s. This complexity was captured by sociologist Charles Liebman in the introduction to his classic 1973 study *The Ambivalent American Jew*:

> The American Jew is torn between two sets of values—those of integration and acceptance into American society and those of Jewish group survival. These values appear to me to be incompatible. But most American Jews do not view them in this way. . . . The behavior of the American Jew is best understood as his unconscious effort to restructure his environment and reorient his own self-definition and perception of reality so as to reduce the tension between these values.[44]

Liebman's theory of ambivalence, and of the conscious and unconscious steps Jews adopted to resolve the tensions of this ambivalence, helps unravel the paradoxes and ironies of postwar American Jewish life. The ambivalence can be detected in every aspect of American Jewish life of the 1970s.

Jews fled to the suburbs to escape settled identity and patterns of life. Suburbia offered the promise of a new beginning, a chance to invent oneself. The separation from ethnic urban neighborhoods, from established patterns of family and friendship relationships, and from established community institutions boded poorly for the preservation of Jewish life. Presumably, Heilman argues, suburban life was an expression of a will to assimilate:

> [The move to suburbia] meant that ultimately tradition, a sense of Jewish uniqueness, tribalism, and ethnic separation, would have to wither, while religion would become diluted into some sort of vague Judeo-Christian mix, a matter of personal choice and no longer an expression of collective destiny. American values and culture would increasingly supplant the Jewish ones in the suburban collective consciousness. But this was essentially what these postwar Jews wanted. Their reinvention of themselves as individuals pursuing happiness dovetailed neatly with the aspirations of all the new suburbanites.[45]

But they moved to Jewish suburbs. Levittown in New York, Cherry Hill in New Jersey, Highland Park in Illinois, and Encino, California, had strong concentrations of Jewish newcomers. Jews moved to be with other Jews. Phillips observes that these neighborhoods resulted in new patterns of acculturation that maintained Jewish identification and participation.[46] As Heilman explains:

> To live in a suburb but to do so with other Jews who Americanized their Jewishness seemed a way of being like other Americans without having to leave the Jewish orbit. It was a reflection of the widespread belief on the part of much of fifties American Jewry that their life choices facilitated cultural change but did not require

wholesale abandonment of their ethnic and religious identity. They believed they could be both genuine Jews and full-fledged citizens of the American suburbs, and that they could pass on this dual heritage to their children.[47]

Finding themselves far from established institutions of Jewish life, the new suburbanites moved to create their own. Religion in the 1950s was an expression of American identity. One needed to belong to the synagogue as an expression of one's American identity, just as the neighbors belonged to their church. The object was to be identified but not too distinct, to be ethnic but not un-American, to be Jewish but not too Jewish. Consequently, one joined the synagogue but did not attend too frequently.

With the rapid expansion of suburbs, the 1950s and 1960s saw an explosion of synagogue building. Historian Jack Wertheimer assembles the statistics:

> In 1957, the Synagogue Council of America estimated a "grand total of 4,200 congregations," more than double the number 50 years earlier, and about 1,000 more than immediately before World War II. The Reform movement's Union of American Hebrew Congregations (UAHC, predecessor of the URJ) grew from 290 temples in 1937 to 698 in 1970, and in the same period the Conservative movement's United Synagogue (US) increased from 250 member congregations to 832. During just one two-year period of the 1950s, 131 new congregations joined the US and 50 affiliated with the UAHC.[48]

But as Wertheimer wryly points out, synagogue construction and affiliation did not necessarily mean synagogue participation:

> A survey conducted by the National Opinion Research Center (NORC) in 1945 found that only 24 percent of Jews claimed to attend religious services at least once a month, compared to 81 percent of Catholics and 62 percent of Protestants; and a mere 9 percent of Jews claimed to attend at least once a week. According to a Gallup survey conducted a decade later, the figure for Jewish once-a-week synagogue attendance rose to 18 percent, as compared to 74 percent for Catholics and 40 percent for Protestants, but research in local communities suggested that the Jewish figure was inflated. By 1970, the National Jewish Population Survey determined that only 8 percent of Jewish household heads attended religious services 50 times a year or more, whereas 55 percent attended fewer than four times a year.[49]

Educating the young was the principal motivation for the establishment of the new suburban synagogue. Jews who were ambivalent about their own Jewish identity still desired to transmit identity to the next generation. Albert Gordon, in his study *Jews in Suburbia*, reproduces the 1948 membership brochure of the new Israel Community Center, in the new suburb of Levittown, New York:

> Many of our people have had little previous contact with synagogue life, having hitherto regarded the synagogue as the province of their elders. Many have not seen the

inside of a "shule" since their Bar Mitzvah. Now, however, they feel that it is time that they "grow up" and they have consequently acquired a renewed interest in synagogue activity. The responsibilities of parenthood have led many to rethink their position with regard to the Jewish heritage which they now seek to maintain in order to be able to transmit it to their children. In Levittown, this "return to Judaism" is facilitated for them through the existence of a synagogue consisting of like-minded young Jewish parents.[50]

In their study of the Lakeville suburb, Sklare and Greenbaum describe the process by which the new synagogue grew out of the informal Sunday school conducted by young suburban mothers. The synagogue remained child-centered so much so that "it is questionable whether the congregation could function at anything like its present level without the religious school. One official of the Temple believes it to be the strongest feature attracting people to the congregation."[51] In surveying the patterns of religious ritual life among Lakeville's Jews, Sklare and Greenbaum conclude that religious ritual is maintained so long as (1) it is capable of effective redefinition in modern terms; (2) it does not demand social isolation or the adoption of a unique lifestyle; (3) it accords with the religious culture of the larger community and provides a "Jewish" alternative when such is felt to be needed; (4) it is centered on the child; and (5) it is performed annually or infrequently.[52]

The paradoxes of the child-centered suburban synagogue are vividly described by Herbert Gans in his 1951 study of the Park Forest community. Like Lakeville's congregation, the Park

Forest synagogue began as a Sunday school. But the community soon split between the men, who wanted an adult-oriented community into which children would be initiated, and the women, who wanted a child-oriented community that would involve adults only tangentially:

> The women feared that the contradictions between the traditional Jewish home, whose features are now incorporated in the Sunday school curriculum, and the American home, which embodies their primary present-day values, would lead to family tensions. So, although they wanted their children to learn about traditional Jewish life, they did not want it brought home. The situation in Park Forest, then, is that many parents reject involvement in the cultural-religious aspects of the Jewish tradition for themselves as adults, while they demand that their children involve themselves to the extent of learning about this tradition, without, however, getting so involved as to wish to practice it.[53]

Park Forest's Jews wanted to integrate seamlessly into American suburban life, but they also wanted to remain distinctively Jewish. The child-centered synagogue offered a way to satisfy both impulses, fulfilling the imperative to transmit Judaism to the next generation without demanding any real behavioral commitment on the part of the adults. The message conveyed to children was that intensive Jewishness led to the celebration of a bar mitzvah and ended thereafter.

Soon after the Six-Day War, a mimeographed monologue entitled "The Last American Jew" circulated among Jewish youth groups across the United States. The monologue imagines a "last American Jew" sitting in a display in the Smithsonian and looking back from the year 2014, recounting the events that led to the disappearance of Jewish life from America—the abandonment of ritual, the estrangement from tradition, the acceptance of assimilation, and finally, the destruction of Israel. The reading, offered with tearful somberness, climaxes:

> How forgetful a people can be! When the people lost their pride in themselves, their religion, their Israel, they lost everything! As it was once said, "If I am not for myself, who will be for me?"
>
> I am the last American Jew. In less than 20 years, I too will die. And never again will another Jew set foot on this planet. My G-d, my G-d, where did we forsake you?[54]

The reading was typically followed by a discussion of the steps to be taken to prevent the calamity and concluded with a promise of personal responsibility for the Jewish people's survival elicited from each teen.

Like the Hollywood Bowl rally, the monologue is redolent with ironies. In lachrymose solemnity, it prophesies the end of American Jewry. But at the moment the reading was being offered, the American Jewish community could count the most synagogues, the most synagogue members, and the greatest number of children enrolled in synagogue schools in its history to date and ever since. The monologue laments the loss of an ethnic culture with Israel at its center and ethnic pride as its most valued emblem. Knowledge of the content of that culture and commitment to its practice were deemed less important than pride. Just like the synagogue one joined but rarely attended, Israel is viewed as a symbol of Jewish resilience, not as a place to go and live or a culture to learn and share. Tradition is cherished as an artifact of culture, an heirloom, not as an engaging way of life. God is not mentioned in the reading until the very last line, which quotes the verse from Psalms uttered famously by Jesus on the cross. And just like the Hollywood Bowl rally, the reading evokes an atmosphere of crisis—the emergency of group survival—as a way of awakening Jewish loyalties. It did not seem to occur to the youth leaders who offered this monologue that presenting an ethnic culture empty of meaning but burdened with collective guilt for its imminent demise might be part of the reason young Jews were abandoning Jewish life.

Harold Schulweis stepped to the bimah to deliver his first address to an overflowing crowd at Valley Beth Shalom in September 1970. What did his congregation expect to hear? As loyal American Jews still enjoying the flush of the post-1967 awakening, they expected their new rabbi to articulate their anxieties about Jewish survival. They expected him to elicit from them a pledge to transmit Jewishness to their children as their primary obligation, evoking pride in Israel and the solemn memories of the horrors of the Holocaust as the emotional hammer behind this pledge. They expected him to reflect warmly on Jewish children and offer his pledge to bring children closer to the synagogue. They expected him to demand a return to tradition, to ritual observance, prayer, and Torah learning. Not that they would ever fulfill such a demand or even consider it with any seriousness. Hearing the rabbi's futile plea for greater commitment and basking in collective guilt was a traditional part of the ritual. And they expected him to condemn the growing narcissism of American culture with its emphasis on self, and call on them to return to a commitment to synagogue and peoplehood.

Schulweis confounded every one of these expectations. He understood well the ambivalence of his congregants' Judaism. His strategy for resolving that ambivalence was to offer his congregation something they had never heard before.

He said nothing about Jewish survival. Survival is not the challenge. Bringing Judaism inward—engaging Jews in Jewish living, offering Jews a reason to choose Jewish life—is the challenge. The rabbi's role is to translate the gifts of Jewish culture into life at this moment, allowing it to find its way into the heart and into life. Survival cannot be pursued as a communal objective. It is a by-product, achieved only when Jews are engaged in Jewish life, when Judaism is lived, celebrated, and internalized. He did not speak about Israel and made no mention of the Holocaust. He would later acknowledge that both are central to Jewish identity and ideology, but they remain secondary to the deeper issue of the personal engagement of Jews in Jewish living.

From his first words, Schulweis spoke to his congregation in an idiom that was shockingly adult. Children were certainly welcome in his sanctuary, so long as they were silent and invisible. This was a decidedly adult place, and his was a decidedly adult Judaism that spoke to the questions of adult life. Children, he communicated, will enter Judaism only when they see their elders practice Judaism with seriousness and fervor. There is no other way to transmit the culture to the young.

He demanded of his new congregants no new commitment to ritual life or even to the synagogue. He proffered no guilt in their lax religious observance. He carefully eschewed the language of "return." Instead, he demonstrated that he lived in their world, appreciated their struggles, and understood their needs. He offered patterns of Jewish thought that would reframe contemporary life and answer its greatest maladies. They had come to suburbia to remake themselves. He took them further. Now was the time to remake Judaism. This was not the time to return to tradition but to move boldly to create a truly modern Judaism that spoke to the futility, the loneliness, the ennui, of modern life. The problem was not the self-absorption of American culture. The problem was a Judaism that had become so focused on the collective that it forgot the person in the Jew. Jewish faith and culture deeply needed *tzimtzum*, contraction and concentration, to turn from the exclusive concern with the communal in order to address the yearning and seeking of the individual Jew.

American Jews were ambivalent, Schulweis believed, only because they had never met the genius of their own culture. And it was his intention to make the introduction.

PART 2

THREE RABBINIC VOICES

CHAPTER 4

The Theological Voice

The Rabbi as Theologian

Once upon a time in the old country, there lived a passionate atheist philosopher who traveled from village to village destroying the faith of believers. No one could resist his sophistry; no faith could withstand his acid skepticism. Soon enough, the philosopher outgrew the challenge of overturning the beliefs of simpleminded villagers, so he set his sights on a higher pursuit. He announced that he would challenge the Rebbe to a disputation. Tearing down the faith of a revered spiritual master would be his life's crowning achievement.

The Rebbe's disciples came to warn him: "Beware this atheist! His arguments are shrewd, his logic is powerful, and his words are seductive. Rebbe, beware this atheist!"

The Rebbe calmly dismissed their concerns. "Let him come. We'll see what he has to say."

The atheist arrived in the Rebbe's town and made his way to the Rebbe's academy. He entered into the Rebbe's chamber and found the old man sitting at a great table piled high with holy books. Just as the atheist prepared to launch into his diatribe, the Rebbe looked up into his eyes and asked him a one-word question in Yiddish:

"Efshar? Is it possible?"

The atheist stopped, his attention immediately arrested. "Efshar? Is it possible?" he repeated to himself. "Is it possible?" His eyes filled with tears. "Is it possible?" Dropping to his knees, he began to weep and then to cry. "Yes, of course, it is possible. It is always possible. It is possible!"

The philosopher, it is said, became a disciple of the Rebbe. And when anyone ever came with doubts, the philosopher would respond, "Remember, it is possible! It is always possible!"

Is faith possible in our time?

Nietzsche famously announced, "God is dead." Not that God was once alive and suddenly expired. The fundamental attitude of Western culture changed. The Enlightenment made faith impossible. Modernity put humanity at the center of the universe. Moderns do not look to God's will to explain their fate. God, if not dead, has been rendered irrelevant. This is the singular challenge facing contemporary religion.

Schulweis' mentor, Mordecai Kaplan, recognized this new reality and responded by reconstructing Jewish life on the foundation of Jewish peoplehood. Though he wrote extensively about theology, Kaplan saw the elevation of belonging over believing, of peoplehood over theology, as his foremost achievement, his "Copernican revolution." In his personal diary Kaplan wrote,

> . . . the main contribution of Reconstructionism . . . is not its humanistic reinterpretation of the tradition but the Copernican revolution it has been seeking to effect in the conception of the relation of the Jewish people to the Jewish religion. So long as we keep on arguing what to do with the Jewish religion and overlook the fact that the Jewish people is moribund, we will accomplish nothing.[1]

Schulweis diverged from his teacher. Belief matters. As post-war American Jewry turned toward peoplehood—Kaplan's "belonging"—as the central element of Jewish identity, Schulweis perceived that the loss of belief was the chief cause of the alienation of contemporary Jews. Kaplan had it backward. Or rather, what was true for Kaplan in the 1930s was now reversed: reviving a moribund Jewish people could not be accomplished without reviving a moribund faith. Schulweis feared that the elevation of belonging without sufficient attention to believing would lead to a Judaism of superficial ethnic pride with no moral foundation. Judaism would become only an identity to be assumed rather than a set of truths to be affirmed or a life to be lived. Belonging, Schulweis argued, rests upon a foundation of believing. Belonging is mediated by believing. Otherwise Judaism is likely to collapse into a hollow ethnic "Jewishness" of kitschy Yiddish phrases, bagels and lox, songs from *Fiddler on the Roof*, but little else.

Through his experience in the pulpit, Schulweis came to recognize what his teacher could not—the dangers of fractured Judaism. From the vantage of the pulpit, he encountered the Kaplanian nightmare—the phenomenon of Jews who belong but do not believe:

> In matters of religion, most people do not ask questions or seek answers. They assume a neither/nor neutrality: neither apostate nor believer; neither denier nor affirmer of their faith. They pay their dues, attend an occasional service, answer yes when pollsters ask them whether they believe in God, and register their children in "Hebrew school." They send their children to know

about religion, not believe; to know about ritual, not to observe; to know how to pray, not to pray; to know something about Jewish history, not to be engaged in the people's way of life.[2]

The contemporary rabbi does not go out to battle a principled atheism, heresy, or *epicorsus* but a benign, contented indifference—a superficial Judaism of ethnic sentimentality attached to no moral or religious truth. This is much more insidious than the conscientious disbelief that Kaplan met in the 1930s.

This alienation of belonging from believing begins in childhood. Children naturally ask religious questions. They ask "really" questions: Did the serpent "really" speak to Eve? Did Noah "really" gather animals into the ark? But these questions are deferred and deflected:

> My first teacher of religion was my grandfather. An erudite man, he taught me how to translate the biblical text and how to pray. He was patient and proud of my questions. Perhaps not all my questions. He was patient with my questions about the meaning of words, grammar, places, dates, facts—questions of "where" or "what" or "how." But my "what for" questions, particularly those that asked for the meaning and purpose of the text, disturbed him. . . . My grandfather would affectionately pinch my cheek and respond "*shpayter*," the Yiddish word for "later."[3]

Questions deferred are questions denied. And questions deferred indefinitely leave a void in their wake. Schulweis' most popular book, his statement of theology, was entitled

For Those Who Can't Believe. The title was his editor's invention. Schulweis' original title for the book was *When You're Older, You'll Understand.* Early in the book, Schulweis introduces the character of David, to whom the book is addressed. David identifies himself as "spiritual" but "not the religious type." David is Schulweis' typology of the contemporary Jew whose religious education was authoritarian, rote, wasteful; whose early experiences of worship were dull and irrelevant; whose experiences of ritual were perfunctory. David absorbed a literal, childish, trivialized reading of religious truths, disconnected from any moral heroism. It is no wonder he is alienated. When asked in recent studies of Jewish identity, "What is your religion?" more than a million Davids, more than a fifth of American Jews, and fully a third of younger Jews answered, "none."[4]

Distant from Judaism, David nevertheless identifies as "spiritual." He represents a generation of seekers who Schulweis identifies as "those who cannot go home again but do not wish to live spiritually homeless." Observes Schulweis, "Home is too important to be abandoned. It must be made habitable again."[5] For Schulweis, reviving the deferred religious questions of youth and addressing them with an adult theology is crucial. It is futile to address issues of Jewish continuity as if they are solely sociological. The core issue is theological—a crisis of faith, the loss of shared belief. The solution involves helping Jews find a Judaism they can believe in, showing them a new way to the sacred.

The Theologian as Rabbi

The Talmud relates that the heretic Elisha ben Abuya lost his faith when he witnessed the death of a child. A boy was sent by his father up to the rafters to retrieve fledglings from a bird's nest. Before taking the chicks, he shooed away the mother bird. In doing so, the boy fulfilled two biblical commandments: honoring his father (Exodus 20:12) and sending away the mother bird (Deuteronomy 22:6–7). Ironically, both commandments appear in Torah with an explicit reward—the promise of long life. But on the way down the ladder the boy fell and died. Witnessing the tragedy, Elisha proclaimed, "*Leit din, v'leit dayan.* There is no Judge and there is no justice" (Talmud, Kiddushin 39b).

Schulweis recorded his own painful Elisha ben Abuya moment:

Right after Yom Kippur I received a frantic telephone call. As I arrived at the home, it was already filled with family and friends. I knew the family very well: serious Jews.

They had been at services during Neilah. Their son, Kenny, whom I also knew from confirmation classes, had suggested that he start out early and break the Yom Kippur fast with friends in Malibu. The parents had insisted that he wait until the end of Neilah. As soon as the shofar was blown, he rushed off in his car, and somewhere on a winding road a drunk driver plowed into his car. Kenny was instantly killed.

I walked into the bedroom where Kenny's father was sitting with his head buried in his hands. He looked up at me, his face grew pale, his fist clenched, and he greeted me with a torrent of curses: cursing me, cursing God, cursing the synagogue, cursing himself. Why in the world had he insisted that Kenny wait until the end of services, he said, when the whole thing was stupid and foolish!

The room was filled with stunned people as Kenny's father continued his curses. Then he told me to leave. "Get him out of my sight," he said. On my way out, his wife grabbed hold of me. "Rabbi," she said, "don't take it personally." But I did take it personally. Kenny's father felt he was cursed by God, and I, his rabbi, represented that God of malediction.[6]

"Rabbi, don't take it personally." But for the rabbi who encounters such moments regularly, it is personal. It is the core of the rabbi's role. In the course of a career, a rabbi will meet every one of the classic theological questions of Jewish belief: the nature of revelation, the truth of scripture, the authority of Jewish law, the efficacy of prayer, the significance of ritual, the meaning of Jewish chosenness, the dialectic between Jewish particularity and universalism, the importance of the land and State of Israel. But no question is as personal and anguished as the question of undeserved suffering, "Why me, Rabbi?" All the other questions can be met with some degree of scholarly distance. Suffering is intensely personal, for the congregant but also for the rabbi:

He didn't want comfort from me. He threw my arm off his shoulders. He didn't want psychology from me. He wanted theology—a mature, ethical, credible theology. His response was extreme, but not unique.

The parents who are sobbing over the infant's crib death, the husband of a young woman afflicted with cancer, the children moaning over the death of a father in an airplane accident—all of them are left with guilt, shame, blame, and anger. Do I not bear some responsibility? Somehow or other, my people have inherited a theology that insinuates that nothing happens by accident; that nothing happens without someone being guilty of some transgression; that catastrophe is *bashert*, fated and decreed. Don't I bear a responsibility as a rabbi?[7]

The problem of theodicy, the justification of God in the face of unwarranted suffering, troubled Schulweis from the beginning of his career. It was the pressing question he asked Martin Buber in their 1952 conversation.[8] In the 1954 textbook on the philosophy of religion he edited with his City College of New York colleague Daniel Bronstein, it was Schulweis who compiled and edited the sections on evil and divine providence. He authored the essay "Suffering and Evil" in the 1964 B'nai B'rith Adult Education volume *Great Jewish Ideas*.[9] It was the topic of his doctoral dissertation in 1971, reprinted as his book *Evil and the Morality of God*. It forms the core chapters of his popular theology *For Those Who Can't Believe* and found its way into many of his sermons and addresses.

He took the question personally. For Schulweis, the question of theodicy was never purely academic. The passion of his writing reveals his deep personal stake in the problem and a deep sense of personal responsibility for its solution. That passion was born of the daily life of a rabbi but was intensified immeasurably by the historical moment. In the introduction to *Evil and the Morality of God*, Schulweis observes that the contemporary loss of faith grows from the coincidence of the horrors of the twentieth century with the process of secularization that began a century earlier:

The implosion sparked by the holocaustal events of our century has exposed serious cracks within the monotheistic faith system itself. Not that the outcry of innocence in the face of genuine evil is new. But the cultural environment in which it is heard is new. . . . The familiar scaffolding of traditional presuppositions surrounding the old questions has fallen. Under such conditions, old questions appear new and old answers must be re-examined again.[10]

Modernity dismantled the structures of faith that once protected belief from the experience of evil. Absent those structures, the horrors of twentieth-century radical evil immeasurably intensified the problem that evil presents faith. Science and its skepticism challenged faith, but it was the phenomenon of radical evil that dealt the blow to faith for moderns:

Contemporary theology cast its eyes elsewhere to search for the cause and remedy of the religious breakdown. In this it was misled. *For most people, the breaking point of traditional monotheistic belief lies not in Darwin or Einstein, but in Dachau and Hiroshima.*[11] [Schulweis' italics]

Scientific skepticism invades religion from without. The problem of evil, Schulweis argues, grows from an internal contradiction deep within monotheism. Ultimately, no theodicy succeeds in reconciling conventional ideas of God with the experience of evil, particularly the radical evil of the Holocaust. Schulweis' colleague and Jewish Theological Seminary classmate Richard Rubenstein reached the same conclusion. A few years before Schulweis completed his dissertation, Rubenstein declared the biblical God dead. The Holocaust confirmed Albert Camus's perception of a cold and absurd universe empty of meaning:

> I believe the greatest single challenge to modern Judaism arises out of the question of God and the death camps. How can Jews believe in an omnipotent, beneficent God after Auschwitz? Traditional Jewish theology maintains that God is the ultimate, omnipotent actor in the historical drama. It has interpreted every major catastrophe in Jewish history as God's punishment of a sinful Israel. I fail to see how this position can be maintained without regarding Hitler and the SS as instruments of God's will. The agony of European Jewry cannot be likened to the testing of Job. To see any purpose in the death camps, the traditional believer is forced to regard the most demonic, antihuman explosion in all history as a meaningful expression of God's purposes. The idea is simply too obscene for me to accept. [Camus] refuses . . . to see man as inevitably and inescapably guilty before God. He accepts the tragedy, the inevitability, and the gratuitous absurdity of suffering, but he refuses to consent to its justice. He would rather live in an absurd, indifferent cosmos in which men suffer and die meaninglessly but still retain a measure of tragic integrity than see every last human event encased in a pitiless framework of meaning which deprives men of even the consolation that suffering, though inevitable, is not entirely merited

or earned. . . . We concur with this choice of an absurd
and ultimately tragic cosmos.[12]

For Rubenstein, the cosmos is absurd and human life ultimately and irredeemably tragic. Under these circumstances,
religion remains valuable as a way of coping with a dark and
senseless world. Schulweis rejected this view. Rubenstein, by
then a professor of theology, could join Camus in proclaiming
the world Godless and meaningless. He could celebrate the
heroism of those who act morally despite the absurdity. Schulweis could not. As a congregational rabbi, Schulweis lived with
ordinary people struggling to live morally and meaningfully
amid the exigencies of real life. He could not abandon them
to Rubenstein's hopelessness. Few possess Camus's heroism.
How were ordinary people to resist the moral cynicism and
despair generated by the normal tragedies of life, much less
radical evil?

In his 1945 graduation essay in the Yeshiva College student
yearbook, *Masmid*, Schulweis posited that the very definition
of religion involves "the general improvement of man, economically, socially, spiritually." Religion "re-affirms man's dignity and innate goodness."[13] Working as a rabbi and living with
people struggling daily to build moral lives only reinforced
Schulweis' innate pragmatism. Like Kaplan, he judged the ade-
quacy of a theology on pragmatic grounds: What sort of moral
personality does a given theology sustain? Does it empower
and inspire human moral action? Does it make a difference
in a human life? As Kaplan taught, this is the function of the
God idea and the sole test of a theology's truth. Schulweis'
pragmatism characterized his thought throughout his career.

For Schulweis, moral courage was the test of any belief. Does a theology sustain or undermine human moral courage?

Rubenstein's theology may have been profound, even poetic, but it was pragmatically unsustainable. In the shadow of the Holocaust, contemporary Jewry desperately needed an idea of God that would support and sustain moral vision and moral action and prevent them from falling into cynicism. This task defined Schulweis' theological mission.

The Failure of Theodicy

All theodicies fail. This was Schulweis' conviction, argued consistently from the beginning of his career. Theodicies fail because the problem of evil presses upon an internal contradiction within the structure of monotheism. Monotheism attempts to unite two ideas of divine perfection: metaphysical perfection, a God who is omnipotent; and moral perfection, a God who is all good. Both of these cannot be maintained together in the face of undeserved human suffering.

Theodicy is conventionally charted as the incongruence of three propositions: (1) God is omnipotent, (2) God is all good, (3) evil exists. To defend God in the face of unwarranted human suffering, one of these propositions must be compromised. At the funeral, the preacher piously intones, "He's in a better place now." Because God is defined as all powerful and all good, evil cannot exist. Suffering is redefined as somehow beneficial. Alternatively, suffering is acknowledged as evil, and God as responsible, because God's goodness is incomprehensible to human beings. The preacher solemnly intones, "We cannot know the ways of God, but we must trust this is God's benevolent plan." Finally, evil may be acknowledged as real, and God as loving and caring, but God is said to be incapable of doing anything about it. At their core, this is how all theodicies function. In the face of evil, one of the propositions must be compromised.

As a philosophical exercise, a theodicy may succeed in explaining suffering. By compromising one of these propositions, a theology may absorb the phenomenon of evil. But what kind of faith is left in its aftermath? The devastating effect on the subsequent life of faith is left unstated in the philosophical evaluation of theodicy. The operation may be successful, but the patient may die. The consequence of a successful theodicy is a truncated faith in a decimated God. The rabbi may walk away satisfied that a cogent and clever argument has been proffered, but the congregant will never again return to the synagogue. No matter how well a rabbi may explain the theology, the congregant is left muttering that any God who can countenance the death of a child does not merit devotion. Thus the philosopher Immanuel Kant's famous dictum that theodicy offers an "apology in which the defense is worse than the charge . . . and may certainly be fully left to the detestation of everyone who has the least sense or spark of morality."[14]

In the Bible, Job suffers and raises his voice in protest. His protest emerges from the beliefs that his suffering comes from God, as do all things in the world, and that God is good. But Job knows he is innocent and therefore unjustly afflicted. How, then, can a good man suffer so? Job's friends rise to defend God. To do so, they indict Job. What appears to be random undeserved suffering, they maintain, is not evil at all but is in fact deserved. Your suffering, they charge, is punishment for some sin. Theodicy's first side effect is to inflict guilt on the sufferer, effectively doubling the pain. At the end of the book, God repudiates Job's friends, which reestablishes the initial dilemma. To answer Job's charges, God asserts that Job has no standing to question God's doings:

> Then the LORD replied to Job out of the tempest and said:
> Who is this who darkens counsel,
> Speaking without knowledge?
> Gird your loins like a man;
> I will ask and you will inform Me.
> Where were you when I laid the earth's foundations?
> Speak if you have understanding. . . .
> Do you know the laws of heaven
> Or impose its authority on earth? . . .
> Shall one who should be disciplined complain against Shaddai?
> He who arraigns God must respond.
> JOB 38:1–4, 33–34; 40:2

Job is told to be silent and accept his fate, for no human being can question God. So, God wins, but what does God win? What sort of religious life is Job left with at the end? Can he worship a God who is metaphysically magnificent but morally vacant? The resolution of the book is the vision of a God who stands beyond human moral judgment and outside of human moral discourse. What is moral for human beings is not moral for God. Intimacy with the personal God is the casualty of theodicy, sacrificed in the defense of God's sovereignty. And most egregious for Schulweis, Job accepts and resigns. His moral sensibility crushed, he ceases to demand justice and surrenders to moral silence.

I know that You can do everything,

that nothing you propose is impossible for You.

Who is this who obscures counsel without knowledge?

Indeed, I spoke without understanding

Of things beyond me, which I did not know.

Hear now, and I will speak;

I will ask, and You will inform me.

I had heard You with my ears,

But now I see You with my eyes;

Therefore, I recant and relent,

being but dust and ashes.

    JOB 42:2–6

In *Evil and the Morality of God,* Schulweis demonstrates that this same pattern is played out in all subsequent theodicies. Every theology, Schulweis argues, is built upon an implicit concept of divine perfection. This concept controls which aspects of divinity are protected and which are relinquished in mounting a theodicy.

Classical Metaphysical Theologies:
Aquinas and Maimonides

Classical metaphysical theologies begin with the presupposition that *being* is good. The moral perfection of the biblical God is transformed into the metaphysical perfection of the philosophical God. As an example, Schulweis cites Aquinas's statement in *Summa Theologica* 1.Q5.1:

The essence of goodness consists in this, that it is in some sense desirable. Hence the philosopher says:

Goodness is what all desire. Now it is clear that a thing is desirable only insofar as it is perfect, for all desire their own perfection. But everything is perfect so far as it is actual. Therefore it is clear that a thing is perfect so far as it is being; for being is the actuality of everything.[15]

Note the syllogism: Goodness = Desirability = Perfection = Actuality. All that is actual, all that is real, is good. It is only the narrowness of human perception, in both space and time, that precludes human beings from appreciating the goodness of the vast divine creation.

In his *Guide of the Perplexed* (3:22), Maimonides interprets God's answer to Job in a similar way. The created universe is perfect. It is only Job's limited human perspective that prevents him from seeing this. Were Job able to see the world through God's eyes and in God's time frame, he would perceive the grand order and perfection in the construction of all things. Job gains equanimity when he realizes it's not about him. It's not personal. His torments are not punishments. The grand machinations of the universe are oblivious to the fate or feelings of one man. His own puny experience is no vantage from which to judge the goodness of creation. So Job surrenders, and God is released from Job's accusations. But at a terrible cost—Job is rendered morally mute. The moral dialogue between God and humanity is silenced. Schulweis concludes,

The normative moral connotation of goodness has been abandoned. The metaphysical ideal of perfection underlies the major arguments of metaphysical theodicy. In its identification with being and actuality, the metaphysical-perfection ideal has removed the moral grounds for criticizing the governance of the universe.[16]

The philosopher wins, but faith loses. God is acquitted of Job's accusations, but Job, and all humanity, is left with a religious life denuded of its moral center. Moral silence becomes the essence of reverence. This surrender of the moral, Schulweis suggests, leaves in its wake no religion at all.

Hartshorne's Process Theology

Classical metaphysics held perfection to be static, unmoved, and unchanging. This makes it difficult to read the Bible's accounts of a God who is moved by prayer, enters into covenant, and is engaged with human beings. Based on philosopher Alfred North Whitehead's metaphysics, philosopher Charles Hartshorne offers a dynamic image of divine perfection much closer to the biblical image: God is the all-inclusive process of knowing, caring, and becoming. God is dipolar: being and becoming, the ideal and the real, past and future. All possibilities are included within the Divine. God's providence sets limits to guide the world toward the development of greater life, persuading and luring creation toward goodness.

Hartshorne's God includes all and cares for all. But, as Schulweis points out, this omnibenevolence has a dark side. He quotes Hartshorne's *The Logic of Perfection*:

> There may be those who think otherwise, who suppose that God can wish well to the sick child in such a fashion as literally not to care about the woes of bacteria causing the sickness. But such persons, in my opinion, are

thinking anthropomorphically about God, who must always relate Himself to absolutely all creatures.[17]

Hartshorne's God cares absolutely for all creatures. God suffers the pain of all creatures. But divine care, in Hartshorne's conception, is impartial. The child and the bacteria, the lion and the lamb, the murderer and his victim, all participate equally and indiscriminately in the flow of the Divine. That is a far cry from the biblical idea of a God who champions moral distinctions:

> The Lord loves the righteous;
> The Lord watches over the stranger;
> He gives courage to the orphan and widow,
> But makes the path of the wicked tortuous.
> PSALM 146:8–9

Hartshorne's loyalty to his metaphysical idea of perfection leads him to compromise the essential element of biblical religion—God's commitment to righteousness. Therefore, Schulweis concludes,

> [Hartshorne's] God is open to change, growth, and suffering, and free from the absolute, passionless, and unchangeable character derived from the Greek idea of perfection. But the crucial element of the biblical ideal of perfection is not evident in his or Whitehead's process conceptualization of deity—the moral character of God, who cares and acts to protect individuals and peoples from the onslaught of evil. Without the moral

ideal of God and the expectations which it engenders, the very question which gives rise to theodicy is crushed. The problem of evil is not solved but dissolved by the transmutation of moral into metaphysical virtue.[18]

Personalist Theologies: Buber and Barth

Theologies, Schulweis asserts, respond to two human impulses: the drive to know and the drive to be known. Metaphysical theologies are rooted in the first. Personalist theologies are rooted in the second. Conceiving of God as Person answers a different human need than conceiving God as being or process, the need to be known, embraced, and comforted. Only a God as Person, who presents us with personality, can meet us in relationship. Personality constitutes a different sort of divine perfection, and personalist theologies wrestle with evil in a different way.

No philosopher celebrates relationship more strongly than Martin Buber. In Buber's philosophy of dialogue, God is the Eternal Thou who can only be met in the I-Thou encounter. Asked by a colleague if he believed in God, Buber replied, "If to believe in God means to be able to talk *about* him in the third person, then I do *not* believe in God. But if to believe in him means to be able to talk *to* him, then I do believe in God."[19] To "believe in" God is to accept a proposition. To "know God" is to enter into relationship. But what happens to that relationship when evil occurs, especially the radical evil of the Holocaust?

Buber himself felt this crisis acutely:

How is life with God still possible in a time in which there is an Oswiecim [Auschwitz]? The estrangement

143

has become too cruel, the hiddenness too deep. . . . Can
one still as an individual and as a people enter into a dialogic relationship with Him? Can one still call to Him?[20]

Buber can only counsel patient waiting and a readiness for
the reappearance of the hidden God: "Though His coming
appearance resembles no other one, we shall recognize again
our cruel and merciful God."[21]

What can such a formulation possibly mean?

In their 1952 interview, Buber promised Schulweis a new
book focusing on issues of good and evil emerging from the
Holocaust.[22] That book, *The Eclipse of God,* arrived later that
year. In his essay "The Love of God and the Idea of Deity,"
Buber articulated an answer.

Buber contrasts philosophical theologies that identify
God with the moral ideal—he is thinking specifically of the
nineteenth-century Jewish Kantian philosopher Hermann
Cohen—with his own theology of dialogue. To enter dialogue,
Buber maintains, God must be personality. But more than
mere personality, Buber understands God as "absolute personality." God may never be encountered as an It. The dialogic
relationship with God sets the paradigm for all I-Thou relationships, thus it is not just good but "supergood." An explanation for radical evil cannot be elicited from God, argues
Buber, because God cannot be forced out of concealment, lest
the relationship be rendered functional and impersonal. God
must be accepted and loved, Buber contends, "in His deepest
concealment. Only through the fear of God does man enter
so deep into the love of God that he cannot be cast out of it."[23]
We can only wait and hope for the resumption of intimacy.

God as supergood absolute personality comes to mean a God beyond questioning, beyond judgment, beyond morality. Schulweis found this deeply frustrating:

> A supergood absolute personality will produce no Jobian discontent. Job will accept every moral incongruity of life without resentment. . . . Faith in an incomprehensible supergood personality may prevent disillusionment, but it is a resolution as desperate as plucking out one's eyes to forestall the possible loss of vision.[24]

What kind of intimacy allows for cruelty but excludes moral accountability? In human parlance, that is called spousal abuse. Who would revere such a God?

Schulweis' ultimate example of personalist theodicy is Karl Barth. Barth is exquisitely faithful to the story of Job. Before his calamity, Job maintained a belief in "Elohim," the benevolent God reflected in his blessed life. Once afflicted, Job protests. He presses his case against God. He knows that his suffering comes from God. And he knows that his sad condition represents a violation of his covenant with that God. It is only then, according to Barth, that Job meets Yahweh, the inscrutable God revealed in the whirlwind. This is not the God of his covenant, the God he has come to understand through his life experience. This manifestation of God, in Barth's interpretation, is autonomous, unhindered, unpredictable, and free to act in the world unbound by human moral ideals:

> For Karl Barth, the need for theodicy is itself a symptom of man's enslavement to moral and logical criteria and

norms irrelevant to the conduct of the divinely unique One. Yahweh neither requires nor asks for Job's "understanding, agreement, or applause." The very question which underlies the alleged need for theodicy is presumptuous. The "message of the cosmos" whispered through the whirlwind informs Job that he is not the center of the universe, that he has nothing to do with its direction, that he is incompetent and irreverent in thinking he can judge its teleology.[25]

Surrendering to this autonomous God is the great triumph of faith: "The divine other is subject personality, not impersonal moral or metaphysical ideals. The divine person cannot be made perceptible to man, reasonable and amenable to human standards without reducing His dignity."[26]

For Barth, the divine personality is the ultimate Subject that can be bound by no predicates. The assignment of any predicated conditions limits God's autonomy and compromises God's perfection. If God is loved because God is good or just or compassionate, Barth would argue, it is not God who is loved, but goodness, justice, and compassion. These ideals belong to human beings, not God, and therefore worship of such a God is a form of self-worship, of idolatry. The only way to genuinely love God is to abandon all predicates and embrace God purely as Divine Subject. In his *Church Dogmatics*, Barth writes,

> Strictly speaking, there is no divine predicate, no idea of God which can have as its special content what God is. There is strictly speaking *only* the Divine Subject as such and in Him the fitness of His divine predicates.[27]

What of God's self-revelations? Does scripture not describe God's character? Scripture reveals a momentary glimpse into an aspect of the Divine. But with divinity as with investments, past performance is no predictor of future results. Like any complex, dynamic personality, a momentary self-revelation does not predict responses in other circumstances. Whatever is taught today may be contradicted tomorrow. And we are not to judge, only to accept. In Søren Kierkegaard's chilling description of the sacrifice of Isaac, God's command to Abraham contradicts previous divine promises, as well as everything Abraham knows of right and wrong. Nevertheless, Abraham resolutely goes forward, the loyal knight of faith, to achieve his "teleological suspension of the ethical." This, held Kierkegaard, is the pinnacle of faith.

Barth's accomplishment, concludes Schulweis, is the complete disjunction of faith and morality. We must choose one or the other:

> Barth calls for man's total allegiance to the divine Ego whose commands will not be deciphered through the moral predicates assigned to Him. The results are clear. The moral predicates have been severed from the subject. Subject and predicates stand over against each other. Faith and morality stand in opposition.[28]

What does it mean to worship a God without attributes? What kind of God is left after all the predicates of divinity are subtracted? Not a God that anyone would venerate. Schulweis cites the British philosopher John Stuart Mill:

If I know nothing about what the attribute is, I cannot tell that it is a proper object of veneration. To say that God's goodness may be different in kind from man's goodness, what is it but saying, with a slight change of phraseology, that God may possibly not be good?[29]

The Eternal Question—Why Me?

All who suffer ask Job's question, "Why me, God?" To protect God from Job's accusations, theologies either compromise God's moral perfection or they counsel human beings to accept suffering in silence. The outcome of theodicy is a God infinitely distanced from humanity. Divine morality and human morality are disjoined. Job's accusation is turned back. Accused of hubris or blasphemy, he is told to acquiesce to his fate. God's integrity is protected at the cost of sacrificing human moral sensibility. The moral dialogue between man and God is silenced. But is it really wrong—or worse, pretentious—to question God after the destruction of a million Jewish children? Or even one?

The radical evil of the Holocaust renders the dilemma of theodicy infinitely more unbearable. It demands of the contemporary rabbi a new theological response. Schulweis concludes his *Evil and the Morality of God* with a citation from Elie Wiesel's novel *The Accident*. Hearing the story of Sarah, a prostitute and tormented victim of the death camps, Wiesel's hero cries out, "Whoever listens to Sarah and doesn't change, whoever enters Sarah's world and does not invent new gods and new religions, deserves death and destruction."[30]

Schulweis felt the inexorable urgency of this task—inventing "new gods and new religion." Traditional theodicy had failed.

The God of those theologies was dead. How could the sacred be recovered "for those who cannot go home again using the old routes, but who choose not to remain homeless?"[31]

Predicate Theology

Consider two lists of propositions, perhaps written on the blackboard of a college classroom:

Column A	Column B
God is just.	Doing justice is Godly.
God is merciful.	Acting mercifully is Godly.
God uplifts the fallen.	Uplifting the fallen is Godly.
God heals the sick.	Healing the sick is Godly.
God loosens the fetters of the bound.	Loosening the fetters of the bound is Godly.

Asks the instructor: Who agrees with column A? A few hands go up. The response is decidedly reluctant and reserved.[32]

Conventional theology affirms a personal God—God as subject. The traditional prayer book is filled with hymns extolling the glories of God. Predicates are offered generously; God is praised as just, merciful, uplifting, and healing. But when belief confronts the phenomenon of evil, as Job sadly discovered, grave doubt sets in. In defense of God, the predicates are snatched away. God's justice, it is said, is not human justice, and God's goodness is not human goodness. To protect God's perfection, the Divine Subject is raised beyond reproach by the endless qualification of God's predicates. It is a kind of religious masochism to maintain allegiance to a God whose goodness and justice we cannot comprehend and whose mercy we cannot perceive. This is the source of the audience's reticence when it comes to column A.

Who agrees with column B? The response is unanimously positive, even enthusiastic. Column A describes God as subject. Column B lists actions, verbs, described as Godly. Column A is descriptive. Column B is normative. While many have trouble affirming the truth of column A, few have hesitation asserting the truth of column B. Schulweis asks, What, then, is the ultimate aim of religion? Is it to enforce faith in God as subject or to elevate a set of predicates to the exalted level of Godliness?

"I propose a shift of focus, from noun to verb, from subject to predicate, from God as person to Godliness, in Hebrew *Elohut*. Not the qualities of divinity but the divinity of the qualities is essential to belief."[33] Inverting the focus from the Divine Subject to the divinity of the predicates, Schulweis attempted to rescue religion from the impossible task of theodicy. This is his predicate theology.

Predicate theology transforms all descriptive propositions about God as subject into normative statements, defining actions as Godly. Metaphysical statements of belief are turned into moral statements of supreme value. Where Barth disjoined morality from faith, Schulweis moves in the opposite direction, collapsing faith into morality:

> To believe in Godliness is to believe in the verbs and
> adverbs that refer to the activities of divinity. To behave
> in a Godly fashion is to realize in one's life the attri-
> butes of Godliness that are potential in all human and
> nonhuman energies. Atheism is not the disbelief in the
> reality and goodness of the noun but disbelief in the

reality and goodness of the attributes. The question to be asked of those who seek God is not whether they believe in a noun that cannot be known but whether they believe in the gerunds of Godliness: healing the sick, feeding the hungry, supporting the fallen, pursuing peace, loving the neighbor.[34]

The normative propositions of Godliness—doing justice is Godly, acting mercifully is Godly, etc.—carry with them the implication that human beings are capable of performing these actions. As Kant famously taught, ought implies can. Asserting that an action is Godly is concomitantly to assert the belief that the action is within human capability. The belief in the human capacity to pursue Godliness is the heart of Schulweis' "theistic humanism."[35]

The heart of Schulweis' religious faith is a belief in the ever-expanding horizon of the human moral self. The Torah begins with the affirmation that the human being is created *b'tzelem Elohim*, in the divine image (Genesis 1:26–27). This verse, according to the second-century sage Shimon ben Azzai, is the Torah's most significant principle (Sifra Kedoshim 4:12). The unfolding of the *tzelem*, the divine image, in a life given to Godliness is Schulweis' conception of God's unfolding presence in the world.

The Torah ends with Moses's affirmation in Deuteronomy 30 that God's moral truth is "not far away . . . it is in your mouth and in your heart to do it" (vv. 11–14). The most proximate connection to divinity is within—within the human being. The God Schulweis worshipped is the "God within." God is found in the human ability to rise above self-interest and self-indulgence toward Godliness.[36] The traditional belief in a transcendent God is translated in Schulweis' theology into faith in the transcendent potential of the human being.

Turning from the God of conventional theology to the God within allows Schulweis to resolve the sharp either/or disjunctions that are so common in contemporary religious discourse: either transcendence or immanence; either universalism or particularism; either scripture is divine revelation or a human product; either prayer is communication with the divine Other or internal human self-talk. A belief in the God within unravels these hard disjunctions by revealing the unifying truth that transforms either/or into both/and. To each forced choice, Schulweis answers, "Yes, both/and": Is prayer communication with God or self-talk? Yes, both/and. Is scripture a divine revelation or a human cultural product? Yes, both/and. Is God transcendent or immanent? Yes, both/and. The God within unites the polarities.

Sources

Schulweis explained that he first derived predicate theology from the traditional Jewish formula of the *bracha*.[37] The traditional formula is a sentence with a subject and a predicate—for example, the traditional prayer over food, "Praised are You, Adonai, Ruler of the universe, who brings bread from the earth." But why the predicate? If the purpose of religion is to exalt the Divine Subject, the prayer formula should properly be truncated as "Praised are You, Adonai, Ruler of the universe." Period. All the more so if, following Maimonides, it is acknowledged that no positive attributes can be properly ascribed to God, or as Barth insisted, that no predicate can ever be attached to the Divine Subject. For Maimonides, the predicates describe not the essence of God but the activities of God. Schulweis goes further. The traditional formula of the *bracha* demonstrates that the purpose of religion is not solely to praise the Divine Subject. The intent of the formula is to elevate certain predicates—bringing forth bread, healing the sick, uplifting the fallen—to the status of divinity.

Maimonides would not disagree. The second source of predicate theology is Maimonides. According to Maimonides, the human being is unique among all the creatures of the world in that humans possess intellect, a quality they share with the Divine. On the first page of *The Guide of the Perplexed*, Maimonides explains that Genesis refers to the intellect when declaring that the human being was created in God's image (1:1). Through the intellect a human being can achieve knowledge of God, which Maimonides understands is the ultimate goal of human existence. *The Guide of the Perplexed*, acknowledged as the greatest work of Jewish philosophy, is a map toward this perfection. The paradigm for the journey to perfection is Moses's ascent of Mt. Sinai. Moses fascinated Maimonides. As his namesake, he modeled his life after Moses—lawgiver, teacher, leader, healer. Moses's ascent of the mountain to stand with God is Maimonides's metaphor for the philosophical quest for perfection of the mind, the ideal of a human life. But one important fact of Moses's story vexed Maimonides's carefully drawn vision: Moses comes down the mountain. Standing face-to-face with God, Moses achieved all that a human being yearns for. Moses realized the full perfection of a human being. But then Moses descends, down to the world, down to his people, and down toward all their troubles. Why doesn't Moses stay on the mountaintop with God?

Only on the very last page of the *Guide* does Maimonides return to this question, and to the most basic question: What is human life for? The thinkers of antiquity, he offers, taught that there are four kinds of perfection that human beings pursue as the purpose of their lives (3:54). He considers them in the order of their popularity:

1. The acquisition of wealth, power, and prestige. Although this is the most popular purpose, the goal toward which most human beings aspire, this notion of perfection is false. Wealth, power, and prestige are transient and remain external to the selfhood of a person. What we own is not what we are. And at any moment, a twist of fate can take it all away.

2. The perfection of the body—physical beauty, health, and well-being. Into this category, Maimonides would include the political stability of a city or country. This is closer to self than the acquisition of wealth. It has value as it includes the moderation of bodily desires, the preservation of physical health, and the protection from social unrest, all of which contribute to the elimination of distractions that might interrupt the life of the mind. But as human purpose, this is also empty, because it affects only the body, which we share with all animals, and does not affect the true uniqueness of the human being.

3. The achievement of moral perfection—the cultivation of character. This is the aim of the Torah's commandments, according to Maimonides. Morality regulates relations among people. In this way, the commandments produce social harmony and peace. As such, they are instrumentally

valuable as a support for the contemplation of the Divine. But imagine a person stranded alone, apart from any human contact. In that circumstance, a perfected moral character would have little value. Morality, held Maimonides, is necessary and useful but still not the highest purpose of human life.

4. Finally, Maimonides arrives at the conclusion, the ultimate and most authentic form of human perfection:

> The fourth kind of perfection is the true perfection of man; the possession of the highest intellectual faculties; the possession of such knowledge which leads to true knowledge of God. With this perfection man has obtained his final object. This is true human perfection; it remains to him alone; it gives him immortality, and on its account he is called man. . . . Your aim must therefore be to attain this [fourth] perfection.[38]

The cultivation of mind that leads to the true knowledge of God is the true purpose of human existence. On this, Maimonides maintains, the prophets and the philosophers agree. Reason and revelation reach the same conclusion. As a proof text, Maimonides cites the prophet Jeremiah:

> Thus said the LORD:
> Let not the wise man glory in his wisdom;
> Let not the strong man glory in his strength;
> Let not the rich man glory in his riches.
> But only in this should one glory:
> In his earnest devotion to Me.

For I the Lord act with kindness,

Justice, and righteousness in the world;

For in these I delight.

Jeremiah 9:22–23, modified per Maimonides[39]

The prophet, Maimonides points out, arranges the perfections in the ascending order of popularity among the masses, which is actually the desceding priority of their true importance—first wisdom, then strength, then riches. The prophet reaches the climax in his affirmation that only devotion to God is worthy of glory. But that is not all the prophet says; he doesn't conclude there. And here is Maimonides's big surprise:

> The prophet does not content himself with explaining that the knowledge of God is the highest kind of perfection; for if this only had been his intention, he would have said, "But only in this should one glory: In his earnest devotion to Me," and would have stopped there . . . He says, however, that man can only glory in the knowledge of God and in the knowledge of His ways and attributes, which are His actions. . . .
>
> We are thus told in this passage that the Divine acts which ought to be known, and ought to serve as a guide for our actions, are *hesed*, kindness, *mishpat*, justice, and *zedakah*, righteousness. . . .
>
> The object of the passage is therefore to declare that the perfection in which man can truly glory is attained by him when he has acquired—as far as this is possible for man—the knowledge of God, the knowledge of God's Providence, and of the manner in which God

156

brings creatures into being and governs them. Having acquired this knowledge, [the perfected human being] will then be determined always to seek kindness, justice, and righteousness, and to imitate the ways of God.[40]

On this last page, in the last paragraphs of the *Guide*, Mai-. monides reveals that the ultimate purpose of human existence is not the perfection of mind and intellectual communion with God after all. Had this been so, Moses would have stayed on the mountaintop. Having reached this pinnacle, Maimonides declares, the perfected human being is determined not just to know God but to imitate the ways of God in the world, to internalize the ways of Godliness and live the Godly life. Knowledge of God brings responsibility to act; it carries an obligation to care for the world. The true object of human development, Maimonides reveals, is to become a living model of Godliness and to bring Godliness into the world.

The last page of Maimonides is the first page of Schulweis.

The concluding chapter of *Evil and the Morality of God*, "Toward a Predicate Theology," begins with an epigraph from the nineteenth-century philosopher Ludwig Andreas von Feuerbach: "Not the attribute of divinity but the divinity of the attributes is the first truly divine being."[41] Feuerbach is the third source of Schulweis' predicate theology.

Feuerbach is often lost in the march of philosophy from Hegel to Marx and beyond, but he is among the most significant religious thinkers of modernity. In his 1841 work *The Essence of Christianity*, Feuerbach proclaimed, "Theology is anthropology."[42] Our ideas of God express the essence of being human:

Consciousness of God is self-consciousness, knowledge of God is self-knowledge. By his God thou knowest the man, and by the man his God; the two are identical. Whatever God is to man, that is his heart and soul; and conversely, God is the manifested inward nature, the expressed self of a man—religion the solemn unveiling of a man's hidden treasures, the revelation of his intimate thoughts, the open confession of his love-secrets. . . . The qualities of God are the essential qualities of man himself.[43]

Human beings, argued Feuerbach, create God in their own idealized image. Fallible, limited, mortal beings, humans are unable to express the true essence of their being—to reach the moral ideals of their dreams. So they project their highest ideals—their human essence—into the sky, reify those ideals into the qualities of a Divine Subject, and reappropriate them under the name God:

In religion man frees himself from the limitations of life; here he throws off what oppresses, impedes, or adversely affects him; God is man's self-awareness, emancipated from all actuality; man feels himself free, happy, blessed only in his religion, because here only does he live in his true genius.[44]

By demystifying religion, Feuerbach aimed to take back that human essence and liberate believers from their alienation. It was the ultimate humanistic project: "While I do reduce theology to anthropology, I exalt anthropology to theology."[45] Karl

Barth, in his introduction to the 1957 edition of *The Essence of Christianity*, celebrates Feuerbach's vision:

> [Feuerbach] only wants the honest confession that the alleged mystery of religion is man: that man is dreaming when he imagines that a Something Other, objectively confronting him, is the ground, that Whence, that necessity and that law, is the source from which his wishes and ideals flow, and is the sea of fulfillment toward which they tend. Man is dreaming instead of recognizing that it is his own being, his desire and duty to live as a man, which he, as a religious man, quite rightly equates with God.[46]

Feuerbach demands a shift of attention from the mysterious Divine Subject to the attributes and qualities, the predicates of divinity, which he took to be the most powerful expression of human moral aspiration. These qualities are what matter in religion. The Divine Subject is merely an imagined vessel created to hold them. Feuerbach used these insights in an effort to dissolve religion into humanism. Schulweis reversed the process. He attempted to restore religion and reestablish a place for God in modernity by elevating the qualities of collective humanistic ideals into Godliness. Feuerbach sought to bring heaven down to earth. Schulweis wished to lift earth up to the heavens.

Answering Evil

By removing the Divine Subject, Schulweis dissolves the task of theodicy. Suffering still exists, but there is no Divine Subject who is responsible. There are only natural causes for phenomena. There is no God to blame or accuse. Suffering is not punishment. No guilt is pressed upon the sufferer. The question "Why me?" has no moral answer. But the question is never silenced. The question is honored as the dignified expression of human conscience.

Predicate theology offers no transcendent purpose for suffering. Human suffering is not part of a divine plan. It is not magically transformed into beneficence. Suffering is the result of the remnant chaos in the universe. Schulweis was fond of quoting the statement in the Talmud, Avodah Zara 54b:

> A pagan philosopher asked a rabbinic elder in Rome, "If your God has no desire for idolatry why does He not abolish it?" The rabbi replied, "If it were something of which the world has no need which was worshipped, God would abolish it. But since people worship the sun, moon, stars, and planets, should He destroy the universe on account of fools? The world pursues its natural course (*olam k'minhago noheg*), and as for fools who act wrongly, they will have to render an account." If a man stole a measure of wheat and went and sowed it in the ground, it would surely be right (*din hu*) that the wheat should not grow. But the world pursues its natural course. If a man has intercourse with his neighbor's wife, it would surely be right (*din hu*) that she should not conceive. But the world pursues its natural course.

In Deuteronomy, nature is the tool of God's justice. So *din hu*, it would be just in the eyes of Deuteronomy for evil acts to bear no fruit. But the Talmud recognizes *olam k'minhago noheg*, the world pursues its own course. Nature is amoral. Nature pays no heed to human intentions. The earthquake, the cancer, and the accident are expressions of the chaos inherent in the world. They are not punishments. They are not deserved. They are not willed by God. Godliness inheres in the benign potentialities of nature awaiting human efforts to transform them into blessings:

> Nature is neutral, potential, and amoral. Godliness is discovered within nature as the indispensable source for our life and in our transformation of its possibilities for human joy. Divinity is not in the acts of nature but in the human control of its floods and destruction.[47]

Predicate theology translates the shock of experiencing evil into a normative prescription. The presence of evil calls forth the imperative to transform the world, not justify its creator. If the world is cruel, fix it. If disease steals life, cure it. If war devastates, teach peace. The presence of God in the world is real, but it is contingent upon human moral action:

> The Job of predicate theology and his friends look elsewhere for explanation and for response. They would examine the "how" and "where" and "what" which brought forth the pain of the situation, in order to call upon the powers of *Elohut* in and between them and the environment so as to bind the bruises and to act so as to avoid repetition of the tragedy.[48]

Revelation

The predicates of Godliness, maintains Schulweis, are not invented but discovered. Traditional religion knows of God through God's self-revelation as recorded in scripture. For Schulweis, there is no Divine Subject who speaks from the mountaintop. The predicates of Godliness are revealed through a community's transaction with history and nature. For Schulweis, revelation is not a one-way communication from on high but an ongoing process of discovery:

> The origin of Torah lies not in an extramundane source which has cast down absolute truths upon a receiving people, nor is it the arbitrary projection of human inventiveness flung upward. Torah is rooted in the matrix of a living organism, in a people which discovers out of its existence with failure and fortune the powers of godliness residing within it and its total environment. Torah as revelation is the product of Israel's creative transaction with history.[49]

Schulweis turns the structure of revelation from vertical to horizontal. The predicates of Godliness are not commanded from on high but wrestled out of a community's collective historical experience, enshrined in its sacred literature, rehearsed on its holy days, and acted upon in the course of its life in the world. In Feuerbach's felicitous description,

> God is for man the commonplace book where he registers his highest feelings and thoughts, the genealogical

album into which he enters the names of the things
most dear and sacred to him.[50]

The truth of revelation is tested pragmatically. It derives
not from its origin in a God who stands outside history and
nature, but in meeting the challenges of real life. Predicates
are transcendent, not because they arrive from above but
because they have been proven to enable human beings to
transcend the narrowness of the human condition and sustain
moral resilience and courage:

> The qualities or predicates are not arbitrary inventions
> of the human spirit. . . . Though their origin may arise
> from human needs, desires, and wants, the qualities are
> tested against the stones of reality. . . . They are carved
> out of the tablets of consequences.[51]

The truth of any revelation is contingent upon the community of the faithful that enacts and lives it. "Individually and collectively we are the verifiers of God's reality. . . . Religious beliefs
are conditional. They demand our behavioral testimony."[52] God
is not "believed in," Schulweis proclaims, God is behaved.

The predicates deemed Godly, Schulweis maintains, are
neither arbitrary nor subjective. Or rather, they are no more
arbitrary and subjective than any report of divine self-revelation.
The rabbis of the Talmud acknowledge as much. In the
celebrated homily of *Pesikta De-Rab Kahana* (12:25),

> Rabbi Levi taught: God appeared [to the Israelites at
> Mt. Sinai] as though He were a statue [alt: a mirror]

with faces on every side. A thousand people may look at the statue, but it would appear to each as though it were looking directly at him. So it is written, "I am the Lord your God." ["your" in the second person singular, not plural]. Rabbi Yosi bar Hanina taught: [At Mt. Sinai] God spoke to each and every person according to his or her own particular ability. And do not wonder at this! For when the manna came down for Israel, each and every person tasted it in his or her own way—infants in their way, the young in their way, the old in their way.[53]

The meaning of revelation is always relative to the listener. Revelation gains objectivity only when gathered together and codified as a communal possession in Torah. So too the predicates of Godliness are discovered through experience, gathered and refined by the religious community, and tested through a community's experiences and exigencies. As Schulweis testifies,

> I know, from the collective experiences of my people, recorded in sacred texts and from my own experiences, only the gerunds, the verbs, of God: healing the sick, clothing the naked, housing the homeless, pursuing peace, loving my people and my neighbors.[54]

As the community changes, and its moral perceptions change, so too does the message of revelation:

> Because discovery and confirmation of divine attributes is an on-going process coterminous with the life of

our people, *Elohut* is not fixed forever. As long as the community of faith is open to life, no predicates reign immutable, no set of predicates can exhaust the changing and expanding character of Godliness.[55]

Schulweis liberates religion from the epistemological puzzles of supernatural revelation. Revelation is an empirical process of learning and teaching carried on by human beings over the course of history. Torah is entirely the product of culture. Its authority derives from its results—it has been tested by a community over time and found worthy.

If pragmatism is the standard, the question is, Does this work? Feuerbach argues that all of religion, including the very idea of God's existence, is the product of projection:

> You believe in love as a divine attribute because you yourself love; you believe that God is a wise, benevolent being because you know nothing better in yourself than benevolence and wisdom; and you believe that God exists, that therefore he is a subject . . . because you yourself exist, you are yourself a subject.[56]

Religion hides this process in order to reify and mythologize the Divine. Schulweis boldly demythologizes religion. But can religious mythology be exploded without losing religion's existential power? Can Godliness fill the place of the personal God in the lives of religious people? Believers come to religion in search of the transcendent, seeking truths that emerge from realms beyond culture and human experience. Schulweis, like Kaplan, sacrifices the metaphysical transcendent.

The only transcendence he acknowledges is the human capacity to grow morally, to transcend the self.

In conventional religion, the believer stands before God and feels called upon to grow out of the narrowness of ego into a bigger, more caring self—to grow the soul. Once the curtain is drawn back and the process of projection is revealed, once the human origins of religious values are acknowledged, can religion inspire? Or do human beings need the transcendent—to confront the Divine as Other—in order to establish a realm of the sacred invested with authority?

Schulweis answered that the opposite was the case:

> Theodicies which house divinity in subject-substantive forms often prevent us from seeing the full moral implications of monotheistic faith for human beings. In demythologizing the ontologizing grammar subject theology, the divinity of the attributes which surround us and of which we are an active part is revealed.[57]

Subject theology, Schulweis insists, has a bigger problem. The total emphasis on the Divine Subject keeps us from appropriating moral predicates. The prayer service, for example, endlessly praises God's righteousness and justice but mutes the imperative to bring righteousness and justice into human life. And theodicy makes it worse. Theodicy distances God morally and negates the possibility of *imitatio dei*. Schulweis, like Feuerbach before him, maintained that liberating the moral predicates from the ontological platform of a subject-God will liberate human moral energies. It will force believers to grow up, relinquish their childish insistence on a projected Father in heaven, and accept a greater degree of moral responsibility for their world. Those seeking connection with the metaphysically transcendent are bound to be disappointed by this theology. But for those disillusioned by the facile formulations of supernatural revelation, predicate theology offers an adult religion of moral aspiration.

Oneness

Most people are trained from childhood to think of God as a "someone," usually located above, who exists, who is real. Is Godliness real? The twentieth-century philosopher Gilbert Ryle once famously hosted a friend on a visit to the university. Shown classrooms, offices, libraries, and laboratories, his friend responded, "Yes, but where is the university?" A university is real, but it is not a thing. It is rather the relationship, pattern, and organization among things that gives them their character. So too is family, community, or any number of other realities embraced as important. Godliness, Schulweis maintains, is such a reality. Godliness is the organization, the pattern, among all the predicates discovered and affirmed by a tradition.[58] The oneness of God, proclaimed daily by religious Jews, is interpreted by Schulweis to affirm that the predicates of Godliness fit together, reinforcing one another. They form a pattern of religious morality. No predicate could be held individually because any particular predicate in isolation from the pattern is morally ambivalent. Too much justice without the tempering of mercy, or mercy without justice, for example, does not yield goodness. Only in their unity and in their proper measure will the predicates prove beneficent.

Prayer

A prayer is recited for a sick friend. In conventional religion, a set of assumptions underlies that prayer: It is believed that the Divine Subject controls the fate of all. The friend's sickness is an expression of that God's will. There is hope that the divine decision might yet be litigated and that healing will soon be decreed. The competence of the physician, the effectiveness of the treatment, the strength of the patient are subordinated to the will of the divine healer. And should healing fail to come, the question will be asked, Why? At that moment, natural explanations—the nature of the disease, the limits of medicine—seem prosaic. Like Job's friends, a moral cause for the tragedy will be sought, falling no doubt upon the sufferer. Perhaps the patient was unworthy of healing. Perhaps God rejected the petition as punishment.

Conventional petitionary prayer reflects conventional theodicy and carries all its flaws. So as Schulweis inverts theology, he inverts prayer. Predicate prayer is not directed toward a Divine Subject. Predicate prayer celebrates the God within. Prayer is reflexive. Prayer is not directed above to the God who heals but within—affirming the divinity of healing and caring, and awakening the resolve to help. The purpose of prayer is to locate and rouse the God within and among human beings and stir a response. Petitions cast upward toward heaven echo back. Schulweis, too, would pray for a sick friend, but he prays in a language that recognizes the divinity of human efforts to help and to heal:

> Where then in this illness is divinity to be found?
> In curative forces discovered within me,
> between us.

In healing powers that form scars
Life-sustaining powers within me
brought forth by men and women,
doctors, nurses, research people
social workers, aides
To relieve the pain—
to lengthen the life
to deepen the moments of joy.[59]

Prayer is not magic. Magic pretends to change the material conditions of existence. Magic is the imagined means to desired ends. The magician pulls rabbits out of a hat, or saws a person in half and then hopefully puts them back together. Prayer engages means, not ends. Prayer changes not the conditions of existence but rather the pray-er. Prayer is normative; it places a claim on the self.

> Prayer . . . is no surrogate for work. Predicate prayer is reflexive in the sense that nothing can be asked another without calling upon the labor of one's own energies. . . . One cannot praise God with arms folded.[60]

Mordecai Kaplan found the traditional prayer book an impediment to prayer, so he edited it heavily and produced his own. Schulweis, in his synagogue, continued to use the Conservative movement's traditional prayer book, but he recommended to his congregation a mental editing of the prayers, an internal translation. "Add two words to your petition: 'through me.' God heal, *through me*. God help, *through me*. God save, *through me*. *Through me*, make peace."[61]

Will Jews pray this way? Schulweis himself had his doubts. Prayer is a deeply emotional, intimate expression of religious life. Will predicate theology suffice?

> It may be reasonably asked whether predicate theology can be emotionally satisfying; whether people can find security in Godly qualities in the same manner that they find it in a personified, individualistic subject; whether predicate theodicy can provide the comfort and consolation which comes from belief in a God who gives and takes away.[62]

Schulweis deflected the challenge. No one asked Maimonides this question, he quips. (Actually, they did.) Faith, he contends, demands thinking, not just poetry. Faith must be morally sound and intellectually whole before it can be emotionally resonant. In a 2010 Rosh Hashanah sermon, "How Do You Pray, Rabbi?" he points out,

> The crisis of prayer is not esthetic, it's theological. Entertainment is no surrogate for belief. It's not a matter of a larger choir, or more musical instruments or even a shorter sermon. It's a matter of belief. . . . Nothing defeats prayer more than to feel superfluous. You can wrap yourself in a tallis and tefillin, but if you are not essential to prayer, you're just turning a prayer wheel, and you feel like a "fifth wheel." When you feel irrelevant, God is irrelevant.[63]

Contemporary Jews complain that the prayer service is too long or the synagogue music is too dull. So the contemporary synagogues rush to apply aesthetic fixes. But the real reason Jews abandon prayer, Schulweis observed, is theological. They cannot believe in the God of the prayer book. Page after page, the prayer book extolls God, but contemporary Jews cannot find themselves in that prayer book. Twentieth-century philosopher George Santayana defined prayer as "poetry believed in." Until Jews are offered something they can believe in, Schulweis observed, they will not choose to pray.

Godliness or Goodness?

Why use God language at all? If the predicates derive from human experience and gain authority as a community's moral cultural heritage, what is added by investing them with the trappings of divinity? Conventionally, divinity implies an ontological or metaphysical judgment—God is real, even more real than an ordinary thing or idea. But Schulweis acknowledges no such ontological status for Godliness. Rather, he eschews metaphysics altogether. The predicates of Godliness are as real as any artifact of culture.

Schulweis offers three explanations for his use of God language: (1) As a value judgment. Activities and values perceived as "merely human" are dismissed as ordinary. Godliness is reserved for those deemed ultimately important for the conduct of a worthy life. (2) As a cultural gesture. Moderns can no longer embrace the religious life of their ancestors. They do not believe in the God once worshipped, nor do they see their lives in the world as their ancestors did. But modern Jews are united in the common possession of a set of core values that define their morality. (3) No one holds a monopoly on religious language. Why *not* use "God"? Concepts of God have evolved continuously over the generations. Holding back new ideas arrests this development.[64]

The effort seems half-hearted. Schulweis' philosophical and rhetorical prowess should have yielded better. More importantly, he deliberately evades the more difficult version of the question: What is the difference between calling a quality "Godly" and calling it "good"? What does "Godly" add to a predicate or quality that is more than "good"? If the ultimate purpose of predicate theology is to escape the traps of conventional theodicy, why not jettison the entire apparatus of theology altogether? If God is so difficult today, who needs God?

Schulweis conceded that the controlling category of Godliness is goodness: "What makes [the predicates] divine is not their lodging in some alleged Subject. They are sacred not because they inhere in any person or super-person but because they are instrumentally or intrinsically good."[65] Alternatively, "What do the qualities which are said to manifest Godliness have in common? They are united in their loyalty to the superordinate ideal of goodness."[66]

All qualities that are Godly are good. Are all qualities that are good also Godly?

Despite concentrating so heavily on the moral implications of theology, Schulweis observes that religion is more than morality:

> Religion includes an entire gamut of cognitive, affective, aesthetic and celebratory values which are vital to its life. They have a significant place among the predicates of divinity. . . . Myth, ritual, the binding of the

community of faith, the mystic and liturgical life are crucial for religion and are interwoven with the fabric of the moral life.[67]

Godliness, it would seem, is a broader category integrating a host of other elements into the moral life.

The question "Why use God language at all?" is not insignificant. It touches upon the integrity of Schulweis' theological project. Whenever Schulweis taught predicate theology, he would be asked pointedly if in fact predicate theology was "just" secular humanism dressed up in religious garb.

Schulweis could have offered a stronger version of his sociological answer. Moral imperatives are developed, refined, taught, and reinforced in the context of a community's culture. They are rooted and expressed in a culture's narratives. These narratives provide a map of existence, of the known world, and a way to the rewards and purposes of life. They guide the conduct of life. Narratives and the imperatives they teach are rehearsed in ritual, encoded in symbols, and celebrated in heroes. Through narrative, imperatives gain emotional resonance. Human beings are taught to feel pride in doing good and shame in doing wrong.

Imperatives rooted in core narratives are deemed sacred. Calling an action or quality "good" is a moral judgment. Calling it "Godly" grounds that action or quality in a culture's map of the world. It is attached to the very purposes of life. Even without a metaphysical sense of transcendence, a predicate deemed Godly carries the quality of sacredness through the power of a culture's narratives. An action deemed good may still be violated. An action deemed Godly carries a sense of taboo, a violation of sacred norms. It is as close to a moral absolute as moderns can reach.

Schulweis could have offered such an answer. And his teacher Mordecai Kaplan would have been very satisfied with this. But typically, Schulweis simply deflected the question. We need moral allies, he maintained.[68] The bigger problem today is nihilism, crass materialism, and moral obliviousness. The secular humanist who lives a morally conscientious life is close enough to the life of Godliness to be counted an ally—closer, in fact, than the traditional religionist whose life is morally indifferent.

The deeper reason Schulweis declined to answer this challenge was existential. Harold Schulweis was a deeply religious man. His life was deeply rooted in the sacred.[69] This was evident to all who came close to him. Godliness was Schuweis' faith. He inhabited that faith with all the fervor and passion of the traditional Jew's reverence for God's commandments. Schulweis experienced the Godly differently than he experienced the good. The imperatives of Godliness were transcendent. They were not obtained from an otherworldly source but from the God within, that part of the human character that commands the human being and the human community to transcend the innate narrow boundaries of ego, tribe, interest, and appetite, to reach morally ever higher. The good can be fulfilled. The Godly can be pursued but never reached. This endless sense of moral demand matched the restlessness of Schulweis' own character. Unlike Moses on Sinai, this mountain can be climbed, but its summit can never be achieved.

Schulweis felt the transcendent demand of Godliness and lived it at every moment. He was driven by it. Just as living without God is inconceivable to the believer, the suggestion that Godliness could be reduced to "just secular humanism" simply made no sense to Schulweis.

I Seek a God I Can't Believe In

The most devastating critique of predicate theology is presented by Schulweis himself, ironically, at the conclusion of his popular *For Those Who Can't Believe.* The entire book is addressed to an imaginary young man, David, who is identified as "a spiritual person who cannot believe." At the book's end, Schulweis offers a surprising confession:

> "Why," he asks, "should I be religious?" I have sought to remove the obstacles to his faith by acknowledging some of the shortcomings of conventional theology and by offering alternative interpretations of beliefs within the tradition. David remains ambivalent. He is drawn to many of the options I have proposed, but he has reservations about the authenticity of these new interpretations.
>
> Paradoxically, the only religious notions he considers authentic are those he cannot believe; the only ones he can believe are those he thinks to be inauthentic.[70]

Schulweis acknowledges that his theology, while intellectually sophisticated and morally inspiring, does not capture David's allegiance. This confession is all the more astonishing considering that the book is specifically intended "for those who can't believe." As a pragmatist searching for a theology that "works," a theology that might bring contemporary Jews back into lives of faith, Schulweis was stung by this rejection. More than the fictional David, this ambivalence was the response he heard whenever he taught predicate theology, even in his own congregation.[71] His theology is philosophically sound but religiously uninviting. To his credit, he acknowledges this in his book.

Schulweis interprets David's reticence as personal obstinacy. David is stuck on the religion of his childhood:

> As far as religion is concerned, David possesses a monolithic mindset. For him, religious belief should be immune from change or reinterpretation. . . . He is precommitted to a sameness of religious belief to which he cannot subscribe . . . [which] makes it easy for him to reject being religious."[72]

This is Schulweis' interpretation of the crisis of contemporary Jewish belief. It is offered with a large dose of exasperation. David wants his rabbi to put forward the supernatural personal God that he was brought up with—a God who benevolently governs all phenomena. But David readily rejects this very belief as childish. He recognizes the intellectual and moral power in Schulweis' concept of Godliness, but he rejects it because it lacks the mythological trappings—the enchantment—of his childhood religion. This is the cognitive trap—what Jews deem authentic they can't believe, and what they can believe they deem inauthentic. It frustrated Schulweis to no end.

Why has David adopted this stance? What causes him to be "precommitted" to a religious belief he cannot abide? Is it just obstinacy or immaturity? Or is something more profound expressed in his attitude?

In an early study of Mordecai Kaplan's "soterics," the salvation theme in Kaplan's thought, Schulweis foreshadowed this very dilemma:

> Those religious personalities committed to a naturalist position cannot afford the luxury of bemoaning the loss of a certain type of morale attendant on the supernaturalist's faith, the more so since many other consequences of such belief are entirely dysfunctional. The reconstructing naturalist needs rather invade new areas of morale and plan new interpretations of symbols and rites so as to compensate for the loss of comfort and ease afforded by facile conformity to convention.[73]

Traditional religion provided "morale"—faith in the possibility—indeed, the inevitability—of redemption. Even Kaplan sensed the need for such morale. For Kaplan, faith in God is precisely the assertion of the possibility of salvation, which he defined as the perfection of the human condition. To believe in God, in Kaplan's famous phrase, is to acknowledge the reality of "the power that makes for salvation":

> The fact that the cosmos possesses the resources and man the abilities—which are themselves part of those resources—to enable him to fulfill his destiny as a human being, or to achieve salvation, is the Godhood of the cosmos. This is the fact which we should have in mind when we worship God and glorify Him."[74]

Kaplan's faith that the world contains the resources for human salvation is a metaphysical judgment, even if it is drawn entirely from his observations of human behavior. Schulweis resisted such judgments, as he resisted all metaphysics. Schulweis asserts that Godliness is potential in all human circumstances, but it is not an assurance of its realization. After the horrors of the Holocaust, Schulweis could not make this claim. He could not repeat the traditional eschatological proposition that redemption, though long in coming, is ultimately inevitable.

Schulweis' aversion to metaphysics rescues him from a host of philosophical dilemmas, but it raises a serious moral problem: Why engage in Godly behaviors if there is no assurance of their ultimate efficacy? Why engage in acts of self-sacrificing morality? What keeps moral behavior from falling into futility?

David, Schulweis' interlocutor, does not really expect his rabbi to offer the God of his childhood. But he does expect his rabbi to offer faith in a morally ordered universe or, at the least, a universe of moral possibilities. This is typically what people expect when they come to religion. Schulweis offers no such universe. Godliness resides in the world, but there is no assurance that the world in any way resonates with human efforts to do good, or that the world is amenable to human moral aspirations. Schulweis felt that predicate theology was the only way to absorb the radical evil of the twentieth century without succumbing to Rubenstein's dark worldview. Godliness was the most he could offer David. But David wants something more.

David's objection is rooted in the very sources of predicate theology. At the end of his very sympathetic introduction to

Feuerbach's *Essence of Christianity*, Karl Barth explains why he pursued a theological pathway diametrically opposite to Feuerbach:

> [Feuerbach] was a true child of his century, a non-knower of death and a mis-knower of evil. In fact, anyone who knew that we men are evil from head to foot, and anyone who reflected that we must die, would recognize it to be the most illusory of all illusions to suppose that the essence of God is the essence of man.[75]

The reality of death and the power of evil sent Barth in search of a theology of grace offered by a mysterious Divine Subject rather than the liberating humanism of Feuerbach. The David of Schulweis' experience expresses a similar sentiment. The same radical evil that compelled Schulweis to abandon faith in a Divine Subject and take up predicate theology sends David in the opposite direction.

In his weekday life, David is fully prepared to agree with Schulweis that there is no supernatural personal God benevolently governing the universe. After reading the morning paper, any reasonable person would. In his daily experience, David appreciates the language of Godliness and the human activism it inspires. He feels the compulsion to heal the world and the warm satisfaction of fulfilling sacred purposes when he does.

But when he enters the synagogue, David wants something different. For David, the synagogue is a place to escape his weekday rationality, to cultivate a "second naiveté" and reappropriate, however temporarily, the enchanted, God-centered, morally ordered universe of tradition.

Religion, for David, is a mode of play. Play is an important part of being human. Play is the willed suspension of the ordinary rational world. Art, sport, drama—all partake of this mode. Play allows human beings to enjoy an alternate reality for some bounded period of time. Religion offers the chance to step out of the ordinary into a different world, an imagined world. David does not want the rabbi to puncture his myths. He comes to synagogue precisely to inhabit them for a little while, a respite from the moral chaos of his everyday experience. He gets plenty of realism from his life outside. He comes to synagogue for a few moments of grace.

It is not his closed mind that keeps David from accepting Schulweis' interpretation of religion. Rather, it is his need for a religious life more enchanted, more mythic, and less rational. But this is something Schulweis cannot provide him. Schulweis' approach to religion, like his character generally, is decidedly cerebral. His religious life begins in the mind. His difficulties with David grow from that orientation. The non-rational elements of conventional religion have no place in Schulweis' theology—a personal God, a transcendent source for ethics, mysticism, religious experience, ecstatic prayer, a sense for the miraculous. His intellectual integrity would not permit this sort of religious life, even if it alienated him from all the Davids he encountered. But by the 1990s, when Schulweis wrote his book, that is where American religious life was turning.

What ultimately separates Schulweis and David is generational. David is a child of the postmodern culture of late twentieth-century America. This culture permits him a complex, layered identity of contradictory narratives. He is comfortable living with the contradictions. Schulweis is thoroughly modernist. He does not comprehend postmodern complexity and is thoroughly exasperated that David does not crave his type of intellectual consistency. Finding himself between the cultural worlds of modernity and postmodernity, Schulweis was sufficiently perceptive to grasp and describe the dilemma of David's generation but not to resolve it. Thus he ends *For Those Who Can't Believe* on a note of resignation. He realizes that he has solved the problem of his own generation but not for the next.

Two Names for God

Tradition has long noted the different names of God presented in scripture. Two in particular dominate: *Elohim* and *Adonai* (YHVH). In the midrashic literature, the names refer to different aspects of divinity: *Elohim* to *midat ha-din* (divine judgment), *Adonai* to *midat ha-rachamim* (divine mercy). Many subsequent theologies, both traditional and modern, fastened upon the multiple names to represent the different ways human beings encounter the Divine. God is one, but God is met in different moments and through different experiences.

In 1986, Schulweis suffered his second major heart attack. This necessitated a triple coronary bypass operation followed by months of rehab. The experience changed his thinking. While he surrendered nothing of his earlier conceptions, Schulweis recognized something missing in his theology. His conception of Godliness carried a dynamic quality. The predicates of divinity call upon human beings to transform their world. Godliness aimed at empowering moral heroism. From his hospital bed Schulweis recognized that not all human circumstances allow for transformation. In some circumstances, the insistence on transformation can be cruel. Schulweis discovered that Godliness can sometimes be found in an ethic of acceptance.

As Schulweis struggled with his heart disease, writer Norman Cousins made headlines with his book *Anatomy of an Illness as Perceived by a Patient*. Cousins suffered from a crippling connective tissue disease and was given only one chance in five hundred of ever recovering. He abandoned his doctor's regimen and took up a routine consisting of watching comedy movies and funny television. Laughter, he maintained, cured him. A few years later, Dr. Bernie Siegel, a pediatric surgeon at Yale University Hospital, published the best seller *Love, Medicine, and Miracles*. Siegel announced that patients could heal themselves if only their attitude was right. Schulweis was enraged by the hubris in these assertions.[76] He recognized in this idea a modern, secular reiteration of the traditional theodicies he had protested his entire career. Laughter, optimism, and positivity might help an ill patient. But when they don't, when the patient's condition worsens, the victim is again blamed: "It's your own fault; you should have had a better attitude."

The theology of Godliness celebrates human empowerment, but not all situations are amenable to transformation. Sometimes heroism is found in acceptance. Acceptance is neither resignation nor surrender, neither passivity nor cynicism. Schulweis would tolerate none of that. Acceptance is not a refusal to engage the world but rather a wise realism that recognizes the limitations of human power. This new note of his theology found its expression in Schulweis' interpretation of God's names.

Elohim is the God who appears in the first chapter of Genesis. *Elohim* is the God of being. When God blesses creation in the first chapter of Genesis, it is because being is good—not morally good but metaphysically good. In identifying *Elohim* in this way, Schulweis incorporates the central insight of the metaphysical theologies without the moral baggage of their theodicies. *Elohim* is the God of the philosophers—Creator, Ground of Being, but unmoved, unaffected, amoral. *Elohim* is the God that Job meets in the whirlwind, the God revealed in nature's majesty. *Elohim* represents the reality principle expressed in the Talmudic dictum *olam k'minhago noheg*, the world pursues its natural course. *Elohim*, like nature, does not represent moral truth. The reverence for *Elohim* means embracing a realism that keeps us from denial, fantasy, or magic. As in Job, *Elohim* demands acceptance, surrender to what is.

Elohim is only one aspect of divinity. To live with *Elohim* alone would be to live a life of resignation, accepting all that is as inevitable, unalterable. However, there is another aspect of divinity: *Adonai*. The tetragrammaton, YHVH, for which Jewish tradition substitutes *Adonai*, appears in scripture only in the second chapter of Genesis and only with the creation of the human being. The human being is charged to till and tend the Garden. *Adonai* is the formal name of Godliness, the imperative to transform the world and heal it. *Adonai* is revealed in human efforts to make the natural world livable, to impose moral order on an indifferent natural universe. In Schulweis' poem,

> Adonai in the vision of a compassionate society.
> Adonai in the transformation of chaos and violence and
> > the void of the universe,
> > into order, sanity, and love.

Adonai in the mending of the universe,
>   the repair of the world,
>   the binding of bruises,
>   the gathering of fragmented sparks
>   buried in the husks of the world.
Adonai revealed in the discovery of the self created in the
>   image of Adonai-Elohim, the Lord God,
>   who breathed into
>   our nostrils and made us a living soul.[77]

Elohim is the God of what is. *Adonai* is the God of what ought to be. The affirmation *Sh'ma Yisrael,* "*Adonai Eloheynu,*" in Schulweis' interpretation, affirms that what ought to be is as real as what is. To recite the *Sh'ma* is to rehearse the commitment to bring those potentialities into reality.

The two dimensions of divinity belong together:

Elohim, the God of nature, and Adonai,
>   the Lord of morality;
Elohim, the God of necessity, and Adonai,
>   the Lord of possibility;
Elohim, the God of what is, and Adonai,
>   the Lord of what ought to be;
Elohim, the God of acceptance, and Adonai,
>   the God of transformation.
Their unity embraces the oneness of reality.
"Ought" is as real as "is."
Without Elohim, the ideals of Adonai are adrift.
Without Adonai, reality is robbed of real possibility
>   and restricted to the status quo.

To live with Elohim alone is to know nature without
   the powers to repair the world as given.
To live with Adonai alone is to live by dreams without
   the hands and feet of reality.
The traditional benediction joins Elohim and Adonai.[78]

Elohim and *Adonai* do not refer to two different gods or to a divided divinity. Like the midrashic application of *midat ha-din* and *midat ha-rachamim,* Schulweis uses the two names for God to evoke two different human experiences of divinity, two stances toward the world. *Elohim* represents the imperative of acceptance; *Adonai,* the imperative of transformation. Religious wisdom guides human beings in deciding between them:

Acceptance and transformation are basic responses to
life rooted in the dual character of divinity. The daunting test of faith lies in determining when acceptance is
appropriate and when it is premature. When are we to
turn to Elohim and when are we to turn to Adonai?[79]

Elohim counsels acceptance. The world is filled with suffering. But suffering is no moral judgment of a human individual. It is part of the physics of living as a body in the world. *Adonai* calls upon us to overcome, transform, and transcend the conditions of existence:

Elohim Adonai,
Acceptance and transformation,
the reality of what is, the reality of what ought to be
the reality of what is yet to be.[80]

God and the Holocaust

The specter of the Holocaust hovers over all of Schulweis'
theology. It filled his nightmares and challenged his thinking.
For Schulweis, the test of a theology's truth is its capacity to
sustain a moral personality and inspire moral courage and
moral action. Does the theology of Godliness pass the test? Or
is Godliness futile in the shadow of Auschwitz?

> The Holocaust mocks my faith. For at the core of that
> faith is the conviction that God breathed into the nos-
> trils of human beings an inviolable human soul, that
> God created the human being in His image and His
> likeness. The taunting dissonance between that faith
> and the facts of the Holocaust disturbs my belief.[81]

To acknowledge *Elohim* is to celebrate the goodness of existence. To acknowledge *Adonai* is to affirm the existence of
goodness. *Adonai* is the locus of predicate theology, the imperatives of Godliness to heal and repair the world. To affirm
Adonai is to affirm the potential of goodness in human existence. *Adonai* is revealed only in human moral action. Linking
Adonai with *Elohim,* as in the *Sh'ma Yisrael,* affirms that human
beings can bring about the world that ought to be. Can this
faith be maintained after the Holocaust? Or has the radical
evil of the Holocaust confirmed the absurdity of human moral
imagination?

> The theological crisis wrought by the Holocaust is radi-
> cal. Not whether God is dead but whether we are dead;

not whether God exists but whether goodness is real or merely the invention of human conceit. . . . "Ye are My witnesses, I am God, says the Lord." To this statement from the book of Isaiah the commentary adds, "If you are my witnesses then I am God. If you are not my witnesses then I am as it were not God." What witness do we have to give from history? What empirical facts as testimony to the character of human nature and of God?[82]

Could faith in Godliness—in human moral potential—be maintained after the Holocaust? The question haunted Schulweis. A relentlessly honest thinker, he could not ignore this question: "If the presence and goodness of God is to be found, it should be uncovered on earth. Where can we search for Godliness among the ashes of Auschwitz?"[83]

In the early 1960s, while attending a Jewish community affair at a hotel in San Francisco, Schulweis was pulled aside by the hotel's owner, the philanthropist Benjamin Swig, who introduced him to the hotel's maintenance supervisor, a German immigrant named Fritz Graebe. Swig urged Graebe to share his story with the rabbi.

During the war, Herman Friederich "Fritz" Graebe was a German national who operated a construction company in the Ukraine under contract with the Nazi government. Graebe had once been a member of the Nazi Party. But witnessing the massacre of Jews in the Ukrainian town of Dubno sickened him, and he grew to hate the Nazis. He formulated a plan to resist. He informed his Nazi supervisors that his projects required large numbers of Jewish slave laborers. Graebe took his workers from the ghettos and concentration camps.

He even took them off trains headed to extermination camps. Graebe inflated his projects so the Nazis would give him more work permits. He exploited every privilege afforded him as a civilian contractor and used all his wealth in a single-minded effort to save Jewish lives. Eventually the Nazis became suspicious, but by the time they came to arrest him, the Allies were closing in and he escaped. Graebe testified at the Nuremberg trials, for which he received death threats, so he moved his family to San Francisco. On the day the war ended, Graebe had five thousand Jews on his payroll. Astonished by what he heard, Schulweis asked Graebe, "What had the Jewish community done to thank you? Why don't we know your story?"[84] Graebe responded that he wanted no recognition. He did only what he thought was right.

Fritz Graebe was the first of many rescuers Schulweis would discover. He was soon introduced to Jacob Gilat, an Israeli nuclear scientist working at the University of California, Berkeley. Gilat and his two brothers were hidden from the Nazis by the heroic efforts of a Polish Christian family, Alex and Mela Roslan. Schulweis learned of Chiune "Sempo" Sugihara, a Japanese diplomat, who saved 3,500 Jews in Kovno, Lithuania; and of the Bulgarian royal family who defied the Gestapo's orders and blocked their efforts to deport Bulgaria's Jews, saving an estimated 50,000. In every land of the Nazi occupation, Schulweis discovered people of every kind—high officials and ordinary townsfolk, ministers and priests and parishioners, peasants and intellectuals, even Nazis—who risked everything to rescue Jews.

The rescuers became Schulweis' obsession. In 1963, he organized the Institute for Righteous Acts at the Judah L.

Magnes Museum (now the Magnes Collection of Jewish Art and Life) in Berkeley to recognize and celebrate the rescuers. Eventually this evolved into a community foundation offering support to rescuers. Founded as part of the Anti-Defamation League, the Foundation for the Righteous became an independent organization in 1986. To date, it has recognized and supported some two thousand rescuers.

For Schulweis, the testimonies of the rescuers were more than inspirational. They were directly connected to his theology. They were, in his mind, divine revelation. The radical evil of the Holocaust destroyed faith in the God who guides history. For Schulweis, the radical goodness of these Christian rescuers verified the truth of Godliness. If even in the darkest place at the darkest moment there were those who found the capacity for heroic goodness, then *Adonai* exists. Godliness is no chimera. No matter how few in number, the rescuers provided testimony to the truth of Godliness. For Schulweis, the accounts of rescuers push back the cynicism and nihilism that grew in the deep darkness of the Holocaust and made faith possible once again.

"Efshar!" It is possible! Graebe, the Roslans, Sugihara, the Bulgarians rescued Jews. For the modern Jew, Schulweis argued, they rescued God.

CHAPTER 5

The Prophetic Voice

In his very last public address, on April 27, 2014, just months before his death, Schulweis spoke to a crowd of thousands at the annual Jewish World Watch Walk to End Genocide. Frail, weak, and with a voice severely strained, he still sounded every bit the prophet:

> A few days after their liberation in April 1945, the survivors of Buchenwald constructed signs with two penetrating words: "Never Again." But the world's indifference, deceit, and mendacity de facto erased the letter "N" from "Never" so that it read "Ever, ever, ever again." How many genocides took place from April 1945 to April 2014? . . . the unspeakable atrocities in Cambodia, Rwanda, Sudan, Darfur, Democratic Republic of Congo. Lest we forget Rwanda's Hutu-led military wiped out 800,000 members of the Tutsi minority in 100 days. . . . Today, we remember ten communities who share a tragic kinship of suffering. We have found each other. We must not let go of each other.[1]

Interviewed that year by the *Jewish Journal* of Los Angeles, Schulweis was asked which of his accomplishments he deemed the most significant. Without hesitation, he responded the Jewish World Watch.[2] Launched in a fiery High Holiday sermon in 2004, Jewish World Watch quickly grew from a circle of Valley Beth Shalom congregants into a coalition of some sixty-two synagogues, churches, and schools dedicated to fighting genocide in Darfur, South Sudan, and the Congo through education, political advocacy, and humanitarian intervention. The yearly Jewish World Watch Walk to End Genocide in Los Angeles attracts more than three thousand participants, many of them teens. The political impact of the Jewish World Watch was confirmed in 2006 when, according to the *Washington Post*, the Sudanese president Omar al-Bashir rejected a United Nations peace initiative, blaming "unnamed Zionist Jewish organizations for stoking public opposition in the United States against his government, through the organizing of nationwide protests against the violence in Darfur."[3]

For Schulweis, the formation of the Jewish World Watch was the culmination of a career of moral passion and activism. In Jewish World Watch the major themes of his moral vision converged: the reframing of the Holocaust narrative, his vision of Judaism as a global religion, and the affirmation of conscience as the beating heart of Jewish life. The biblical prophets mediated a divine moral vision to a people often oblivious and indifferent. Rabbis, Schulweis remonstrated, must speak in the very same voice. Jewish World Watch was the crescendo of Schulweis' prophetic career. Those who witnessed this final address that April afternoon could feel his prophetic urgency. If the discovery of Christian rescuers verified Schulweis' theology of Godliness, the success of the Jewish World Watch substantiated his faith in the efficacy of Jewish global moral activism. The Holocaust rescuers redeemed his idea of God. Through Jewish World Watch, Schulweis birthed a new generation of rescuers.

The Rabbi as Prophet

In his 1980 Rosh Hashanah sermon, later published in *Moment Magazine*, Schulweis posed the questions: "What does Judaism tell me about the way that I am supposed to live my life? What is of ultimate importance in Jewish life?"[4]

Schulweis first addressed these questions as a twenty-year-old senior at Yeshiva University. In his senior yearbook essay, he argued that the purpose and aim of religion is moral development. Religion in its truest form, wrote Schulweis in 1945,

> cries out for the welfare of Man, not men; it strives to make him a better man; it asserts his G-d-given rights to economic, political, and social justice; it reaffirms man's dignity and innate goodness. . . . Religion can be tested on empirical grounds. The sincerity of religious theory is to be manifested in human behavior, in the relationship between man and his neighbor.[5]

In his 1980 sermon, he weighed the value of each mode of Jewish life. Is the ultimate goal of Jewish life the cultivation of learning? Is it a life of piety or the practice of ritual observance? Each of these, Schulweis affirms, is valuable but not of ultimate value. In practice, they each point to a higher Jewish value:

> So what is the end, what is the "what for?" The answer is the cultivation of a *yiddisher neshomo,* a soul and a

character of *rachmanut,* of *erlichkeit,* of *eidelkeit,* of sensitivity, of dignity, of care, of compassion. Otherwise, every
one of our wonderful symbols becomes but dead wood.[6]

The highest value of Jewish life, its teleology (a word he
loved to use), is the cultivation of moral character. Judaism
projects a specific image of the moral personality as its ultimate aspiration, its goal. All the gestures of Jewish culture and
faith are intended to cultivate, nurture, and reinforce that
moral personality.

Schulweis' use of Yiddish in the sermons was deliberate. He
was aware that the question he asked was subversive and his
answer at odds with what his audience expected their rabbi
to say. The prevailing narrative of Jewish life dealt with Jewish
continuity, Jewish survival. His congregation, like most American Jews of that moment, had been conditioned to view Jewish continuity as an ultimate, self-justified Jewish value. No one
asked, Why survive? At least within the walls of the synagogue,
they viewed ritual observance, Torah study, and prayer as the
core gestures of authentic Jewish being. Their mental image
of piety was a Jewish grandfather with beard, *payos, davening*
in his *kappata* and *shtreimel.* No one was ready for the rabbi to
declare that personal morality is the goal of Jewish existence.
So Schulweis chose an internal Jewish cultural vocabulary to
demonstrate that the cultivation of moral character is the highest purpose of authentic Jewish life. Morality is *mama loshen,* the
distinctive essence of Jewish tradition. And he chose Yiddish
because that was the language in which he communicated with
his own father and grandfather. The sermon was directed as
much to them as it was to the congregation sitting before him.

The question is not whether you believe in morality *or* you believe in ritual, the question is not whether you believe in ethics *or* you believe in kashrut, the question is not either/or, but the question is whether you understand the end, the purpose, the meaning, the thrust. Because if you do, you will daven, but differently, you'll keep kosher, but differently, you'll come to the synagogue, but differently, you will even say the blessings differently: "Blessed art Thou O Lord our God who has commanded us by Thy commandments and has made us *sanctified*." I am a sanctifying power, a hallowing power. There is holiness in me because I can be moved to tears. I can be stirred into action when I see bitterness, helplessness—that is my pride, and that is the answer to the question, "Who are you?"[7]

The moral personality is the goal of Jewish life. Schulweis' favorite proof text for this conviction was the *haftarah* text chosen by the rabbinic tradition for the morning of Yom Kippur—Isaiah chapter 58. In the midst of the most intensive day of Jewish ritual, the rabbis asserted the priority of morality. Schulweis saw himself in the role of Isaiah. The prophet witnessed majestic rites of the Day of Atonement performed with precision and dutiful care in Jerusalem's Holy Temple. Outwardly, such ritual conscientiousness suggested a community of deep devotion:

To be sure, they seek Me daily,
Eager to learn My ways.
Like a nation that does what is right,

That has not abandoned the laws of its God,

They ask Me for the right way,

They are eager for the nearness of God.

    ISAIAH 58:2

But looking deeper, the prophet perceived the emptiness of it all. Separated from real life and performed without regard to the covenantal vision of social justice, the rites amount to nothing but a charade. God does not need these rituals. God needs righteousness:

On your fast day

You see to your business

And oppress all your laborers!

Because you fast in strife and contention,

And you strike with a wicked fist! . . .

Is such the fast I desire?

    ISAIAH 58:3–5

The purpose of religious life is the cultivation of moral behavior. The covenant did not demand spectacular feats of moral self-sacrifice but a consistent assertion of human solidarity in the daily conduct of life—to recognize the needs of those who live among us and to respond.

To unlock fetters of wickedness,

And untie the cords of the yoke

To let the oppressed go free;

To break off every yoke.

It is to share your bread with the hungry,

And to take the wretched poor into your home;

When you see the naked, to clothe him,

And not to ignore your own kin.

ISAIAH 58:6–7

Neither the prophet nor Schulweis denied the significance of ritual. Ritual has value but not intrinsic or ultimate value. Ritual is a language for expressing devotion to God—devotion that is realized through patterns of moral behavior. Ritual is infrastructure—scaffolding—supporting moral growth and moral education. Ritual becomes problematic when its mystery and magic conceal its true function as symbol and framework. When it is split off from moral responsibilty and invested with reverence, ritual becomes an empty gesture at best and a form of idolatry at worst. Schulweis watched this split take root in his generation. It was the reason so many intellectuals of his generation abandoned religious Judaism.

The popular culture presented a vivid example. In 1997, journalist Mitch Albom published *Tuesdays with Morrie,* a touching tribute to Morrie Schwartz, his sociology professor at Brandeis University. In the book, made wildly popular on television by Oprah Winfrey, Albom describes his weekly visits with Schwartz during his decline and death from ALS. With great tenderness, Albom shares all the wisdom the beloved teacher imparted in those last days.

Although they never met, Schulweis recognized Morrie Schwartz as a *landsmann*—raised in the same Bronx neighborhood, in the same rich culture of Yiddishkeit and socialist ethics. Morrie expressed Jewish values but without Jewish language and with no awareness that these values emanated from centuries of Jewish culture. This frustrated Schulweis intensely. Morrie represented an entire generation of cultural Jews and political Jews who bore no appreciation for the Jewish religious roots of their ethics. The Jewish religion of their upbringing was formal, ritualistic, and cold. It failed to touch on the ethical life. Having never met the idea that Jewish religion was a cultural mechanism for cultivating moral character, an entire generation—including Morrie Schwartz, Sidney Hook, and not incidentlally Schulweis' own father—was lost to the Jewish people:

> I was saddened because I think that the synagogue bears some responsibility for the loss of Morrie. . . . Didn't the synagogue ever teach Morrie the religious roots of his humanism, the theological foundations of his moral sensibility, the rootedness of Yiddishkeit in the soil of Judaism, the ethics of Jewish ritual?[8]

Interviewed shortly before his death by the journalist Ted Koppel, Morrie Schwartz was asked to reflect on the meaning of life and death. He quoted Marcus Aurelius. The tragedy, Schulweis perceived, is that Morrie has no language of his own with which to face death. Schulweis mourned Morrie and the Judaism Morrie never knew, the Jewish moral language Morrie never learned. He mourned the failure of his generation to teach that language:

> Morrie didn't get it, because Morrie wasn't taught. The ethics of Yiddishkeit, of Jewish humanism, did not come out of the air. Jewish conscience is implanted in

the ethics of ritual and the ritual of ethics. The philan-
thropy of the Jewish people is a cultivated conscience.[9]

In the last decade of his own life, Schulweis' ideas on morality and faith coalesced in his conception of conscience. Conscience, Schulweis acknowledged, is an elusive phenomenon,
better illustrated than defined. "Nevertheless, conscience is
the subterranean wellspring beneath the stream of Jewish law,
ethics, and theology."[10]

Schulweis never offered a clear definition of conscience.
He pointed to the linguistic map of the concept in Jewish
sources. There is no word in biblical Hebrew that directly
translates "conscience." Modern Hebrew coined the word
matzpun, which is related to the word *matzpen*, for "compass."
Both are derived from the word *tzafun*, meaning "hidden,"
because they point to hidden forces within us and within the
world. Alternatively, they are related to *tzafon*, or "north," the
magnetic direction that enables us to navigate our world. Conscience is the moral compass carried within, directing human
beings toward the good.

While there is no word for conscience in the Bible, Schulweis suggested that the biblical analog is the word *yirah*, usually translated as "fear."[11] In the Bible, the terms *yirat elohim*
and *yirat Adonai*, the fear of God, connote emotions of awe,
reverence, and submission before the Divine and are often
connected to morality. Consider four settings of the term:

1. In Genesis 20, Abraham passed off his wife as his sister
   (for the second time!). When the ruse was discovered,
   Abimelech, king of Gerar, confronted Abraham. Abraham
   expressed his fear that this was a place without *yirah*:

"What, then," Abimelech demanded of Abraham, "was your purpose in doing this thing?" "I thought," said Abraham, "surely there is no fear of God [*yirat elohim*] in this place, and they will kill me because of my wife." (Genesis 20:10–11)

2. Joseph appeared before his brothers in the guise of the Egyptian premier. They could trust his word, he assured them, because he was a man of *yirah*:

On the third day Joseph said to them, "Do this and you shall live, for I am a God-fearing man [*et-ha-elohim ani yareh*]." (Genesis 42:18)

3. The midwives of Egypt, Shifra and Puah, disobeyed Pharaoh's order to destroy the sons of the Israelites. The Torah locates the source of their courageous resistance in *yirah*:

The midwives, fearing God [*va'tirena ha-miyaldot et ha-elohim*], did not do as the king of Egypt had told them; they let the boys live. . . . And because the midwives feared God, He established households for them. (Exodus 1:17, 21)

4. Jethro, Moses's father-in-law, the priest of Midian, instructed Moses to choose leaders for the people who display the quality of *yirah*:

You shall also seek out from among all the people capable men who fear God [*yirei Elohim*], trustworthy men who spurn ill-gotten gain. (Exodus 18:21)

Each story describes a transaction between Israelites and non-Israelites. In each, *yirat elohim* is understood to connote integrity, honesty, common decency. *Yirat elohim* is the Bible's term for a universal moral sensibility shared by people of all nations. It is not a product of revelation. It belongs to no particular culture. It is rather the common possession of all civilized people, and it provides them a common moral language and moral standard.

The Holiness Code in Leviticus appeals to this same sense of common decency—and not to a special revelation to Israel—when commanding certain behaviors, affirming that these are expressions of the conduct all decent people are expected to abide:

> You shall not insult the deaf, or place a stumbling block before the blind. You shall fear your God [*v'yareita me'elohecha*]: I am the LORD. . . . You shall rise before the aged and show deference to the old; you shall fear your God [*v'yareita me'elohecha*]: I am the LORD.
> LEVITICUS 19:14, 32

Elsewhere in the Bible is a related phrase, *yirat Adonai*. This phrase goes beyond fundamental common decency and reflects the quest for a higher morality. *Yirat Adonai* is the language of moral aspiration. In Psalm 34:

> Come, my children, listen to me;
> I will teach you what it is to fear the LORD [*yirat Adonai*].
> Who is the man who is eager for life, who desires years
>   of good fortune?

Guard your tongue from evil, your lips from deceitful speech.
Shun evil and do good, seek amity and pursue it.
  PSALM 34:12–15

And the instruction of Psalm 111:

The beginning of wisdom is the fear of the LORD [*yirat Adonai*];
all who practice it gain sound understanding.
  PSALM 111:10

This linguistic map of *yirah* fills in Schulweis' concept of conscience. Conscience begins in a basic sense of moral decency that is universal. It constitutes a common moral language grasped by decent people of all cultures. Conscience confronts us and lays demands upon us. It bears a quality of authority that is transcendent—it is in us and of us, but it is also beyond us and claims our submission. Conscience is teleological. It grows into a dynamic force, as an impetus to moral aspiration and moral growth.

Conscience, Schulweis argues, is inborn, but only in potentiality. It requires realization and cultivation. The chief function of a Jewish religious culture is to develop, direct, refine, and reinforce conscience:

It is always becoming. How? By interaction between commandments, mitzvot, by biblical, rabbinic, liturgical texts of four millennia. You read them but not blindly, mechanically, impersonally. You have to allow the narratives of your ancestors, the patriarchs and matriarchs, the priests and sages, to pour into you. But you are not

a passive receptacle. Your soul is a filter through which
the culture of four millennia flows.[12]

Conscience requires a carefully constructed pedagogy.
Judaism, at is essence, is a curriculum for the cultivation of
conscience. This was the source of Schulweis' love and passion for Jewish life and the key to his interpretation of Judaism. Schulweis found conscience in every expression of Jewish
life—in every text, ritual, and symbol.

Conscience, however, has its enemies. Just as a culture can
cultivate conscience, it can also stifle or warp conscience. The
psychological experiments of Stanley Milgram and Philip Zim-
bardo demonstrated the "banality of evil," how ordinarily good
people could very quickly be turned into agents of cruelty.
Schulweis engaged in an ongoing battle with those in his Jewish world who would deny conscience. In each decade of his
career he was met by a different adversary, and in each decade
he introduced a new facet of the Jewish life of conscience.

The 1970s: The Holocaust Dybbuk

Beginning in the the early 1960s, Schulweis spoke widely to
Jewish and Christian audiences about the remarkable Christian heroes who rescued Jews during the Holocaust. His efforts
were featured on a 1990 episode of the CBS news program
60 Minutes entitled "My Brother's Keeper." Christians welcomed his message. But when he spoke before Jewish groups,
he received harsh castigation. Holocaust survivors felt he sul-
lied the memory of their torments and emphasized the significance of the few rescuers over the multitude of the victims.
Others in the Jewish community found it impossible to hear of

the moral heroism of Christians. Many in the Jewish community were deeply offended by Schulweis' transformation of the narrative, turning a story of Jewish suffering into a narrative of Christian righteousness and reframing the unmitigated darkness into a story of hope and moral redemption. The animosity he faced from Jews, typically expressed with strong emotions, never ceased to shock him. What should have been welcomed as uplifting testimony of moral courage and benevolence was bitterly rejected. What should have been good news—that Christians risked their lives and fortunes to rescue Jews from Nazi terror—was somehow difficult to hear. The Jewish community, he concluded, was possessed by what he called "the Holocaust dybbuk," which exerted a strong warping effect on Jewish moral sensibilities. The narrative of the Holocaust was destroying the Jewish people's moral vision.

As early as 1963, well before the Holocaust found its place as a central theme of American Jewish culture, Schulweis expressed concern about the way the Holocaust was being taught to children.[13] Contemporary Jews bear an obligation, he argued, to share with the next generation the realities of history. But this must be accomplished without destroying their moral vision, without inducing a sense of moral despair, without destroying all vestiges of hope:

> I find myself wondering: "What am I doing to their morale, to their will to live as Jews in the world, to their trust and belief in God and man, to their moral strength?" . . . I grow uneasy with the suspicion that I may myself be leading my people to succumb to a view of history raised to the heights of metaphysical fatalism.

"This is the way of the world. This is the way it was and is and will always be. We and they. We who suffer and they who persecute." Against my every intention I seem to endow hatred of the Jew with an immortality and ubiquity, and prepare the ground for acceptance of the Jew as the world's eternal victim.[14]

By the mid-1970s, the Holocaust had become central to the core narrative of American Jewish identity. Every Jewish communal cause evoked the memory of the six million as a motivation and justification. Commitment to Israel, loyalty to the Jewish future, the imperative to transmit Judaism to the next generation, and the opposition to intermarriage all found their driving impetus in the Holocaust. Emil Fackenheim's celebrated "614th commandment"—the prohibition against giving Hitler posthumous victories—became the chief rationale for Jewish existence. The American Jewish community, it seemed, having lost its faith in God and covenant, replaced that faith with an assertion of contempt for Hitler.

Schulweis' apprehensions were realized. The popular Holocaust narrative advanced a fatalistic view of the Jewish people as history's eternal victim, never to escape the world's demonic designs. The narrative portrayed the isolation of the Jewish people as a metaphysical reality. A popular Israeli song in 1967 proclaimed "*kol ha-olam negdaynu,*" the whole world is against us. In 1973, novelist Cynthia Ozick published a widely read article in *Esquire* entitled "All the World Wants the Jews Dead."

The conventional Holocaust narrative permitted no room for hope. There were no heroes, only perpetrators and their victims. All the institutions of the Western world, it was told, conspired to destroy the Jews: the Nazis who built the concentration camps; the ordinary Germans, Poles, and Ukrainians who acted as willing accomplices; the Allies who closed their borders to Jewish refugees; the church, which remained indifferent; the university, which stood aloof. And, of course, a God who was silent.

Most disturbing to Schulweis was the way the Holocaust had become the chief motivational tool for Jewish education. Instead of touching the emotions of Jewish youngsters with the joys of Jewish life, Jewish educators resorted to gruesome images of Jewish death. Through graphic films, grim literary accounts, and even educational games simulating the experience of victims, the Jewish young were forced to internalize the darkness of the Holocaust narrative as their special inheritance. What is the cumulative effect on the next generation, Schulweis wondered, of this constant reiteration of the Holocaust narrative but the deadening of the Jewish heart?

> If anti-Semitism is endowed with immortality, if the paranoia mounts, if the common wisdom prevails, "scratch a gentile, find an anti-Semite," if pogrom, persecution, inquisition, crematoria are the sole lenses through which we will view our destiny, if all roads lead to Auschwitz, we have foreclosed all options for a happier future. . . . We owe our children more than a past of litanies and a future of isolation. We owe them a way of looking at the world not as an immutable conspiracy against us and at themselves not as caught in a leprous circle.[15]

The popular Holocaust narrative induced a sense of despair that was both psychologically untenable and profoundly un-Jewish. The next generation of Jews, he foresaw, would turn away from a community obsessed with death and gripped by despair. Anti-anti-Semitism is no basis for Jewish identity. He perceived the ironic upshot of Fackenheim's formula—a Judaism built upon spite for Hitler ultimately undermines its own moral foundations. A Judaism of moral fatalism, communal isolation, cynicism, and despair is no Judaism.

Schulweis turned to the stories of Christian rescuers as a strategy for reframing the Holocaust narrative. In place of the despair evoked by the popular narrative's fatalism, the accounts of the rescuers opened a way to celebrate the efficacy of moral heroism and the possibilities of moral courage. In place of a vision of the Jewish people eternally isolated and threatened, the rescuers' narratives affirmed the possibility of solidarity with the decent and the righteous who abide in every corner of the world. In place of despair, the narratives of rescuers demonstrated how redemption might yet be achieved, if even step by tiny step. Schulweis felt he owed this corrective to the memory of those destroyed. "To be so haunted by their death that we are crippled for life offers no honor to those whose ambition for us was at the very least that we overcome the past and reaffirm our fidelity to life."[16]

Still, Jewish audiences did not want to hear it. It took Schulweis twenty years before a national Jewish organization would place the recognition of Christian rescuers on its agenda. It took twenty-five years before he could persuade the social science community to study the phenomenon of altruism as thoroughly as they had analyzed totalitarianism and the authoritarian personality. The result was the groundbreaking research of sociologists Samuel P. Oliner and Pearl Oliner, founders of the Altruistic Personality and Prosocial Behavior Institute at California's Humboldt State University.[17]

Invariably, Schulweis met stiff resistance. In 1976, Cynthia Ozick launched a bitter attack in the pages of *Moment Magazine*, accusing him of Holocaust denial:

> When Rabbi Schulweis asks us to manipulate the past by playing up one aspect of memory more than another— by stressing a handful of righteous Christians, for instance, who saved Jewish lives during the Holocaust ("no matter," he says, "how small the number of these moral heroes may be") [her quotations], rather than the incriminated multitude—he is asking us to declaim to the past for pragmatic reasons, to appeal to it out of prudence, rather than allowing history its free and truthful tongue.[18]

History, Schulweis responded, does not speak on its own. History is a narrative constructed to achieve certain moral aims. The truths of the Holocaust must be told. But it is ours to determine how they should be interpreted and what lessons should be drawn. The rabbis of the Mishna made Passover the celebration of liberation, deliberately understating the horrors of Egyptian slavery so as not to induce a sense of despair. Only one item on the traditional seder plate is bitter, and even that is always eaten together with the sweet:

> Jews, witnesses to the capabilities of human beings to torture and destroy, are also witnesses to the human capacities to save and rebuild. That double witness is

vital for healing the traumatized conscience of humanity. . . . The precarious imbalance that places all weight
of evidence on the depressive side of the scale may
be corrected by the empirical evidence of human
benevolence.[19]

Jews are very good at reciting the history of their persecu-
tion. But *hakarat ha-tov*, recognizing and celebrating the good,
is also an essential Jewish value. The acknowledgment of the
good is the basis of hope. And hope must remain the center
of the Jewish reading of history, otherwise the aspirations of
conscience are futile. There is a surrealistic tone to Schulweis'
controversy with Cynthia Ozick. It was a Manichean battle:
the great novelist desperately and derisively defending a dark,
despairing worldview, and the rabbi pleading to allow some
light into the narrative and into the Jewish world. Schulweis
perceived a moral obligation to modify the prevailing Holocaust narrative no matter how stubbornly the community
clung to its endless darkness.

The 1980s: Out of the Cave

According to the celebrated Talmudic tale, the second-century
sage Rabbi Shimon bar Yohai, running from a death sentence
decreed by the Romans, withdrew into a cave for twelve years
and sat, buried up to his neck in sand, learning divine secrets
with his son (Talmud, Shabbat 33b). Rabbi Shimon, having
witnessed the horrific death of his master, Rabbi Akiba, could
see absolutely nothing redeemable in Roman civilization. He
saw no way to share the world with Rome without imbibing
its moral poison. For twelve years, Rabbi Shimon retreated

from the world, even from his own physical existence, sub-
sisting solely as a disembodied, thinking head. To protect the
purity of his soul from the coarse brutality of the Roman world
around him, he withdrew, sharply dividing body from spirit,
worldliness from holiness, us from them.

Schulweis witnessed a similar phenomenon. Infused with
the trauma of the Holocaust, the American Jewish community
escaped into the cave, turning inward, away from the world.
The communal agenda of the 1970s and 1980s was dominated
exclusively by concerns of Jewish particularity.[20] American
Jews worried about their communal survival, what came to be
called "Jewish continuity." They were anxious about the rising rates of intermarriage and the indifference of the young.
And they obsessed about the survival of the State of Israel.
There was little patience for universalist, moral matters. When
your house is on fire, you don't worry about the neighbors'
problems.

Jewish communal discourse fell into a set of forced either/
or choices: either the commitment to universalism or loyalty to
particularism, either activism in the world or devotion to the
Jewish people, either love of Israel or concern for the world,
either you worry about your own or no one does. Which are you
first, a Jew or a human being? Each of these, Schulweis strongly
insisted, is a false choice. Genuine loyalty to Jewish tradition
demands a response of both/and. Loyalty to Judaism demanded
a love for our own, together with a deep sense of responsibility
for the world. Particularist concerns for survival, continuity, and
cultural distinctiveness are significant, Schulweis argued, but
none can be addressed by focusing exclusively inward. To the
contrary, the survival of Jewish community and culture can

only be achieved by turning outward toward the world. Out-reach, he taught, is the best in-reach.

The other escape route was into materialism. By the 1980s, Schulweis' neighborhood of Encino emerged as a center of affluence, and Valley Beth Shalom as a community of considerable prosperity. Schulweis reminded his congregation that Judaism did not condemn the accumulation of wealth. Judaism condemned the obsession with wealth, the elevation of wealth into life's highest value and standard. Our aspiration, he quipped, points toward the Garden of Eden, not the Garden of Gucci. Jews confused middle-class values for Jewish values. Jewish tradition values education, but not as a means of achieving material success. Education is a spiritual pursuit, a way to refine the soul and sharpen moral vision.[21] Escaping into the cave of opulent indifference, he declared, extinguishes the Jewish soul.

At the end of the Talmudic tale, the tradition chose the world and rejected the cave. Rabbi Shimon's monasticism is repudiated. God commands him to leave the cave and enter the world. But in the shadow of catastrophe, Rabbi Shimon's cave continued to beckon the generations to come. The temptation to follow Rabbi Shimon into the cave of moral surrender and spiritual isolation worried Schulweis.

In the early 1960s, Schulweis visited Germany at the invitation of the West German government. Just after visiting Dachau, he was invited to meet with the great German church leader Otto Dibelius, bishop of Berlin. He asked,

"Bishop, what did you do on Kristallnacht when the synagogues and temples and houses were destroyed by the Nazis? What did you do when so many Jews were placed in jail?" The Bishop looked at me and said, "You are a rabbi, and you should know that it is my first obligation to protect the well-being of my church. . . . As a Bishop, my primary concern was with my church and its people." I came home from Germany having learned a most valuable lesson: beware of spiritual narcissism and overcome religious selfishness and religious tribalism.[22]

Pulling the Jewish community out of the cave of spiritual narcissism and religious tribalism became a central task of Schulweis' rabbinate:

> For a Jew, to love Judaism is to love humanity. That is basic Jewish theology. The God of Israel is global not tribal. The traditional formula for our liturgy reads, "Blessed are Thou O Lord our God, King of the universe." *Melech ha-olam.* We are the custodians of the world and its inhabitants.[23]

Jewish universalism and Jewish particularism are dialectically connected. They cannot be disjoined. Forcing a choice between them is a false interpretation of the Jewish tradition and a false perception of the contemporary Jewish condition. Particularism is the necessary foundation for universalist commitments. The cultivation of a universalist concern for the entire world is the goal of Jewish morality:

> Compassion and justice are not like pieces of pie. Cut a slice for yourself; you take away from the other. Your pie

is too small. Your God is too small. True love and mercy are inclusive, expansive, embracing, enlarging. . . . Like charity, love begins at home, but it must not end there. If it ends there, it's not love and charity but tribal narcissism. . . . It is a false choice: Do you love your children or the children of others? On the contrary, because we love our children, we love other children. Because we love our families, we love other families. Because we mourn our Holocaust, we mourn the holocausts of the world.[24]

Judaism, Schulweis declared, is a global religion. Its concern is for the entire world. This is the principal implication of Jewish monotheism. Loyalty to the Creator of all demands concomitant responsibility for all humanity. Anything short of that turns God into a parochial, tribal idol:

> This Jewish vision of God enlarges us, elevates us, exalts us. To believe in God the Creator of the universe means that nothing in this world, that no people in this world, is foreign to our concerns. Because of our belief in God, the whole world is relevant to us: Israel, of course, Israel is the apple of our eye. Israel is the chief of our joys and concerns but also Somalia, Bosnia, Rwanda, China. Is it too much to place on our Jewish agenda? Then it is we who are too small for the God of creation.[25]

The universal vision of Jewish morality, Schulweis argued, is the most magnificent product of Jewish culture. It is the uniqueness of Judaism among world cultures.

> Judaism gave the world not ziggurats or pyramids
> or mausoleums, but compassion and responsibility.
> We gave the world a sacred humanitarianism. . . . We
> gave to the world a sacred universalism that remains at
> the foundation of our relationship with the world.[26]

A column in the *New York Times* in 2004 by columnist Nicholas Kristof described the horrors of genocide in the Sudanese province of Darfur. This article touched Schulweis deeply. As a global religion, he declared, Judaism must inspire a sense of global responsibility. In the shadow of the Holocaust and after the horrors of Rwanda, Somalia, and Bosnia, he could not remain silent about Darfur:

> I say: "Never again!" Was this vow only to protect Jews
> from genocide? Don't I remember what you and I said
> and preached and taught and heard: "Where are the
> nations of the world? Where are the churches of the
> world? Where are the priests, pastors, the bishops and
> the Pope?" And will my children and grandchildren ask
> of me, "And where was the Synagogue, where were the
> rabbis, and where were you during Rwanda, when geno-
> cide took place in 1994?"[27]

Jewish World Watch was launched as an act of *tshuvah*, personal repentance. Having spent forty years telling the stories of Christian rescuers during the Holocaust, Schulweis suddenly found himself in the very same position—an outsider, living in safety, witness to genocide, and facing the daunting challenge to respond. The crisis could not be ignored.

Once he articulated the vision, Schulweis went looking for a leader to work out the practicalities. Janice Kamenir-Reznik, a member of Schulweis' congregation, was a celebrated lawyer and respected community leader who recently retired from her law practice to pursue more personal interests. Schulweis caught her at just the right moment, and Kamenir-Reznik became Schulweis' partner in launching Jewish World Watch. Together they built an organizational infrastructure, gaining community financial and volunteer support, joining more than sixty-two congregations and schools in activities of education, advocacy, and direct political action.

An unforeseen consequence of Jewish World Watch was the enthusiasm it generated among the young. Thousands of teens participated in Jewish World Watch programs, walks, and projects. The narrowing of Jewish moral concern—the communal pulling inward in the name of Jewish continuity—not only violates the deepest truth of Jewish tradition but, ironically, it also actually threatens the Jewish future. A narrowly particularistic worldview, Schulweis argued, drives young Jews away from Judaism:

> Today, our children ask real questions. Why should we be Jews and why should we be loyal to Judaism? They live in a new world. Don't give them yesterday's failed answers. . . . Our children don't want to live in a cave. They yearn for idealism. They yearn for sacrifice, for altruism, for passion, and they want to find it in Judaism.[28]

The global moral vision of Jewish World Watch engaged young Jews in a way that the dark narratives of the Holocaust could never do. It offered hope, an affirmation of the efficacy of moral and political action, and a practical way to respond. It offered a vision of human solidarity. This was Godliness at its best, and it was the young who got the message most powerfully.

Not everyone in the community resonated with Schulweis' message. Each time he articulated the mission of Jewish World Watch in the synagogue, his critics asked, Why is this a Jewish problem? Why does this matter to us? They were enraged by his appropriation of Holocaust imagery and language to describe the tragedy of Darfur. The most strident critcs charged that it is sacrilege to apply Holocaust images to another people's plight. The Holocaust belongs exclusively to the Jewish people. To speak of Darfur with reference to the Holocaust desecrates the sacred memory of the six million martyrs.

In response, Schulweis pointed to the thousands of young people who came to march against genocide, raise funds for medical clinics and water wells, and participate in educational programs about Darfur and the Congo. Their actions were tesitmony that the way to ensure the continuity of the Jewish people in the next century, and in so doing, to honor the sacred memory of Holocaust, is to affirm Judaism's vision as a global religion. Jewish responsibility for the world is the Torah's deepest truth. The true lesson of the Holocaust is not the exclusivity of Jewish victimhood but rather a renewed commitment to the urgency of human solidarity.

Ultimately Schulweis did not have to answer his critics. The thousands of young people who cheered him at Jewish World Watch rallies did it for him. They announced to the Jewish community that the moment had come to leave the dark cave and stand in the light of the world.

The 1990s: The Stenosis of Halachah

Sometime in the 1970s, Schulweis delivered a sermon about homosexuality. He quoted the verses from Leviticus condemning homosexuality as a *toevah*, an abomination. In the sermon, he conceded that homosexuality, while not necessarily a moral perversion, was most certainly a form of mental illness.[29] Twenty years later, during the spring of 1992, a woman from the congregation came to see him to share the story of her son.

The son was always a peculiar child, but his parents hoped he would grow less awkward with maturity. He went off to university, and when he returned home for the winter break, he informed his parents that he was gay and had had several encounters with other men. His parents were horrified. They sent him to a psychiatrist, who referred the young man to a clinic that promised to "reprogram" and cure him of his homosexuality. After completing the program, the young man began to date women and entered into an intimate relationship with a girlfriend. But soon he fell into a deep depression. One night, the young man committed suicide. At this point in the story, the mother turned to Rabbi Schulweis and asked him directly, "Rabbi, was my son an abomination? Did God punish him? Is that why he died?"

The conversation shook Schulweis deeply. He began to research the history of homosexuality, what science understood about it, and how it was met in halachah, the Jewish legal tradition. At the same time, he sought out other members of the congregation who had gay or lesbian children. He was surprised at how many he found, including the son of his associate rabbi, Jerry Danzig, and the daughter of the immediate past president of the congregation, Sylvia Bernstein. Schulweis came to believe that the castigation of gays and lesbians by the Jewish community needed to be removed. At a retreat for the congregation's board of directors during the spring of 1992, he announced that he would speak about homosexuality in his upcoming Rosh Hashanah sermon. He would welcome gay and lesbian Jews into the synagogue and would establish a new support organization at Valley Beth Shalom for their families. In the sermon, delivered on September 27, 1992, he reviewed the scientific evidence demonstrating that homosexuality is not a chosen lifestyle but biologically determined. He acknowledged the condemnation of homosexuality in Jewish tradition beginning in the Torah, but he argued that rabbis historically met and overcame halachic precedents they found immoral. A rabbinic decree of the nineteenth century, for example, overturned the Talmudic prohibition forbidding a deaf person to serve as a witness in a Jewish court, count in a minyan, or officiate a wedding. It was within the prerogative of a rabbi to declare a halachah, a Jewish religious law, even an explicit law of the Torah, morally wrong and set it aside. Turning to those who sat before him, he concluded with deep emotion:

> You who are invisible and inaudible, I want you to know, for myself, that this is your home and that these are your people, that I am your rabbi and that this is our God and that you are welcome here and that the synagogue is open to you and that nothing should be deprived to you. You are part of the family. You are part of the *min-yan.* You are part of the blessings.[30]

It was the only time in Schulweis' career that a sermon received a standing ovation.

Schulweis was challenged by traditional members of his congregation who threatened to resign from the synagogue over the issue. He invited them to sit with him and discuss the matter. Some did. Others left. The next year he returned to the topic and continued to spell out his position. Again he weighed the scientific evidence on the origins of homosexuality and the various mechanisms for challenging settled halachah. In the end, he deemed this a moral argument that superseded the normal channels of halachic change and development. It was a communal moral emergency and demanded a bold step:

> The underlying issue is moral, not textual. We cannot, as thinking, feeling Jews, base our judgment on a verse or two in the Bible. There is an entire corpus of religious text and spiritual principles that forms rabbinic conscience. . . .
>
> The community and its rabbinic leadership have powers to turn the earth into a living heaven or hell. Over some issues we mortals have little control. We have little control over natural catastrophes: earthquakes, floods, hurricanes, tornadoes. But there are catastrophes over which we have control because we have created them. The curse upon the gay person we have pronounced. This tragedy we have imposed on our children is not the will of God. It is our doing. The blessing and curse, life and death given us is our choice. We are not coerced to silence.[31]

In March 1993, Schulweis was once again invited to offer the keynote address to the national convention of the Rabbinical Assembly gathered in Los Angeles. He chose to speak about halachah and morality. He noted the paradox that characterizes the Conservative movement, a movement that trumpets its loyalty to halachah as its religious core but generates so little passion for halachic observance among its laity. The principal reason for this, Schulweis argued, is the growing separation between halachah and morality:

> I am concerned about the direction that Jewish law has taken within our movement. I fear that the *halachah* is becoming increasingly isolated from the moral idealism of Judaism. I fear that *halachah*, as it has been presented, suffers from a stenosis, and dangerous narrowing that has cut itself off from its moral and spiritual vitality, that it has become more an exercise of legal virtuosity, and in the process lost sight of its soul and goal.[32]

As an example, Schulweis cited a recent scholarly article from the eminent Talmudist David Weiss Halivni, who had just left his position on the faculty of the Jewish Theological Seminary, Conservative Judaism's flagship. In his article "Can a Religious Law Be Immoral?" Halivni argues that the rabbis of the Talmud never consciously abrogated a biblical law for moral reasons even when they acknowledged the law was immoral.[33] Schulweis adamantly rejected Halivni's conception of an amoral halachah, decided solely on the basis of technical textual exegesis. Over the generations of Jewish life, he insisted, rabbis always brought moral insights to bear on their interpretations of the law. Separating halachah from moral-ity paralyzes halachah and renders rabbis mute in the face of pressing moral crises.

> Morality cannot be pushed aside as another extra-legal datum. Morality is the essential attribute of *halachah* . . . the healing of our institutional schisms depends upon our integration of *halachah* as a wholistic moral and spir-itual expression . . . what unites us as a religious move-ment is not our legal expertise but our moral sense.[34]

The religious status of homosexuality presents a poignant and painful case of halachic paralysis. Defending the religious castigation of homosexuality solely because the Bible says so reveals a stunning moral blindness and disturbing rabbinic cowardice.

> One of the major arguments affirming the biblical stig-matization of homosexuality is predicated on preserv-ing the integrity of the biblical law no matter what. . . . No matter what kind of evidence you can bring—psy-chological, biological, socio-organic or ethical—even if the evidence is absolutely correct, even if the Torah misunderstood the nature of homosexuality, there can be no cogent or compelling reason to overturn the law.[35]

This moral blindness undercut the religious integrity of Conservative Judaism, Schulwies concluded, and alienated its lay constituency from halachic observance.

The speech received a mixed reaction from the audience
of rabbis. The next day, Ismar Schorsch, the chancellor of the
Jewish Theological Seminary, requested the floor to offer a
retort. In a brief address, Schorsch bitterly blasted Schulweis.
The Conservative laity, he argued, does not want morality.
They want an assertion of tradition's authority from their rabbis. Morality, Schorsch announced, is irrelevant to the inner
life of Conservative Judaism:

> While [the laity's] observance is selective, they rarely
> presume to impose their momentary predilections on
> the wisdom of a tradition born in revelation and tem-
> pered by time. Nor do they come at us with ethical
> imperatives, for that has never been the universe of
> discourse in Conservative Judaism or, for that matter,
> in Judaism. The ash heap of history is cluttered with
> proposals for reform rejected by our movement despite
> the fact that they were bathed in the bathos of ethical
> imperatives.[36]

Defending Halivni's conclusion, Schorsch declared that
textual exegesis, completely independent of moral consider-
ations, determines the shape of Jewish religion. Morality has
nothing to do with it. With uncharacteristic passion, Schorsch
declared,

> The era of ethical imperatives ended with the proph-
> ets. The rabbis declared prophecy a marvel of the
> past and closed the canon. . . . The rabbis rightly sus-
> pected ethical imperatives as subjective, arbitrary and

impermanent, a prescription for anarchy. For better
or worse, contemporary Judaism is heir to the rabbinic
tradition. We are no longer biblical but rabbinic Jews,
the products of a religious culture that has made of
intertextuality a sacred dialogue and exegesis a way of
thinking.[37]

Schorsch's attack was not ultimately about homosexuality
or the nature of halachic decision-making or even the ideology
of the Conservative movement. In declaiming ethical imperatives as "subjective, arbitrary and impermanent, a prescription for anarchy," Schorsch not only rejected Schulweis' call
for a moral halachah but also revealed his own deep fear of
the antinomian quality of conscience. He was afraid of losing
control, afraid that his religious universe would be infected by
the anarchy of drifting cultural fads masquerading as morality. He was zealously defending his personal sense of religious
security and certainty from the moral relativism of modernity.[38]

A decade later, in his book *Conscience*, Schulweis recognized
that his debate with Schorsch emerged from a deep chasm
within Jewish religion. What stood between Schulweis and
Schorsch were two models of covenant.

According to a celebrated rabbinic midrash, when the people Israel arrived at Mt. Sinai, God held the mountain above
them and declared, "If you accept My laws, you will live. And
if not, this shall be your grave." The people Israel responded,
"All that the Lord has commanded, we will do" (Talmud, Shabbat 88a). This midrash describes a model of the covenant that
is vertical in its orientation: the all-powerful, commanding
God delivering the law from above; the people Israel below

passively receiving God's law. This authoritarian model of covenant demands submission and obedience before God. Rebellion, dissent, and questioning are stigmatized. The model for this religious attitude is the narrative of *Akedat Yitzchak*, the Binding of Isaac. In the story told in Genesis 22, Abraham, the truly lonely man of faith, overcomes all his reservations—his fatherly love for his son, his loyalty to his wife, his concern for his posterity, and most especially his own conscience—to faithfully fulfill God's will. Sacrificing everything he values out of obedience to the Divine earns him God's blessing:

> Because you have done this and have not withheld your son, your favored one, I will bestow My blessing upon you and make your descendants as numerous as the stars of heaven and the sands on the seashore; and your descendants shall seize the gates of their foes. All the nations of the earth shall bless themselves by your descendants, because you have obeyed My command.
> GENESIS 22:16–18

Joseph B. Soloveitchik constructed his theology on the *Akedah* narrative as a model of ultimate surrender to God. Drawing upon Kierkegaard's conviction that Abraham's sacrifice of his conscience in obedience to God's command was the highest expression of faith, Soloveitchik portrayed covenanted man as a hero who aspires to complete self-denial and self-negation in the presence of the divine commandment.[39] Devotion is affirmed in the careful observance of all of halachah but most especially the *hukkim*, the apparently arbitrary laws of Torah. These commandments are valued above all others because they are performed not out of deference to moral rules or social practice but solely as a gesture of surrender to the divine commander.

This vertical model of covenant offers the believer an experience of the transcendent. It offers certainty and security. Its dictates are permanent, safe, and objective. They are not subject to the shifting tides of culture. This model satisfies the believer's need for a secure, unchanging faith. Schorsch's attack reflected the ferocity with which a believer will defend this kind of faith. He fears moral relativism, antinomianism, and the denigration of established tradition. He is terrified of the moral insecurity brought on by change. He looks with trepidation down the slippery slope leading into an abyss of endless compromise, assimilation, and cultural disintegration, a descent that leaves him a stranger in a strange world—a lonely man of faith.[40]

Schulweis recognized the authenticity of this model of covenant. But it disturbed him deeply. He read the *Akedah* narrative differently. At the end of the story, God rescinds the command. That, Schulweis explained, was the voice of conscience reasserting itself. Read from the end, the story does not celebrate ultimate obedience but rather the ultimate triumph of conscience over commandment.

> The sickness of our age is the failure of conscience. Too many listen to the voices of . . . others who would make slavish followers of us. . . . Jews should never contemplate the suspension of the ethical. If the commandment is not ethical, then it cannot come from God. If the commandment is not ethical, it cannot be validated by

halachah. If it is not ethical, we must have heard wrong. And we must test our hearing. If the commandment is not ethical, then the source is not the commander we are to follow. It is no act of piety to raise our children to be followers without question. To do so would be to bind our own children on the altar, to kill their critical minds.[41]

The vertical model of covenant is authentically Jewish. But it is not the entirety of Judaism. Traditional Judaism embraced another model of covenant, a horizontal model, rooted in a different biblical narrative—Abraham's challenge to God over the fate of Sodom:

> Abraham came forward and said, "Will You sweep away the innocent along with the guilty? What if there should be fifty innocent within the city; will You then wipe out the place and not forgive it for the sake of the innocent fifty who are in it? Far be it from You to do such a thing, to bring death upon the innocent as well as the guilty, so that innocent and guilty fare alike. Far be it from You! Shall not the Judge of all the earth deal justly?"
> GENESIS 18:23–25

What religious world is described by a tale in which a human being challenges God? This narrative affirms that human beings possess a moral sensibility independent of God. And upon the basis of that moral sensibility, the human being may question God's moral judgment and get away with it. Abraham appeals to the conscience within God. God takes no offense but welcomes the challenge. This model of covenant embraces and sanctifies dissent as part of a process of refining revelation. Man is a partner, not only in the creation of the world as the Talmud teaches but also in the construction of religious truth. This vision of human possibility represents a revolution in human religious consciousness—a horizontal covenant, the covenant of conscience:

> Conscience is the inner witness to the covenant that carries the divine and human signatures. Despite the apparent contradictions to God's word, conscience appeals to the God within God. Therefore, God registers no insult or anger against the challenge of conscience directed to Him. On the contrary, God recognizes in the holy dissent of the prophetic heroes His own truth.[42]

Schulweis discovered evidence of this model of covenant throughout the texts of the rabbinic tradition. In a startling tale related in the rabbinic midrash Bamidbar Rabbah (Hukkat 19, 33), Moses challenges the ten commandment's warning that God "visits the iniquity of the fathers upon the children to the third and fourth generation" (Exodus 20:5). Moses demonstrates to God the immorality of the stricture, and God responds:

> By your life Moses, you have instructed Me. Therefore I will nullify My words and confirm yours. Thus it says, "The fathers shall not be put to death for the children, neither shall the children be put to death for the fathers."[43]

In the Talmud, the rabbis challenged the morality of the law of *ben sorrer u'moreh*, the rebellious child, found in Deuteronomy 21:18–21. They twisted and turned the law, interpreting it out of existence, and proudly declared, "*Lo haya, v'lo atid lehiyot*"—there never was such a case, and there never will be (Talmud, Sanhedrin 71a).

In these and many other cases, the rabbinic tradition celebrates a unique religious personality—not the obsequious servant of an overbearing divine master but a partner invited to share the task of shaping moral truth. This conception changes the notion of revelation:

> Revelation is not a one-way directive from above or a human projection from below. Revelation is the dialogue of reciprocal covenant, an ongoing process of listening and interpreting, of receiving and giving. Awareness of having entered the covenant makes it impossible to separate the divine and human element in the encounter of revelation. Conscience is the hyphen of the human-divine covenant that runs both ways.[44]

Schulweis' argument with Schorsch, with all its attendant passion, represents the confrontation of these two models of covenant. For Schorsch, the argument reflected his deep fear of a religious world drifting farther and farther away from the secure moorings of tradition. For Schulweis, it reflected his fight for the moral dignity of his religion. It presented a stark question for Jewish religion: Which religious personality is normative—the obedient Abraham of the *Akedah* or the Abraham of moral chutzpah at Sodom? Which has priority? World events would soon come to address this question.

2000: The Duty to Obey, the Duty to Disobey

Schulweis' last book was entitled *Conscience: The Duty to Obey and the Duty to Disobey*. The issue of obedience and disobedience in religion arose not only from arguments within the Jewish community but more so from world events. Like so many Americans, the tragedy of September 11, 2001, shook Schulweis. He was deeply disturbed by the devastation and by the fact that this horrific terrorism was a religious act. The attack on 9/11 was mass murder in the name of faith, in the service of God. Suddenly the debate with Schorsch took on a terrifying weight well beyond the Jewish community. Can religion sanction immoral behavior? Does conscience have a role in faith? What is religion's responsibility for promulgating acts of evil?

Schulweis insisted that his religious vision was not a formula for anarchy.

> [The call for conscience is] no brief for antinomianism—for a society freed from the discipline of law and the duty to obey. No society can long endure without the duty to obey the collective wisdom of religion, which provides society with the continuity of inherited values in a time of indisputable chaos.[45]

But religion, he contended, has become complicit in teaching "the absolutism and inflexibility of the uncritical duty to obey."[46]

The duty to disobey must also be promoted by religion, because it is not really disobedience. It represents the courage to challenge authority out of obedience to the dictates

229

of conscience. Schulweis draws a line from Abraham's challenge to God over the fate of Sodom, to the refusal of the Egyptian midwives Shifra and Puah to murder Israelite children, to the rabbis who rewrote the Bible's teachings on the rebellious child, to the Christian rescuers Herman "Fritz" Graebe and Alex Roslan—together forming a tradition of holy rebels who stood against the power of authority in the name of conscience.

The interaction between the two models of covenant, Schulweis writes, is dialectical, like a pendulum swinging between two poles. The arc of the pendulum describes truth. As long as the pendulum swings freely, the tradition remains vital, and religion contributes fruitfully to the welfare of humanity. But arrested along its way, the pendulum stops and points to a partial truth, which is inevitably a lie. The pendulum must swing freely between the right-hand pole of authoritarianism and the left-hand pole of anarchy. But today, Schulweis warns,

> The pendulum is frozen on the right side. An overall view of religion, politics, and ethics suggests the overwhelming bias toward the duty to obey. It disproportionately favors authoritarian religion and authoritarian policies of the state.[47]

Shoving the pendulum back into motion was Schulweis' task. He saw the heroic religious rebel, willing to challenge authority in the name of conscience, as the necessary corrective to a culture of increasing authoritarianism. And he saw himself in that role. The rabbi as prophet is responsible to promulgate conscience against all its adversaries. In this the rabbi assumes an exalted position in religious life. It pained him how much of Jewish life was devoted to following rules, obeying dicta, and conforming to the expectations of tradition. It pained him that those devoted to the preservation and perpetuation of Jewish tradition perceived the cultivation of conscience as tangential, peripheral, or worse, as a threat. *Conscience* was Schulweis' last book and among the last things he wrote. The book's first manuscript ends with a personal confession of his faith, Schulweis' own epitaph:

> Civilization cannot endure without conscience. With the death of conscience, civilization is imperiled. Conscience has many foes and many obstacles. But as the prophets of all ages testify, conscience is irrepressible. That blessed obduracy is the hope of our moral sanity and survival. "It has been told to you, O man, what is good and what the Lord requires of you; only to do justice and to love goodness and to walk modestly with your God; then will your name achieve wisdom" (Micah 6:8).[48]

CHAPTER 6

The Voice of Community

In April 1964, *Look* magazine prominently featured an article entitled "The Vanishing American Jew: Leaders Fear Threat to Jewish Survival in Today's 'Crisis of Freedom.'" *Look* senior editor Thomas B. Morgan assembled the results of recent demographic studies of American Jews that revealed sharply rising rates of intermarriage, falling birth rates, and a widespread abandonment of Jewish identification. American Jews were disappearing, concluded Morgan.

By the time Schulweis arrived in Encino in 1970, the narrative of a Jewish future threatened by forces of assimilation and secularization had become firmly entrenched in the American Jewish community's identity. This narrative fit well into the perennial Jewish narrative of the "ever-dying people." For community fundraising and rabbis' sermons, it offered a convenient emotional foil. The specter of anti-Semitism could no longer be invoked to flog the community and motivate Jewish identification and generosity, as postwar American Jews enjoyed unprecedented security and prosperity. But here was a new reason to start worrying—American freedom was destroying the Jewish future! Assimilation and intermarriage were completing the job Hitler left unfinished! In the opening address to the third national conference of the Young

Leadership Cabinet of the United Jewish Appeal, cabinet chair Edward Robin (who would, years later, become a member of Schulweis' Encino congregation) expressed the community's narrative concisely:

> Can our generation of American Jews break through the cycle of security, comfort, and reluctance, and forge a genuine impact on the future of our people? . . . Here in the *goldene medine*, under the constant threat of assimilation and loss of identity, we face the question whether the Jewish people can retain its uniqueness in a free society. In the face of this challenge, we have created the greatest philanthropic movement in history and have begun to build for ourselves a creative Jewish existence of learning and observance, concern and love.[1]

Not everyone in the Jewish community accepted the narrative. In his address to the 1965 General Assembly of Jewish Welfare Federations, Abraham Joshua Heschel objected. Survival, he argued, is not a goal. It is not an objective worthy of Judaism:

> There are two words I should like to strike from our vocabulary: "surveys" and "survival." Our community is in spiritual distress, and our organizations are too concerned with digits. Our disease is loss of character and commitment, and the cure cannot be derived from charts and diagrams. The significance of Judaism does not lie in its being conducive to the mere survival but rather in its being a source of spiritual wealth, and

source of meaning relevant to all peoples. Survival, mere continuation of being, is a condition man has in common with animals. Characteristic of humanity is concern for what to do with survival. To be or not to be is not the question. How to be and how not to be is the question.[2]

Schulweis objected as well. The narrative of assimilation and secularization did not fully account for the reality he witnessed within his congregation. It was true that Jews, particularly younger Jews, were abandoning Judaism, but not for secular lives. Young people were joining cults, following new religious movements—"Moonies," Hare Krishna, Maharishi Mahesh Yogi, popular forms of Buddhism, and Jews for Jesus. Adults flocked to encounter groups, growth centers, and human potentiality movements such as Scientology, transcendental meditation, the Arica School, Synanon, Daytop, Gestalt, personal actualization, and EST. Rooted in psychology, these groups functioned as "secular religions," offering their own doctrines, rituals, charismatic leaders, and promises of redemption.[3] Those who stayed within the Jewish community sought a new kind of Judaism in the Jewish counterculture—a Judaism that was mystical, expressive, and emotional. For as many who would come to hear Schulweis' lectures and sermons, even more flocked to Shlomo Carlebach's concerts.

Schulweis' people were searching for something. He sensed the presence of real needs that defied the accepted narrative of assimilation and secularization. These were religious needs. But they were not met by contemporary Jewish life. It was neither assimilation nor secularization that threatened the Jewish future, Schulweis concluded, but rather the irrelevance of the synagogue—its indifference to the personal needs of Jews:

> The synagogue became an empty shell called the sanctuary. . . . That sanctuary was not filled with the concerns of people. People would say, "The last place I would come to is the synagogue when I'm in trouble." It should be the first; it should respond to needs which are real but which are often dismissed as selfish.[4]

That there were Jews who disagreed with his politics, theology, or interpretations of Judaism did not bother Schulweis. He welcomed vigorous argument. But to be found irrelevant was intolerable to him. Schulweis went in search of a theory that might offer more insight into the lives and needs of contemporary Jews than the accepted narrative of assimilation and secularization. He went looking for a theory of contemporary Jewish identity that might generate a new focus for the synagogue and the reorganization of Jewish community life. Heschel ended his 1965 address with the call: "We need a revolution in Jewish life." Schulweis was determined to incite that revolution.

The Psychological Jew

Schulweis found the backbone of his theory in the writing of social theorist Philip Rieff. Rieff taught at the University of Pennsylvania for most of his career and was best known for his work on Sigmund Freud. He edited a ten-volume edition of Freud's papers, and he produced two landmark analyses of Freud's impact on Western culture, *Freud: The Mind of the Moralist* and *The Triumph of the Therapeutic.* The last chapter of *Freud: The Mind of the Moralist,* entitled "The Emergence of Psychological Man," is considered a classic in modern social theory.

Rieff maintained that Freud signaled the arrival of a new character type in Western culture—"the psychological man." Three character types have dominated Western civilization: "political man," formed by classical antiquity; "religious man," promulgated by Judaism and Christianity and dominant in the Middle Ages; and "economic man," generated by the Enlightenment. This last model turned out to be only transitional, leading to the emergence of a new character type, the psychological man. Both political man and religious man perceived themselves embedded in community—the polis or the church. They endowed their respective communities with sanctity. They could not conceive of a self apart from the community. When life was in disarray, their culture offered forms of therapy to restore the self to its proper place within the community. Economic man emerged from the Enlightenment's revolt against the authority of sacralized community in the name of autonomous individuality. With the advent of modernity, the sacred community was transformed into the secular marketplace. Unlike the polis or the church, the marketplace demands no commitment beyond self-interest. Nothing is asked of economic man except the pursuit of his own self-interest and satisfaction.

Freud's signal accomplishment was to introject marketplace morality—the calculated self-conscious pursuit of satisfaction—into the inner life. Psychological man is acutely aware of his inner life and consumed by the economy of his own satisfactions:

The psychological man of the twentieth-century [is] a child not of nature but of technology. He is not the pagan ideal, political man, for he is not committed to the public life. He is most unlike the religious man. We will recognize in the case history of psychological man the nervous habit of his father, economic man: he is anti-heroic, shrewd, carefully counting his satisfactions and dissatisfactions, studying unprofitable commitments as the sins most to be avoided. From this immediate ancestor, psychological man has constituted his own careful economy of the inner life.[5]

Freudian psychology taught psychological man to be wary of participation and commitment in public life. Public life carries frustrations. Public life places claims upon the self that can upset one's inner equilibrium and interfere with the pursuit of personal satisfaction, the principal objective of life:

The successful patient has learned to withdraw from the painful tension of assent and dissent in his relation to society by relating himself more affirmatively to his depths. His newly acquired health entails a self-concern that takes precedence over social concern and encourages an attitude of ironic insight on the part of the self toward all that is not self. Thus the psychoanalyzed man is inwardly alienated even if he is often outwardly reconciled, for he is no longer defined essentially by his social relations.[6]

Psychological man is essentially a "privatist," finding his identity and satisfaction apart from community and commitment.

This was Freud's moral revolution—dividing human character from participation in relationships. What is humanly valuable comes from within. Human connections are confining and are therefore dangerous:

> All binding engagements to communal purpose may be considered, in the wisdom of therapeutic doctrines, too extreme. . . . It is in this sense that the contemporary moral revolution is anti-political . . . representing a calm and profoundly reasonable revolt of the private man against all doctrinal traditions urging the salvation of self through identification with the purposes of community.[7]

The morality of psychological man, Rieff argued, generates its own culture, its own institutions, its own forms of expression:

> Where the family and nation once stood or Church and party, there will be hospital and theater too, the normative institutions of the next culture. . . . Religious man was born to be saved, psychological man is born to be pleased. The difference was established long ago when "I believe," the cry of the ascetic, lost precedence to "one feels," the caveat of the therapeutic. And if the therapeutic is to win out, then surely the psychoanalyst will be his secular spiritual guide.[8]

Rieff's description of the displacement of religion by psychology—with its own clergy of psychotherapists, its own rites, and its own vision of redemption—captured Schulweis' attention.

He found in Rieff's typology the theory that explained the dilemma of the Jewish community. The criticisms leveled at the contemporary synagogue—that the synagogue is cold, lifeless, and irrelevant—could not be resolved with superficial remedies such as new melodies, new prayer books, or more engaging sermons. Instead, he argued, rabbis must recognize the new kind of Jew who sits before them in the synagogue, "the psychological Jew":

> We are confronted with a new character ideal, with a radically different kind of Jew, the newest sociological phenomenon in our history. We face the emerging "psychological Jew." Our rhetoric, our allusions, our claims presuppose a set of experiences, values, and basic categories which, in fact, belong to another Jewish typology. We appeal to "God, Torah, and Israel" and experience the shock of non-recognition when the triadic sancta are addressed to our new audience. We sense vaguely that we have lost the power to bind and to loosen, to move our people, to seriously affect their behavior.[9]

Psychological Jews are nonideological, uncommitted as a matter of principle. They are not Orthodox, Conservative, or Reform, neither Zionist nor anti-Zionist. They are loyal only to their own satisfaction and wary of any commitment that might bind or claim the self. Most adamantly, the psychological Jew is a privatist, unbound by community:

> For this post-religious, post-ideological Jew, all community is suspect. He may not have read Freud or Marcuse

or Brown, but a meta-psychology has filtered down to warn him that civilization is regressive. Psychological wisdom counsels that community, whether in the shape of religious faith or political ideology, robs him of his private satisfactions, his privacy and individualism. In our times, the danger to ourselves comes from the suffocating demands of community. And while community in part is useful, it must be kept at a safe distance lest it drain our energies and desiccate our joys.[10]

When psychological Jews come to synagogue, it is not out of devotion to faith, community, or peoplehood, but for its salutary effects—it is good for their children to be exposed to religion. The quintessential ritual expression of the psychological Jew is the private bar or bat mitzvah celebrated on Shabbat afternoon, apart from the larger community. The invitation list is restricted to friends and family. Why should this most special family moment be shared with a congregation of strangers? The psychological Jew will have "his rabbi," she will engage "her cantor," showering attention exclusively on their family and celebrating the extraordinary talents of this unique child in the exclusive intimate presence of invited family and friends. Talk of community and obligation does not penetrate.

Rabbis, notes Schulweis, constantly flagellate themselves for their inability to reach their congregants, for their failure to build true community and change patterns of ritual behavior. They often feel, in the words of Rabbi Mordecai Waxman, that they are "plowing water."[11] This sense of futility, counsels Schulweis, is not due to a lack of talent or effort but because they have misperceived the congregation they address. Rabbis were trained to speak the language of character types that no longer predominate in their congregations. In the past, the Jewish community was populated by religious Jews and ideological Jews. Both defined themselves by the community to which they belonged and welcomed the claims laid upon them by the community.

The religious Jew submitted every gesture of life, from the most trivial to the most profound, to the authority of tradition. Schulweis' grandfather was the paradigmatic religious Jew. When his wife, Schulweis' grandmother, fell ill, the community offered prayers tying her fate to the community: "May she be healed together with all the sick of Israel." When she died, words of consolation were likewise connected to community: "May God comfort you together with the mourners of Zion and Jerusalem." When the holiday of Sukkot interrupted the period of shiva, his grandfather rose from his grief without protest or complaint to join the community in its festival joy, because he understood instinctively that his wife's immortality was linked with the community's eternity.[12]

The secular ideological Jew rejected the strictures of tradition. The ideological Jew perceived the tradition's faith in the coming of the Messiah as an expression of Jewish impotence and victimhood. In place of the tradition's Messiah, he affirmed a vision of this-world redemption. Whether Zionist, Yiddishist, nationalist, socialist, Bundist, or ethical culturalist, the ideological Jew was claimed fully by the plight of one's people and a vision of their salvation. A quintessential ideological Jew, Schulweis' father, like his mentor Chaim Zhitlovsky, was driven by his social idealism and dedication to the redemption of his people.

Rabbis enter the synagogue prepared to talk to religious Jews and ideological Jews. But the congregation that sits before them is fundamentally different. The congregation is populated by psychological Jews who bear neither the devotion of the religious Jew nor the commitments of the ideological Jew. In fact, Schulweis points out, it is not a congregation at all but an audience of disjoined individualists:

> The rabbi then is addressing not a Jewish congregation but an audience of Jews. He commits "a fallacy of composition" who assumes that an assembly of Jews is a Jewish assembly. A congregation is made up of people who share experiences and values which transcend their private perceptions. An audience is comprised of separate egos who have come together for reasons of their own and dissolve into discrete bodies after the event is over.[13]

Having been rigorously trained to answer questions germane to communal Jewish life and Jewish peoplehood, the rabbi finds himself or herself terribly alone. Neither shared faith nor shared ideology bind the rabbi's audience together into a community. Alienated from traditional faith, no one asks the religious questions the rabbi was trained to answer. So the rabbi is forced to play pulpit ventriloquist, throwing his or her voice to create the illusion that someone is asking. Pathetically, rabbis simulate dialogue to pretend to themselves that someone in the room inhabits his or her universe of discourse. This inevitably leaves the rabbi with a gnawing sense of futility. And it leaves the psychological Jew with a yet deeper impression of the moral emptiness and spiritual irrelevance of the synagogue.

The character of psychological man, according to Rieff, was generated by the advent of a transitional character, economic man. The psychological Jew, according to Schulweis, is born of the Jewish version of economic man, the middle-class Jewish family. The middle-class Jewish family, Schulweis argues, confuses middle-class bourgeois values for Jewish values, infusing those middle-class values with religious sanctity. They pursue material success with singular religious devotion. This family typology—the stuff of *Goodbye, Columbus* and so many other twentieth-century novels and films—is presented by Schulweis as a parody of the warm Jewish family sentimentally celebrated in *Fiddler on the Roof.*

The middle-class papa is no Tevye. He is not "master of the house, who has the final word at home." He is, in fact, master of no house and bears no words:

> He has been sucked into the vortex of career, business or profession. By his own account, "he has a tiger by the tail." Papa feels driven by some mysterious, ubiquitous power that makes him expand to stay alive, because if not, his murderous competitors will eat him up alive. The demands on the middle-class father are limitless. . . . Success's demands are omnivorous. They devour every moment of his life.[14]

The middle-class father, left with neither time nor tenderness for his family, hires surrogate fathers to raise his children—athletic coaches, scout leaders, camp counselors, and the rabbi. He buys his children's loyalty, offering every toy and prerogative except his own loving presence, which has been stolen by his success.

The middle-class mama, prefeminism, lives a terrible contradiction. Unmarried, she is a failure. Once married, she is expected to give up her plans, her dreams, her life to care for husband and children.

> Her glorious years, her best years, will be in pregnancy, when the children are two or three years old, and she is needed. When the children grow older and enter the school years, she turns into the family teamster, the perennial chauffeur, driving for the growth of others. With the children's adolescence, a tug of war begins. The adolescent child wants autonomy and mama needs purpose.[15]

With the children's growing independence, mama faces the prospect of psychological unemployment. A victim of "postparental depression," she holds on tighter and tighter:

> Mama had to live for everybody except herself. What was her success? Her success was the success of others. And so she became a nagging, demanding, driving woman. She became the Minority Whip of the House.[16]

And should mama ever consider changing her role, moving into the world to derive satisfaction from her own endeavors, the classic Yiddish folksong *My Yiddishe Momme* hammers home the culture's expectation for her:

> How few were her pleasures.
> She never cared for fashion styles.
> Her jewels and treasures

She found them in her baby's smile.

Oh, I know that I owe what I am today

To that dear little lady so old and so gray,

To that wonderful, *Yiddishe momme, momme* mine.[17]

The first product of this strained family is the middle-class Jewish son. The son is subjected to a particularly Jewish form of child abuse called "disappointment." The fear of disappointing his parents drives the middle-class Jewish son to be a star at everything—lead in the school play, first violin in the orchestra, honor student, captain of the team. How else can he repay a father who works so hard and a mother who loves so selflessly? The middle-class Jewish son is "a *nachas*-producing machine," always performing, achieving, reaching:

> From infancy on, he is measured by silver and gold stars, regent exams, SAT, 3.8, 4.0 averages, summa cum laude, Phi Beta Kappa societies. . . . How high is "up" for the upwardly mobile? The incorporated drive to achieve according to one's best efforts is insatiable.[18]

If challenged, his parents will protest, "We only want him to work up to his potential!" But that's the trap. Potential is an ever-expanding horizon, an asymptotic goal beyond reach. It is a sly way of communicating that no degree of achievement is ever enough. From a very young age, the son is admonished that education is a sacred Jewish value, that success in school is a religious imperative. Hidden from the son is the radical divergence between the middle-class idea of the value of education and the traditional Jewish idea. For the middle class,

246

education is the golden pathway to material success and prestige. For Judaism, education is the vehicle for character development. *Ain Torah ain derech eretz*—without Torah learning, there is no right conduct, teaches Pirke Avot 3:17. The middle-class family, by contrast, fails to recognize any value in the child's character. Qualities of kindness, generosity, selflessness, and devotion are overlooked, because they are unrelated to material achievement. Parents will boast of a child's acceptance to an Ivy League school. Very few parents, Schulweis sadly notes, boast of a child's inner goodness or gentility.[19]

The middle-class Jewish daughter is caught in every trap. Should she strive to achieve, as her brother is expected to do, she is deemed pushy, aggressive. She is warned that she is making herself unmarriageable, cutting off her only way to happiness. Should she turn demure and reserved, burying her abilities and ambitions to qualify for marriage, she will find herself burdened with a terrible sense of inauthenticity. The common pejorative stereotype of the Jewish American princess—vapid, spoiled, narcissistic, entitled—is the weaponized stereotype deployed against the middle-class Jewish daughter who demands her autonomy, her authenticity, her own voice, her own place in the world.

Schulweis' portrait of the family is certainly dated. It is specific to mid-twentieth-century second- and third-generation American Jewish families. Feminism, changing images of masculinity, diverse models of marriage and child-rearing, and a changing economy altered this portrait substantially through the end of the twentieth century and the beginning of the twenty-first. What is noteworthy is how much of the model remains intact: the crushing pressure to invest endless hours in one's career, the agonizing choice between career and family, the assignment of status based on material success, the expectations of perfection laid upon children, and the cruel mixed messages delivered to women.

Growing up in this family, Schulweis observed, the middle-class Jewish child comes to feel that he or she is loved only conditionally. As a result, the child grows insecure in the world and suspicious of attachments. The middle-class Jewish child:

> carries within him unresolved ambivalences of respect and contempt, of love and fear. . . . He bears the scars of parental pressures to excel and "make it." It is against the background of this middle-class transitional figure that the ambiguities of the psychological Jew can best be understood. He is a product of his middle-class upbringing.[20]

In a family where middle-class values were confused with Jewish values, the middle-class Jewish child comes to associate with Judaism so much of what he or she resents in the family—the pressures, roles, and expectations, together with the unrelenting guilt that enforces them. The middle-class Jewish home was emptied of moral purpose, ritual beauty, and spiritual transcendence:

> The ethos of material success has overwhelmed the family and left it bereft of memory and imagination. The bourgeois Jewish home is devoid of ritual poetry and myth; its institutions appeal to no system of heroics whereby the life of performance and acquisition may be

transcended. Both have succumbed to a banal utilitari-
anism, a pan-technical world of means and instrumen-
talities. With the loss of superordinate ends, the young
adult feels himself pressured but for not great purpose.[21]

Raised on relentless images of what a "good Jewish boy"
ought to be, or how a "nice Jewish girl" ought to behave, the
middle-class Jewish child grows up to become the psychological Jew, acutely aware of the imbalances and contradictions
sown into the inner life, seeking liberation from the roles and
expectations and their attendant guilt, suspicious of attachments, most especially Jewish attachments. Why do "good Jewish kids" join strange cults?

> They are love-starved persons escaping a society at home
> and at school dominated by obsessive compulsions to
> make it. They are entrapped by a smile and cordial invi-
> tation to a song-fest because they seek refuge from an
> unsmiling, competitive and tough society. Their rever-
> sion to child-like play and simplistic formulas in the cult
> environment is not a revolt of anti-intellectualism. It is
> a rejection of the analytic, depersonalizing, dispassion-
> ate, achievement-oriented academic atmosphere from
> which they seek refuge.[22]

Joining a cult is not a rejection of Judaism as much as it
is a rejection of the middle-class values the Jewish family has
relentlessly promulgated.

Looking into the lives of his congregation through lenses
provided by Rieff, Schulweis developed his theory of the

psychological Jew. He planned a book on this discovery and prepared the first four chapters of "The Psychological Jew," but he was interrupted by his first heart attack in 1983. He published the outline of his typology in his sermons and addresses through the 1970s. Schulweis' typology anticipated the findings of Robert N. Bellah and his associates in the landmark *Habits of the Heart*, published first in 1985, and of Steven M. Cohen and Arnold M. Eisen in *The Jew Within*, published in 2000. Bellah introduced his study by noting Alexis de Tocqueville's warning that individualism "might eventually isolate Americans one from another and thereby undermine the conditions of freedom."[23] Cohen and Eisen found similar patterns in Jewish life:

> The American Jews we interviewed overwhelmingly follow the pattern described by Bellah and his co-authors fifteen years ago in *Habits of the Heart*. The "first language" that our subjects speak is by and large one of profound individualism. Their language is universalist, liberal and personalist. Community—though a buzzword in our interviews, a felt need, even a real hunger for some—is a "second language," subordinate to the first. Our subjects, like Americans more generally today, do not speak it as often or as well. . . .
>
> Community and commitment, in fact, are repeatedly redefined and apprehended by our subjects in terms acceptable to sovereign ever-questing selves. Only in those terms is commitment possible and community permitted to obligate the self.[24]

Cohen and Eisen's portrait of the "sovereign ever-questing self" as the dominant character type among American Jews was

derived empirically from extensive interviews and the findings
of recent demographic studies and based on Bellah's studies.
Their portrait is strikingly parallel to Schulweis' typology of
the psychological Jew, which was drawn from Rieff and from
his personal encounters with his Encino congregation.

Mediating Structures: The Synagogue *Havurah*

Psychological Jews come to the synagogue for a few hours
on the High Holidays. They politely follow the prayer service, listen to the rabbi's sermon, mingle with acquaintances,
and then return home to resume life as before. The experience remains superficial. The privatism—the deep suspicion
of attachments—shields the psychological Jew from being
touched by the holiday's theology, the cantor's melodies, or
the rabbi's teaching. On the surface, the psychological Jew
appears sanguine, satisfied with life. But deep within, Schulweis sensed disequilibrium. In his conversations with psychological Jews, Schulweis discovered emptiness, a longing for
community, and a hunger for connection:

> The psychological Jew and all of his therapeutic
> wisdom has backfired against him. . . . His vaunted
> individualism has borne fruits of loneliness. His non-
> involvement in the community and its commitment
> and claims have resulted in nausea and boredom.
> Behind the mask of autonomy and of self-sufficiency,
> and his detachedness into a terrifying anonymity, lies
> the longing for belonging, the craving for community
> and purpose.[25]

A life turned exclusively toward the self and its satisfactions inevitably leads to loneliness and purposelessness. But when the psychological Jew encounters the synagogue, he or she finds no remedy. The synagogue presents itself as another cold institution—impersonal, faceless, and uncaring. Rabbis are trained to answer religious questions and address personal issues, Schulweis quipped. But the issue most frequently posed by congregants is, "Rabbi, I bet you don't remember my name." This is not a test of the rabbi's retentive memory. It is a challenge to the anonymity of the congregation. So long as the synagogue mirrors the soulless anomie of the society at large, it remains irrelevant to the psychological Jew.

In 1973, Schulweis delivered the keynote address to the Rabbinical Assembly Convention, the national meeting of Conservative rabbis. The moment was heavy with irony. The beginning of the 1970s saw the zenith of the Conservative movement's expansion and influence. Congregations coast to coast were flourishing. But the rabbis were uneasy.

Conservative rabbis were succeeding institutionally but failing spiritually. They were not reaching into the lives of their congregants. They were not changing behavior. The norms of observance, prayer, and learning preached by Conservative Judaism held little sway over the lives of the Conservative laity. Rabbi Max J. Routtenberg had testified to the rabbis' unease just a few years earlier in his presidential address to the 1965 Rabbinical Assembly Convention:

> During these past decades we have grown, we have prospered, we have become a powerful religious establishment. I am, however, haunted by the fear that

somewhere along the way we have become lost; our
direction is not clear, and the many promises we made
to ourselves and our people have not been fulfilled. We
are in danger of not having anything significant to say
to our congregants, to the best of our youth, to all those
who are seeking a dynamic adventurous faith that can
elicit sacrifice and that can transform lives.[26]

No technical fix would remedy this problem, Schulweis
declared. None of the ploys that rabbis were so fond of—the
"creative services," movie reviews from the pulpit, contemporary melodies for prayers (Simon and Garfunkel tunes were
particularly popular), "relevant" sermons—would effectively
reshape the lives of Conservative Jews. What was needed was a
thorough transformation of synagogue life. To touch the lives
of Jews, the synagogue must become a real community, a network of close, personal, caring relationships. In the absence of
real community, Judaism remains only an abstraction:

> Without the matrix of community, one cannot speak of
> peoplehood or of the wisdom, ethics and aspirations of
> that people. Without the concreteness of inter-personal
> relationship, the rhetoric of I-Thou dialogue between
> man and man and between God and man is vacuous . . .
> The primary task on the agenda of the synagogue is the
> humanization and personalization of the temple. To over-
> come the interpersonal irrelevance of synagogue affilia-
> tion is a task prior to believing and ritual behaving. To
> experience true belonging is an imperative prerequisite
> for the cultivation of religious and moral sensibilities.[27]

The anonymity of the synagogue, Schulweis pointed out, reflects a larger problem of modernity: contemporary society is "underinstitutionalized." Schulweis drew this insight and language from the writing of sociologist Peter Berger, who in turn drew upon the German sociologist Arnold Gehlen. Gehlen argued that modernity hollowed out the space between the family and the state, leaving little support for the cultivation of culture.[28] The nineteenth-century French sociologist Emile Durkheim labeled this layer of society its "intermediate institutions," the network of communal organizations, trade associations, and religious communities that provide a sense of belonging and identity to the individual. Modernity was missing what Berger called "mediating structures," those institutions, organizations, and associations standing between the personal life of individuals and the impersonal institutions of a society. The social connectivity that mediates a culture's values, orientation, and sense of meaning into individual lives was missing.[29]

Schulweis perceived that the synagogue itself required its own mediating structures to push back the impersonal institutionalization of the synagogue and build a warm, face-to-face community. The synagogue required a new layer of mediating structure connecting the lonely psychological Jew and the larger synagogue institution. In his 1972 Rosh Hashanah sermon, Schulweis proposed the creation of synagogue *havurot*. The *havurah* was a cell of ten families, couples, or singles, at roughly the same stage and status of life—singles with other singles, young couples, families with children of similar ages, seniors—who gathered regularly to share Jewish life. The synagogue, Schulweis imagined, would then become a *havurah* of *havurot*, with its membership rooted in the close, personal connections of the *havurah* experience.

It was important to Schulweis that the entire *havurah* project be led by the laity. To allow room for Jews to assume responsibility for their own spiritual lives, the rabbi needed to practice a form of professional *tzimtzum*, contraction. Though the rabbi was available as a resource, each *havurah* determined its own program. The *havurah*'s Jewish learning, ritual observance, and mutual support would be organized and offered entirely by lay Jews to one another. In this way, they would learn to turn toward one another rather than reflexively looking to the rabbi for leadership. Schulweis learned from Buber's description of the Hasidic community. The genius of the Hasidic master was to turn the attention and loyalty of his Hasidim toward one another, creating a circle of intimacy, mutual concern, and support:

> We are challenged to decentralize the synagogue and deprofessionalize Jewish living so that the individual Jew is brought back into a circle of shared Jewish experience. My experience with the *havurazation* of the synagogue strengthens my conviction that we can help the psychological Jew meet his genuine needs for autonomy and help overcome his depersonalization by providing a way towards authentic community.[30]

Schulweis insisted that the idea of synagogue *havurot* came to him from his readings in Buber, but many of its core features were in the air.[31] The communitarian, participatory, "do-it-yourself" culture of Schulweis' synagogue *havurot*, along with the very term *havurah,* reflected the countercultural *havurah* movement of the late 1960s.[32] In 1973, the same year Schulweis shared his vision of synagogue *havurot* at the Rabbinical Assembly Convention, the *Jewish Catalog* was published. A product of the *havurah* movement, the *Catalog* was a resource guide to the kind of grassroots "do-it-yourself Judaism" that Schulweis envisioned growing within synagogue *havurot.* Removed from its setting in the rebellious youth culture, Schulweis located *havurah* culture in the heart of the "establishment," the synagogue. In doing so, he created a revolutionary new form of Jewish religious life.

A committee was established at Valley Beth Shalom to form *havurot* and to offer guidance on activities and programs. By the following year, fully nine hundred families were involved in some ninety-five *havurot.*[33]

Havurah activities varied. Some *havurot* took up Jewish study. Others were purely recreational. Most adopted a program that mixed Jewish and social activities. Holidays and life-cycle rituals were celebrated together. *Havurot* met monthly, generally on Saturday or Sunday evenings, in members' homes. The *havurah* succeeded in breaking down the walls that isolated suburban families. This brought Judaism out of the synagogue and back into Jewish homes. Schulweis painted a poignant image of a circle of Jewish adults, standing arm in arm in a living room, chanting the *havdallah* prayers, while children peered out from their bedroom doors.[34] For the first time in their lives, children saw adults engaging in Jewish behaviors for their own spiritual satisfaction and without a rabbi's guidance.

In 1974, E. Anderman, a graduate student at the UCLA School of Social Welfare, studied the Valley Beth Shalom *havurah* experience and concluded, "There are strong indications that through discussion and study, shared ritual observance, and through interaction with one another, *havurah* members experience an enhancement of their identification as Jews."[35]

Why did *havurot* succeed at Valley Beth Shalom? Schulweis maintained that the *havurah* mediated an experience of true community to the wary psychological Jew, allowing for personal autonomy and offering an opportunity to bond with a circle of new friends in a safe environment. Other factors were involved as well. The community of Valley Beth Shalom in 1973 was made up primarily of newcomers to the neighborhood, newly separated from extended family and friendship networks. Far from siblings, parents, and cousins on the East Coast or in the Midwest, the *havurah* became a surrogate extended family. UCLA professor Harry Wasserman studied the *havurot* at Valley Beth Shalom and four other synagogues between 1974 and 1979. He observed that

> the *havurot* tend to become extended families in varying degrees. They undertake such activities as visiting the sick members of the *havurah*, filling the familial roles of afflicted persons (providing sustenance and care to a husband and children when a mother is hospitalized), providing emotional support to the bereaved in fulfilling the traditional practice of the *Shivah*, gathering together of all *haverim* and their children for the festive holidays, and the communal celebration of *B'nai* and *B'not Mitzvah, Hannukat Habayit*, etc. In these kind of extended family activities, the *havurot* behave as human

support systems, providing a context of sharing joys on proper occasions and a matrix of people who give mutual aid through the provision of succor and care when illness and death strike.[36]

A second factor in the success of Valley Beth Shalom *havurah* was the army of talented, energetic women who were not working outside their homes and who welcomed the opportunity to lead and organize *havurah* activities.[37]

Finally, a related third factor was leadership. Schulweis was uninterested in professional administration. He believed that synagogue programs should be run by lay leaders. The individuals he found at Valley Beth Shalom to launch the *havurah* program fortuitously turned out to be uniquely dedicated, insightful, and diligent.[38]

While it was women who primarily organized *havurot*, Wasserman found that it was men who most benefited from the *havurah*. For many, it was truly life-changing:

> For some of the male respondents, the *havurah* experience provides a content of social intimacy which either had been lost or had not been deeply felt for many years. Men in particular seem to restrict their social worlds to their families, to business and professional associates, and to impersonal, formal organizations. *Havurah* provides a network of relationships in which feelings of acceptance and belonging are enhanced, and where human warmth outside the family circle is a normal, comfortable feeling. These men are surprised that they have the capacity within themselves to enjoy a

warm group experience. More poignantly, they may not have ever been aware that they had suppressed the need for social intimacy since the days of childhood.[39]

The *havurah* program thrived through the end of the 1990s. But as the supporting factors changed in the next generation, *havurot* at Valley Beth Shalom began to wane. Members who were newcomers in 1971 settled and raised a new generation. By the 1990s, many synagogue members had extended families living in the neighborhood. The need for a surrogate family diminished. The presence of real extended family compromised the *havurah*—"Where do we go for Passover seder or Hanukah, to the *havurah* or to Grandma's?"

Also, by the 1990s, economic pressures and the next generation of feminism sent the army of talented, energetic women who had once led *havurot* out of the home and into the workforce. Women could no longer devote hours to planning *havurah* activities. Families had less time to devote to *havurah* activities.

Finally, one of the principal features of the *havurah* experience was the opportunity for laypeople to learn from one another. The 1980s and 1990s saw the flowering of what cultural critics termed the *cult of the expert*. Americans turned to experts for advice on child-rearing, sex, health, nutrition, exercise, and personal fulfillment. American Jews, likewise, wanted to be taught by experts; they had little patience for amateurs.

Though *havurah* membership eventually waned, the introduction of *havurot* had a profound lasting effect on congregational life. The *havurah* introduced the experience of genuine, warm, supportive communal life to a generation of psycholog-ical Jews deeply suspicious of binding social commitments and deeply ambivalent about their Judaism. It raised expectations for congregational life. Synagogues everywhere were now expected to provide not just worship services, Torah learning, and the traditional expressions of Jewish life but also warm, personal, supportive human connection. Ultimately, *havurot* gave real meaning to the cliché of "Jewish community." The phrase was no longer solely sociological but came to refer to a powerful experiential reality.

Mediating Structures: Paraprofessional Counselors and Para-Rabbinics

The *havurah* was Schulweis' first answer to the lonely individu-alism of the psychological Jew. But he soon saw that it was not enough. As important as it was to bring the psychological Jew into the community, it was equally important that the com-munity acknowledge the needs of the psychological Jew. The psychological Jew was asking for personal attention. But the community had no way to answer. There was a striking dis-symmetry between the needs of the psychological Jew and the resources of the Jewish community. In his 1979 Rosh Hashanah sermon, "What Hurts the Jew," reprinted in *Moment Magazine*, Schulweis records the dialogue between the plaintive psycho-logical Jew and his hapless rabbi. Cries the psychological Jew,

> "Help me. . . . Pay attention to my personal life. I am
> falling apart. Stop telling me what I can do for the sake
> of Judaism, for the sake of the synagogue, for Zion's
> sake, for the sake of mitzvot. Tell me instead, oh tell me,

what Judaism can do for me, what the synagogue can do for me, what the Jewish community can do for me, what mitzvot can do for me. Tell me what *you* can do for me, you, rabbi.

"Look at *me*, in my despairing particularity, in my existential loneliness, in my deadening boredom, in my inability to celebrate, to laugh, to cry, to feel."

Answers the rabbi:

"Dear friends, I understand your personal needs, your anxieties, your quest for meaning and intimacy. But here in the synagogue we are concerned with other things—with prayer and with ritual observance, with study and the celebrations of weddings and coming of age. For what you want, you must go elsewhere." And that is where they are going.[40]

The psychological Jew speaks the language of personal need. The community responds in the language of communal obligation. Playing on traditional Talmudic legal terms, Schulweis explains, the psychological Jew inhabits *reshut ha-yachid*, the domain of the personal, while the community inhabits *reshut ha-rabim*, the concerns of the collective:

The psychological Jew has his private holocausts and they are being ignored by the community. He is exhausted by his own envies and self-doubts, and his inability to relate to his spouse, children, parents, self. Were we to give voice to his silent broodings, we would hear a half-angry, half-pleading protestation against the super-personal concerns of the community which ignores his distress. "Do not tell me to support the synagogue, tell me what the synagogue does to support me. . . . Do not tell me to preserve Jewish continuity, show me how it can preserve my integrity."[41]

Psychological Jews must not be abandoned, argues Schulweis. They must not be condemned or caricatured or dismissed as insignificant by-products of the "me decade." Their needs are real, and collectively they represent a significant constituency of contemporary Jewry. Told that there is nothing for them in the Jewish community, they go elsewhere—to the psychological movements, religious cults, and alternative spiritual communities that promise to take the inner life seriously.

Schulweis' personal encounters with psychological Jews and their needs, often in the privacy of his study, awakened this new sensitivity. In the privacy of his study, psychological Jews revealed their existential suffering to him. Decades later, he noted sardonically that in the synagogue sanctuary, people say, "Rabbi, please keep it short." But no one says that in the rabbi's study, where the topic of conversation is the self.[42] The rabbi's private study is the domain of searching individuals. But the rabbi feels unequipped to respond.

The needs of the psychological Jew confound the rabbi, not because the rabbi is unlearned or indifferent but because traditional Judaism never developed a robust language of the individual life. It is a lacuna within Judaism itself. Schulweis drew this insight from his reading of contemporary Jewish thinkers. With the notable exception of Kaplan, all the

greatest contemporary Jewish thinkers decried the absence of
the individual from traditional Judaism. They reflect the same
frustration Schulweis experienced when meeting the psychological Jew: Judaism has no language for *reshut ha-yahid*, the
inner life of an anguished soul.

Joseph B. Soloveitchik, the revered "Rav" of Modern
Orthodoxy, opens his landmark 1965 essay, "The Lonely Man
of Faith," with a startling confession: "I am lonely."[43] This is
astonishing: What traditional Jewish thinker ever spoke in the
first-person singular? What Jewish religious master ever confessed the anguish of his inner life? Since when is loneliness a
Jewish problem, a rabbi's problem? Soloveitchik's confession
is remarkable both for its content and for its idiom:

> I am lonely. Let me emphasize, however, that by stat-
> ing "I am lonely" I do not intend to convey to you the
> impression that I am alone. I, thank God, do enjoy
> the love and friendship of many. I meet people, talk,
> preach, argue, reason; I am surrounded by comrades
> and acquaintances. And yet, companionship and friend-
> ship do not alleviate the passional experience of loneli-
> ness which trails me constantly. I am lonely because at
> times I feel rejected and thrust away by everybody, not
> excluding my most intimate friends . . . my "desolate,
> howling solitude."[44]

How can it be, wondered Schulweis, that the most exalted
figure in Orthodox Judaism complains of loneliness? And
more, why did he express his loneliness in secular philosophical language and not Jewish language? Why is the rich

language of traditional Judaism so inadequate that Soloveit-chik is driven to the idiom of existentialist philosophy?

> What is missing in Jewish life to satisfy the longing of the soul? Is halachah not enough? Is Jewish ritual not enough? Is Jewish philosophy not enough? . . . What of the interior life, *bein adam l'atzmo*—between man and himself?[45]

Judaism has no language to describe the existential "I," the experience of the lone individual struggling with life. Jewish language is built on the premise that there is no "I" without a "we." But the "I" without a "we" is precisely the condition of modernity. That alienation is what made Soloveitchik a "lonely man of faith."

Schulweis found the same theme in the writing of Martin Buber, Franz Rosenzweig, and Hermann Cohen. He found Abraham Joshua Heschel's formulation of the problem most poignant:

> Torah speaks in the language of men. But the sages have overlooked *the man in the Jew*. They gained no insight into his difficulties and failed to understand his dilemma. Every generation has its own problems. Every man is burdened with anxieties. But the sages remained silent: they did not guide the perplexed and showed no regard for the new problems that arose.[46]

The testimony of so many contemporary thinkers com-pelled Schulweis to reconsider the psychological Jew's condition. The psychological Jew needed more than a way into community life. Psychological Jews needed Jewish language to describe their personal anguish and Jewish answers to address their condition. This required another new mediating structure. The rabbi could not do this alone.

As rabbi of a congregation whose membership surpassed one thousand families, Schulweis realized the impossibility of personally meeting the individual needs of all his members. He needed help. In 1972, Schulweis launched a paraprofessional counseling center at Valley Beth Shalom. The model of paraprofessional psychological counseling had been developed in a number of large churches. Under the direction of Dr. Arthur Sorosky, a psychiatrist and congregant at Valley Beth Shalom, Schulweis gathered a group of committed laypeople who devoted themselves to two full years of intensive training and ongoing supervision. He also gathered a group of mental health professionals to guide them. The VBS Counseling Center opened in May 1975 and operates to this day, offering psychological counseling to individuals, couples, and families, as well as support groups for cancer patients, the newly widowed, men meeting midlife, and others in need, all led by paraprofessional volunteers. The services of the VBS Counseling Center are available to synagogue members and others in the community regardless of religious affiliation. The center has become a model for programs in synagogues and churches nationwide.

In the success of the VBS Counseling Center—both in meeting a felt need in the community and in attracting an enthusiastic cadre of committed volunteers—Schulweis came to see a new model for the outreach needed to touch the lives of psychological Jews. The psychological Jew does not need a new ideology, a new holy text, a new sacred rite. The psychological Jew needs a human connection.

> How are we to begin? We have been called people of the book, but it will not happen by books alone. There is no dearth of texts in Jewish life; there is a dearth of persons. . . . Jews need Jews to be Jewish. Jews are hungry for the warmth and sympathetic intelligence of other Jews.[47]

From the experience of the VBS Counseling Center, Schulweis developed the idea of "para-rabbinics"—volunteers training to assist fellow congregants in their religious lives.

The most intimate moments of Jewish life, Schulweis observed, are the liminal life-cycle events: birth, maturity, marriage, and death. It is precisely at those moments that the synagogue fails most egregiously. The rituals are performed by rabbis and cantors with professional precision but often without heart and sensitivity for the inner life of celebrants. The bar or bat mitzvah is trained to read a Torah portion with exactitude, but who speaks with the family about the messy challenges of parenting an adolescent, or with the child about the meaning of adulthood? The shiva is led with smooth proficiency, but who holds the hand of the mourner? Families too frequently experience "rite-less passages and passage-less rites."[48]

As a response, Schulweis envisioned a group of trained lay volunteers who would offer counseling, guidance, and support to new parents anticipating the arrival of a child, to the family celebrating a child's coming of age, to the couple preparing to marry, to the family enduring divorce, to the newly bereaved. He recruited a group of volunteers, many from the synagogue board, and put them through an intensive two-year program of learning about the traditions of life-cycle rituals as well as the psychological implications of these moments.

For many of the volunteers, the training was the best Jewish education they had ever experienced.[49] But when it came to deploying para-rabbinics, the results were mixed. Those assigned to meet bar and bat mitzvah families found great success. Bar mitzvah counselors guided families through the preparations for their celebrations. Families found it helpful to discuss their questions about the ceremony, as well as their anxieties about their child's impending adolescence, with someone who had been through the experience. Similarly, those assigned as bereavement counselors were very effective in conveying to congregational families the assurance that their community was with them at a difficult time.

Others registered disappointment.

Always averse to magic in religion, Schulweis underestimated the symbolic magical power of the rabbi's presence, especially to those coping with trying personal circumstances. In moments of distress, people want their rabbi. Few in the congregation were willing to divulge intimate, personal issues to a fellow congregant who was a stranger. In the end, many of those chosen as para-rabbinics enjoyed an extraordinary measure of the rabbi's time and attention and deeply valued the training but found it frustrating that they were rarely called upon to actually serve.

While the para-rabbinic program had mixed success in addressing the inner life of psychological Jews, it did succeed in forever changing the lives of the para-rabbinics. The same symbolic rabbinical magic that precluded success in touching lives in the congregation cemented a uniquely close relationship between Schulweis and his para-rabbinics. Out of the first classes of para-rabbinics, Schulweis drew an entire corps of new synagogue lay leaders, including most of the subsequent presidents and officers of the synagogue. Invited into the rabbi's sacred domain to share his holy responsibilities, the para-rabbinics came to identify with the rabbi's vision of the synagogue and his leadership. They bonded with the rabbi with an intimacy and loyalty that lasted years. As a way of addressing the needs of the psychological Jew, the para-rabbinic program had only mixed results. As a way of tapping the latent creative energies of a congregation, it succeeded beyond Schulweis' dreams.

Poetry

Harold Schulweis believed in programs. He believed he could invent a program to address every spiritual problem he met. Every Rosh Hashanah, his congregation at Valley Beth Shalom came to synagogue expecting to hear the debut of some new initiative or program. His retelling of the prevailing narrative of the Holocaust found expression in the Foundation for the Righteous. His theology of Godliness would be embodied in MAZON: A Jewish Response to Hunger, launched with Leonard Fein. His prophetic vision of Jewish universalism drove the Jewish World Watch. The alienation of the psychological Jew found its solution in *havurot* and para-rabbinics. For every problem, there was a program.

The para-rabbinic program met some success in correcting the "rite-less passages and passage-less rites." But the deeper issue Schulweis identified—finding a Jewish language to speak to the inner life of the psychological Jew—was not a problem of sociology. Schulweis came to recognize that the loneliness of the psychological Jew was not amenable to any programmatic remedy. It required more than a mediating structure. It demanded a different kind of Judaism, a new Jewish language. In his 1994 sermon "The Individual in the Jew," Schulweis reflected on what he learned listening to Jews who met him not in the public space of the synagogue sanctuary but in the privacy of his study:

> In the study, I understand the limits of sanctuary culture. The individual has been lost sight of. Vicarious living won't do. Vicarious prayers won't do. Vicarious identity won't do. I cannot define his Jewishness on the basis of his ancestry or his descendants. I cannot help them spiritually by telling her "Be Jewish out of respect for Zayde or be Jewish out of regard for your children." Proxy religion will not do—quotational Judaism will not do. I have learned from them—You will not live Jewishly through your ancestors or through your children. Sam Levinson once wrote, "When I was a child I used to do what my parents wanted. Now that I am a parent I do what my children want. My problem is, when do I do what I want?"[50]

Following Kaplan, Schulweis once pointed to supernaturalism as the core problem plaguing Judaism in modernity. Now, having served in the pulpit for more than four decades, he discovered the problem of "superpersonalism," the Jewish tradition's neglect of the suffering individual:

> Superpersonalism, more than supernaturalism, proves
> an embarrassment to modern Jewish theology. Its pro-
> testation against the dead hand of impersonalism in
> philosophy, prayer and communal life expresses, on
> a profounder level, much the same disaffections of the
> psychological Jew in his search for self and spirituality.[51]

It was his own moment of existential crisis that changed Schulweis' orientation. In 1986, he suffered his second heart attack and underwent risky open-heart surgery. The confrontation with his own mortality changed Schulweis. The search for a Jewish language to address the most intimate elements of life became his personal project. Schuweis' entire career was focused on the communal. He once proclaimed that the primary task ahead was the humanization and personalization of the synagogue. Now he came to realize that the truly critical need was to humanize and personalize Judaism itself—to overcome the insensitivity of Judaism to the inner life of the individual.

Beginning in 1986, Schulweis began to write poetry. It did not come easy. He had always expressed himself in the first-person plural. Now he needed to find his voice in the grammatical singular. Trained in the discursive philosophic discourse of the mind, it took a life-and-death crisis to move him into the realm of the emotions. The intellect was the idiom of his public self; emotions were kept private. In sermons and addresses, he shared his ideas but rarely his inner self. He was a thoughtful pastor and personal counselor, demonstrating care for his congregants when they stepped into his study, but in social settings, he kept his distance. He was personable and welcoming but not naturally gregarious. Only in the small circle of very close friends would he truly open himself. This all changed with his health crises of 1986. In his words, "Nudged by the surgeon's scalpel, my hand turned to poetry."[52]

Poetry became his opening and idiom for the inner life. It reflected his discovery that something important was omitted from his own training as well as from the idiom of traditional Judaism. In reality, it was something he had suppressed in his own life. He explained this discovery in the introduction to the published collection *Living Our Legacy*:

> I imbibed from my studies, secular or religious, a winking condescension toward poetry. At the yeshiva, seminary, and university, poetry lacked the status of analytic prose. . . . Poetry lacked the rigor of syllogistic argument, the precision of linear thinking and the grammar of intellectual debate. The life of the emotions had no place in the academy, but were better left at the door of the private self, where spontaneity and subjectivity could reign. . . .
>
> Socrates and Maimonides were tough-minded. I needed to balance that with tender-mindedness. . . . [Poetry] opened unsuspected dreams and passions of my own. . . . With poetry came a greater softness, a more empathic intelligence.[53]

Schulweis' poetry deals primarily with life-cycle moments for the very same reason that he directed the para-rabbinics toward those rites—they are the liminal moments, the turning points, the moments of openness, the most revealing and personally significant moments of human life. His poetry captures the very personal meanings in these life moments and interprets them in very Jewish language. Two samples, from birth to death:

From Where Did You Come?

From where did you arrive?
Out of the womb of Eve and the seed of Adam
Angels showed your unborn soul
The secret of heaven and earth
Your soul pleaded with God not to push you
From the comfort of the womb.

And God answered:
Do not cry
Do not be afraid
The world you enter is the better world
You have lived in innocence.

Here, you will be My ally, My witness
My co-creator, My co-sanctifier
Here is your place
Here, confirm My name
Here, bring strength to those who inhabit the world
Here, offer testimony of My goodness
Welcome to this world.[54]

For Those Beloved Who Survive Me

Mourn me not with tears, ashes or sackcloth

Nor dwell in darkness, sadness or remorse

Remember that I love you, and wish for you a life of
song

My immortality, if there be such for me, is not in tears,
blame

or self-recrimination

But in the joy you give to others, in raising the fallen

and loosening the fetters of the bound

In your loyalty to God's special children—the widow,
the orphan,

the poor, the stranger in your gates, the weak—I take
pride.

The fringes of the tallit placed on my body are torn,
for the dead cannot praise You, O Lord

The dead have no mitzvot

But your tallit is whole and you are alive
and alive you are called to mitzvot

You can choose, you can act, you can transform the
world.

My immortality is bound up with God's eternity
with God's justice, truth and righteousness

And that eternity is strengthened by your loyalty and
your love

Honor me with laughter and with goodness

With these, the better part of me lives beyond the
grave.[55]

Through poetry Schulweis found a way to touch the inner life of psychological Jews with the life-wisdom of the Jewish tradition. The turn to poetry signaled his recognition that Judaism needed to take account of the emotional life:

> Your heart has wisdom. The heart can teach. What can you learn from emotion, intuition, feelings, temperament? Nothing except that some of the most important decisions of your life and mine are matters of the heart: Whether to marry, whom to marry, and when to marry; what kind of friends to cultivate and learn to keep, and what kind to avoid; what vocation and what profession to pursue and what not to seek; what kind of life, what meaning, what purpose, do we choose? How much Judaism to put into your home? All matters of the heart and wisdom.[56]

As one of the last public statements that Schulweis delivered to his congregation, this acknowledgment of the emotional life is also a final testimony that contemporary Judaism must speak to the whole person. The dry intellectuality of Mordecai Kaplan was not sufficient to reach the modern Jew. But neither was the ecstatic emotional expressivity of Shlomo Carlebach. A lifetime of caring for Jews at the most intense moments of their lives, together with his own experiences of life and death, displaced his relentless intellect and opened Schulweis to the fullness of the human experience: "There are two sanctuaries in us: mind and heart. When they are split apart, the twin tablets are shattered. When they are united, mind and heart give birth to wisdom. It is a Jewish wisdom."[57]

Reinventing the Rabbinate

A parable:

> Once an old Jew lost his snuff box made of the horn of
> a goat. "I've lost my snuff box made of horn," he wailed.
> And then the old Jew came upon a sacred goat that was
> pacing the earth and the tips of his black horns touched
> the stars. When the goat heard the old Jew lamenting,
> he leaned down to him and said, "Cut a piece from my
> horns—whatever you need to make a new snuff box."
> The old Jew did this, made a new snuffbox and filled it
> with tobacco. When he returned to the House of Study,
> he offered everyone a pinch of tobacco. Everyone was
> awed by the scent: "What a wonderful tobacco! It must
> be because of the box. Where did you get it?" And the
> old man told them about the sacred goat. Then one after
> the other, they went out onto the street and looked for
> the sacred goat. The sacred goat was pacing the earth
> and the tips of his black horns touched the stars. One
> after the other they went up to him and begged permis-
> sion to cut off a bit of his horns. And time after time the
> sacred goat leaned down to grant the request. Box after
> box was made, and the fame of the boxes spread far and
> wide. Now the sacred goat still paces the earth—but he
> has no horns.[58]

This folktale, first told by the Hasidic master Menachem
Mendel of Kotzk, was a favorite of Schulweis. He shared it in his
2003 Selichot sermon. It is an astoundingly honest confession

of the plight of the spiritual leader who sacrifices himself piece by piece to the needs of the community. Schulweis took this tale to heart, literally—he had suffered three heart attacks in the course of his late adulthood. His synagogue initiatives—*havurot*, para-rabbinics, and many others—not only changed the culture of the synagogue for the congregant but also represented a reinvention of the rabbi's role as leader of the congregation. This came at a critical historical moment.

Postwar rabbis, particularly Conservative rabbis, experienced a deep crisis of morale. In his brief history of the Conservative rabbinate for Jacob R. Marcus and Abraham Peck's *The American Rabbinate,* historian and rabbi Abraham J. Karp describes the heady optimism that filled the hearts of newly ordained rabbis in the first years of postwar America, including his own class at the Jewish Theological Seminary in 1945:

> In his address at the first postwar commencement exercises of the Jewish Theological Seminary, Judge Simon H. Rifkind observed that, whereas in Europe the rabbis were the products of the community they served, in America the community is shaped by the rabbis who serve it. The newly ordained rabbis accepted the judge's observation as issuing a challenge and pointing to an opportunity. The new American Jewish community would be fashioned in the decades ahead, and the rabbis would be its architects.[59]

Karp documents how this optimism melted into despair over the ensuing decades. The ideological ambiguities of Conservative Judaism, the institutional challenges of synagogue life, and the painful gap between the Judaism taught at the Jewish Theological Seminary and the Judaism practiced by the Conservative laity turned rabbis into sacred goats. Karp cites Milton Himmelfarb, writing in 1958:

> How are we to explain the Conservative rabbis' readiness to put up with the inconsistencies, contradictions, and ambiguities they have to live with? These things hurt. One of the ways in which the rabbis try to soothe the hurt, unavailing but revealing, is to change congregations; the Conservative rabbinate is a restless body of men. . . . The average Conservative rabbi dislikes his job and dislikes the intellectual muddle.[60]

Karp confirms Himmelfarb's sad observation: during one year, 40 percent of the rabbis who held Conservative pulpits applied to the placement commission of the Rabbinical Assembly for new positions. In a paper delivered to the 1970 conference of the Rabbinical Assembly, Karp disclosed the frustrations that leading Conservative rabbis had shared with him:

> We preach to congregants about kashrut, Shabbat, halakhah in general, knowing that the vast majority neither keeps them nor feel any compunctions over ignoring these rules. The fraud is open, mutually recognized, with all the implicit contempt and self-contempt it engenders.[61]

Arthur Hertzberg reiterated this theme in his 1975 address to the Rabbinical Assembly:

We [Conservative rabbis] are, if we are honest with ourselves, in the most difficult and loneliest situation in
Jewish history. We are rabbis who have nothing going
for us except our own passion, our own conviction, our
own lives, and what we are willing to put them on the
line for.[62]

In 1980, the Rabbinical Assembly convened a Blue Ribbon
Committee on the life of the rabbi. The committee reported,

Many rabbis are not happy with the role that the congregations have assigned to them ... [they] feel over-
worked by a multitude of tasks which only minimally
contribute to the realization of their personal and
professional goals ... [which] leaves meager time and
energy for what was once regarded as the primary function of the rabbinate: teaching and studying.... Rabbinic burn-out ... a reversal of the process that begins
with high enthusiasm and dedication, but which ends in
depression and alienation.[63]

By century's end, it was no better. In 2000, researchers Daniel J. Elazar and Rela Mintz Geffen found that

rabbis seem to be suffering ever more than in the past
from the stress and frustration associated with their
positions, with the amount of stress and frustration
growing in proportion to the dedication of the person
involved.... Rabbis have great difficulty because of the
role conflicts they find thrust upon them.[64]

How can this crisis of rabbinic morale be understood? Postwar American Jewry experienced remarkable success. No community in the history of the Jewish diaspora had ever enjoyed as much freedom, security, and material prosperity as postwar American Jewry. An unprecedented number of synagogues, seminaries, schools, summer camps, and communal institutions were built since the end of World War II. Unprecedented numbers of American Jews joined synagogues and sent their children to Jewish schools. Why were rabbis so unhappy?

Organizational psychologist Edgar H. Schein observed that professionals form their own specific subcultures, which may be separate from, and often opposed to, the culture of the institutions in which they work. People carry into the workplace implicit sets of assumptions and attitudes that "derive from common origins, common educational background, the requirements of a given occupation such as the licenses that have to be obtained to practice, and the shared contact with others in the occupation."[65] Schein insightfully demonstrated how people working in the same setting and often on the very same tasks look upon the world with very different eyes, carry very different expectations, and measure themselves by very different standards. He warns that the misalignment of these subcultures—with one another as well as with an organization's institutional culture—can severely impede an organization's effectiveness and eventually destroy the organization.

Like other professionals, rabbis inhabit a subculture—a set of shared, implicit assumptions about their identity, their world, and their tasks—that may differ from the culture of the institutions and communities they serve. By the mid-1970s, Schulweis perceived that this rabbinic subculture was badly misaligned with the realities of American Jewish life, detrimental to the community, and deeply self-destructive for rabbis themselves. Schulweis' synagogue initiatives not only changed the lives of his congregants but they also constituted a revolt against the subculture of the rabbinate and redefined the role of the congregational rabbi.

American rabbis, particularly those of Schulweis' generation, were trained to see their world in distinctly hierarchical terms. Conservative rabbis, such as Schulweis, were schooled in halachah, Jewish law. They were trained to serve as a community's *mara d'atra*, literally, "master of the place." Historian Abraham Karp concludes, "The emphasis on halachah in his rabbinic training apotheosizes rabbinic authority."[66] Even though they do not adhere to halachah, liberal congregations adopted similar hierarchical leadership models, often taken from the corporate world, with the rabbi assuming the role of CEO.[67]

This hierarchical orientation had deep psychological roots. Rabbis of Schulweis' generation were taught in seminary by legendary scholars who represented models of piety, learning, and authenticity that their students knew they could never achieve. When these rabbis left the seminary and entered congregational life, they looked down upon their congregants the way their teachers had looked down upon them. According to the prevailing rabbinic subculture, the rabbi is the authority. The rabbi knows; the congregant is ignorant. The rabbi teaches; the congregant passively and gratefully absorbs the rabbi's truth. Above all, the rabbi maintains control of the transaction. The physical architecture of synagogues said it all: rabbis preaching from high above to congregants listening passively far below. Rabbis were never taught to speak *with* laypeople, only to preach to them. The laity were relegated to passive recipients of the rabbi's wisdom.[68] To protect their privileged position, rabbis were taught to keep the laity at arm's length. They feared and disdained any lay intrusion upon their authority. Consequently, the relationship between rabbi and congregant, and most especially between the rabbi and a congregation's lay leadership, was not untypically marked by mutual mistrust, resentment, and animosity. Sylvia Bernstein Tregub, a young lay leader at Valley Beth Shalom in 1971, frequently spoke in neighboring congregations about the Valley Beth Shalom experience with *havurot*:

> Everywhere I went, they thought we were crazy. The rabbis especially had a hard time with this. They'd ask me: "You mean you send them out of the synagogue, out of the sanctuary, outside the rabbi's supervision, to do Judaism on their own? How do you know they're doing it right? What if they never come back?"[69]

Schulweis perceived how deeply destructive the misalignment of cultures had become. Rabbis were trained to preach the truth down to an obedient congregation. But psychological Jews do not want instruction from on high. They do not care for preaching. More than anything else, psychological Jews want to be heard, listened to, validated. Psychological Jews want to be personally acknowledged by the rabbi. Rendered a passive audience, the congregation will never change the way they live and will never grow spiritually. Very soon, they simply stop listening. Consequently, rabbis grow increasingly tired, disappointed, and bitter, perceiving themselves as failures. Standing far above the community, demanding reverence as the *mara d'atra*, the rabbi is the loneliest person in a congregation of lonely people:

> The fatal paradox is: the more indispensible I grow, the more irrelevant I become; the more active I become, the more passive the congregation; the more ubiquitous I am, the greater the Jewish distance between myself and the congregation. . . . Where the community does not function, the Rabbi becomes functionary; where the community is absent, the Rabbi becomes omnipresent.[70]

Schulweis' introduction of *havurot* and para-rabbinics changed the model of rabbinic leadership from hierarchical to collaborative. In the same way that his conception of Godliness transformed theology from a vertical to horizontal metaphor, he changed the structure of rabbinic leadership from a vertical model of control to a horizontal model of cooperation. He redefined the relationship between rabbi and laity:

> The rabbi needs Jewish allies. He needs lay colleagues to relate Judaism to Jews face-to-face. Realistically, no rabbi has the time or energy to engage the individual Jew person-to-person and to sustain such a relationship. The rabbi needs to enter into a collegiality with lay leaders dedicated to serve the synagogue community as para-Judaic counselors. He needs to train *"baale-batim,"* not as custodians of the material culture of the temple, but as Judaic counselors concerned with the spiritual life of the individual Jew.[71]

Such a change is much more than just organizational. Surrendering control is emotionally risky. Professionals do not typically relinquish authority to nonexperts. For rabbis who deem themselves *klei kodesh*, vessels of holiness, it is unheard of. Schulweis himself was personally secure enough and held enough faith in the native wisdom of his congregants to step back and empower his laity to share his authority. He intentionally determined that *havurot* would be lay led. Rabbis would not interfere. He trusted his laity enough to hand over the management of life-cycle rites to para-rabbinics. On Shabbat mornings, he did not preach but engaged his congregants in dialogue about the lessons of Torah. He listened as much as he taught:

> There is much untapped energy and idealism in our laity. For the sake of Judaism and our sacred tasks, that laity cannot be allowed to remain as passive critics, spectator, and audience outside the circle of commitment. They must be brought into our confidence, to share the gravity of our calling and to help us. We cannot afford to continue the distance which grows between us. Rabbis need allies. We need collegiality with our laity.[72]

In welcoming the voices and energies of the laity, Schulweis pioneered in the synagogue what would come to be described as collaborative community leadership. As defined by William Drath and Charles Palus of the Center for Creative Leadership:

> The purpose of the process of leadership . . . is to offer legitimate channels for members to act in ways that

will increase their feelings of significance and their actual importance to the community. The question for an individual in a position of authority is no longer how to get people to do what is needed but how to participate in a process of structuring the activity and practice of the community so that people marginal to its practice are afforded the means to move toward the center of that practice. In other words, how can the contribution of each person in the community of practice be made increasingly important and increasingly appreciated for its importance.[73]

Schulweis' new style of leadership introduced a revolution into American synagogue life. Harvard scholar Ronald Heifetz distinguishes between technical problems that can be solved from within a system and adaptive problems that demand that the system be reconfigured, its assumptions rethought, and its processes reimagined.[74] Synagogues typically seek technical solutions that do not threaten established institutional patterns. The perennial problems of synagogue life—attracting membership, building community, involving younger members, and raising funds—are thought to be amenable to some technical fix: a new brochure, a spiffy website, a new marketing campaign, a new adult education program, or new melodies for the prayer services.[75] These initiatives are safe—they maintain the institutional structure. But they always fail.

In the 1990s, the American Jewish community launched some forty different synagogue transformation initiatives.[76] Schulweis anticipated all of them by twenty years. He perceived in 1970 what all the subsequent transformation initiatives discovered in the 1990s and beyond: The problems that beset the American synagogue are not technical, they are adaptive. There is no readily available technical solution to the alienation of American Jews from their synagogues. Only a thorough process of transformative, adaptive change will bring about the kind of synagogue contemporary Jews will support.

And Schulweis understood in 1970 what the synagogue transformation initiatives of the 1990s came to discover unfortunately too late: that no matter how dysfunctional and ineffective a synagogue, the resistance to changing the synagogue culture is powerful and devious. The secret to transformational change is to engage the community itself as a change agent. This demands a special kind of leadership. Transformational adaptive change, according to Heifetz, demands that a leader cast light upon a problem and open discussion of new possibilities by holding the system in the tension of the problem long enough to unfreeze its thinking. Then, "the job of leadership is to orchestrate the conflict that arises in those discussions and develop experiments to find out how to push the frontier forward in an evolutionary way."[77] Schein interprets the task in psychological terms. Change only occurs when a leader "can reduce learning anxiety by increasing the learner's sense of psychological safety."[78]

Schulweis trusted his laity enough to resist the temptation to affect change by himself. Instead, he engaged the laity in the process. In Heifetz's terms, he held his synagogue community in creative tension by constantly pointing out the ways in which the old narratives of Jewish identity and affiliation no longer held true. With ruthless honesty, he described how the synagogue had failed to connect with its members. He did this repeatedly, almost doggedly. But unlike so many other rabbis, he did not stop there. That wasn't the end of the sermon. He did not criticize his people as bad Jews. He did not subject the congregation to jeremiads against assimilation and Jewish alienation. Nor did he piously prescribe a return to an earlier generation's faith and loyalty, again as so many rabbis did (and continue to do). Instead, he invited the laity to join him in the search for new forms of community life and empowered them as his partners in the process. He used his formidable oratory, in an idiom redolent with allusions to tradition, together with the enormous symbolic power of his rabbinic persona, to provide the reassurance of safety for this process to proceed. Secure enough in his own authority, he allowed the process to proceed outside his control. As a result, he released deep resources of energy, wisdom, leadership, and loyalty latent in the lay community. This, in turn, made it possible not only for the synagogue to evolve but also for a rabbi of his vast ambition and aspiration to find a home in a congregation without experiencing the burnout and despair suffered by so many of his colleagues.

During the installation of one of his assistant rabbis, Schulweis disclosed his vision of collaborative rabbinic leadership:

> When the rabbi does it all, when the cantor does it all, they become performers, this becomes a theater, you become spectators, and Judaism a spectator sport which basically is moribund and dies. The joy of the rabbi is the creation of lay people who are paraprofessionals, who can serve as counselors and advisors and helpers and instructors in order to help people in their lives. That has to be the joy of the rabbi.

Is the ego of the rabbi threatened? You think that I now feel less important, less significant, less a rabbi because I am in fact less indispensable? The answer is yes. For that, I have a congregation of friends who share my worries, who are worried with me, who are frightened about certain things, but who also want to do something to change the quality of their lives and the lives of that community.[79]

The ultimate result of Schulweis' leadership was a synagogue that became a model for creative congregational change that was studied and replicated in congregations across the continent. At the same time, he shaped a rabbinate he could inhabit with considerable joy for more than fifty years. Speaking to his new young assistant, Schulweis affirmed,

There is no profession but literally no profession in which there is greater opportunity for growth. There is no profession in which there is a greater opportunity for service. There is no profession in which there is a greater opportunity for joy and honor than the rabbi. It is not only a very fine job for a Jewish boy but . . . also for a fine Jewish girl. I would say in general, there are very few positions which are more intellectually, morally and spiritually fulfilling and satisfying than the rabbi.[80]

Harold Schulweis refused to succumb to the ambiance of pessimism and frustration that surrounded the Conservative rabbinate of his time. He felt all the incongruent expectations and demands that came with the contemporary rabbinate. In response, he proceeded to reinvent his rabbinate. Like the legendary rabbis of the preceding generation—Wise, Silver, Leventhal, and the others—Schulweis welcomed the mandate to experiment, improvise, and reshape his rabbinate. Of all his ambitious innovations, programs, and projects, this was ultimately his most successful.

EPILOGUE

In his 1943 book *The Hero in History*, Sidney Hook, Schulweis' professor and mentor at New York University, pondered the classic question—Is a hero shaped by the times or the times by the hero? While acknowledging the dialectic, Hook comes down firmly on the side of heroism. Historical conditions, he asserts, present opportunities, but it is the hero who shapes the progress of events:

> In such situations the great man is a relatively indepen-
> dent historical influence—*independent of the conditions*
> *that determine the alternatives* [emphasis in the original]—
> and that on these occasions the influence of all other
> relevant factors is of subordinate weight in enabling us
> to understand or to predict which one of the possible
> alternatives will be actualized.[1]

Schulweis internalized this conviction. Heroic historical figures can transcend the conditions of their times to shape the outcome of historical moments. Embracing this heroic role, Schulweis demonstrated a rabbi's capacity to shape the character of Judaism, the institutions of Jewish life, and the structure of rabbinic leadership.

Schulweis is most renowned for the programmatic innovations he introduced into synagogue life—*havurot* and para-rabbinics—and for the communal institutions he launched—the Foundation for the Righteous, MAZON, and Jewish World Watch. His true genius, however, was in the conceptual step prior to the invention of these programs— in his ability to recognize the weaknesses in the narratives governing Jewish life of his time and in his capacity to imagine and put forward alternative narratives. The programs he introduced were, in reality, his method of introducing new narratives into Jewish communal life. It is on the level of narrative that Schulweis demonstrated his creative genius.

Schulweis evinced an allergic reaction to "split thinking," the reduction of complex issues into simplistic either/or binaries. Every sharp disjunction, he taught, always conceals a transcending truth that unifies the polarities. It was the split thinking that he detected in the commonly held narratives of Jewish life that he rejected most fiercely. These include:

- *The split between belonging and believing, which reduced Judaism to "Jewish identity"*—a shallow ethnic affiliation that left an entire generation with a Judaism that demanded allegiance but had little to say to the deep moral questions of human existence and no response to the historic crises of the twentieth century. In his theological voice, Schulweis provided a pathway to the core of sacred moral truth at the heart of the Jewish tradition.
- *The split between the Jewish faith and the reality of the Holocaust.* Schulweis resonated with Richard Rubenstein's scream of protest—How does Jewish religious life go on

as if the Holocaust never happened? He refused to hide from the question. But he sought a better answer, an alternative to Rubenstein's cold atheism. In *Godliness*, Schulweis proposed a theology that could face the reality of the Holocaust without succumbing to despair or resorting to irrational fundamentalism. Celebrating the sanctity of human moral responsibility, *Godliness* provided a renewed sense of the sacred that does not compromise the believer's intellectual and moral maturity.

- *The split between a God "up there" and human beings "down here."* Divine moral truth, taught Deuteronomy, "is very close to you, in your mouth and in your heart" (30:14). God is within. God is revealed in the human capacity to transcend the narrow self and reach toward the moral ideals of Godliness. Worship is not a petition place before a distant divine judge but the search for the means within to transcend—to grow, heal, help, give, care.

- *The split between Jewish universalism and Jewish particularism, between commitment to "us" and concern for "them."* The Jewish community, Schulweis maintained, drew the wrong lessons from the Holocaust. Turning inward, away from the world, and splitting Jewish particularism from Jewish universalism corrupts the fundamental moral truth of Judaism. Judaism is a global religion teaching responsibility for the world. And especially for a Jewish community anxious over declining numbers and diminishing participation, the split between universalism and particularism is strategically unwise. The way to engage a younger generation of Jews in Jewish life is to celebrate a Jewish moral vision of global responsibility.

- *The split between ritual and morality, halachah and conscience.* As the prophet Isaiah preached, an adherence to ritual observance that is insulated from the imperatives of conscience is blasphemous. Whether out of reverence for tradition or fear of the new, this split leaves Judaism with precepts and practices that are discernably immoral. Obedience to conscience is loyalty to God. Religion consists of both a duty to obey and a duty to disobey. Both must be observed. Conscience is the mediating factor that brings them together.

- *The split between self and community.* The most corrosive force in Jewish life is the modern culture of individualism that divides the "privatist" psychological Jew from the life of the community. Equally egregious is the complicity of the community's institutions in this division. The greatest contemporary religious problem is human loneliness. Humanizing the community by creating real human connection is the first priority of Jewish institutions.

- *The split between the rabbi and the laity.* A misalignment of roles, expectations, and values has left the rabbi the loneliest, most frustrated person in the congregation. It blocks the rabbi from engaging the energies of the congregation. A reinvention of the community entails a reorientation of rabbinic authority from a vertical model of traditional authority to a horizontal model of collaborative communal leadership. This will engender a new fruitful relationship between a community's rabbi and its lay members.

- Finally, *the split between Judaism and modernity.* Schulweis refused to accept the conventional narrative of the "vanishing American Jew" that presented a bleak future for the American Jewish community. Assimilation, alienation, and the disappearance of American Jewry are neither inevitable nor inexorable, provided the community welcomes new interpretations of Jewish belief, new approaches to Jewish practice, and new forms of Jewish belonging. The "ever-dying people" is also an ever-renewing people.

Locating the hidden truth that unifies and integrates the polarities and resolves the conventions of split thinking, Schulweis reshaped the Jewish community's narratives and reimagined Jewish life for a new generation.

Rabbi Harold Schulweis passed away on December 18, 2014. At his funeral, speakers shared a story Schulweis told often. He maintained the story came from traditional midrash. No one has been able to find the source:

> When the angels of heaven learned of God's plan to create the human being *b'tzelem elohim*, in the divine image, they were aghast.
>
> "How can God place something as pure and holy as the *tzelem*, the divine image, in a creature as deceitful, base, and corrupt as the human being?" So they conspired to steal it and hide it from the human. But where, where to hide the holy *tzelem?* The angels met in urgent council to decide.
>
> "Hide it on the top of the highest mountain," suggested one angel. But no, "One day, he will climb that mountain and find it."
>
> "Hide it beneath the deepest sea," suggested another. But no, "Someday, he will plumb those depths and find it."

"Put it at the farthest edge of the most forbidding wilderness," another offered. But no, "He will learn to traverse the wilderness some day and will find it."

Finally, the shrewdest of the angels stepped forward. "We will place it deep in his heart. He will never look for it there."

Divinity, taught Schulweis, is not far away. It is not up there or out there. God abides here, hidden within us. Only, human beings do not know that. Just as no human being can see his or her own face unaided, we do not recognize the divinity within us. The task of the rabbi, Schulweis taught, is to hold up a mirror. That mirror is Torah, the sacred moral wisdom of the Jeiwsh tradition.

The story concludes:

> God always follows the counsel of the angels. So God created the human being and planted the *tzelem* deep within the human heart. Deeper than anyone can find it alone. But not so deep that those who love us and share life with us can't find it for us.

God, taught Schulweis, is known in moments of self-transcendence—in loving, caring, healing, giving. God speaks in the voice of conscience, drawing human beings upward to be better, drawing us outward to be loving, drawing us forward to be giving. God lives in the connections that unite us, in the space between I and Thou, between the self and the other. Judaism is a language of self-transcendence. The synagogue is the central institution teaching self-transcendence. The Jew is the one who constantly asks not what is but what ought to be.

A NOTE ON SOURCES

In his writing and speaking, Schulweis revealed the processes of his own creativity and reflection. He often quipped that the pulpit was the best form of psychotherapy. His sermons were the confessions of his inner life. For Schulweis, the sermon was never a simple homily. The sermon was his revolutionary praxis—his vehicle for working out his understanding of the world and his prescriptions for healing that world. Once perfected, sermons became articles, and articles were gathered into books.

This study calls upon these books, both in their published forms and in unpublished manuscripts found in Schulweis' personal files. The perusal of those files turned up treasures. For example, Martin Buber's handwritten corrections and comments on Schulweis' master's thesis, reflecting Buber's frustrations with the young Schulweis' relentless rationalism. As well, a folder containing more than thirty years of personal correspondence between Schulweis and Mordecai Kaplan, reflecting the warm affection Kaplan always held for his prized student.

Upon the occasion of his eightieth birthday, friends and admirers of Rabbi Schulweis established the Harold M. Schulweis Institute. One of the principal functions of the institute is the collection and dissemination of Schulweis' sermons, articles, and poetry. There is no comprehensive collection of recordings or transcripts of the sermons. The institute has devoted the past fifteen years to gathering, editing, and transcribing as many as can be found. These were often found on scratchy cassette tapes recorded surreptitiously by congregants during religious services. The sermons dating back to 1970 are now available in written and audio form on the websites of the Harold M. Schulweis Institute (www.hmsi.info) and of Valley Beth Shalom (www.vbs.org).

In addition to his writing, this study is based on an extensive set of interviews conducted in 2008 in celebration of the fortieth anniversary of Schulweis' tenure at Valley Beth Shalom. Eleven hours of videotaped interviews were conducted by the author. They engaged Schulweis in a process of reflection on his career and thought with a specific interest in his creative process—the sources of his most important ideas and the inspiration for his innovations, as well as the failures he encountered. The video recordings of these interviews are available on the Harold M. Schulweis Institute website.

As well, this study is based on extensive interviews conducted with Schulweis family members, notably his wife, Malkah; rabbinic colleagues, notably Rabbi Jerry Danzig, who served as his assistant rabbi and executive director both in Oakland and Encino; lay leaders and congregants from his congregations in Oakland, notably Samuel Shafer and "Pinky" and Agnes Pencovic, who served as leaders of the congregation for many years, and in Encino, notably Sylvia Bernstein Tregub, Elaine and David Gill, and Richard and Barbara Braun; and community leaders who worked alongside Schulweis in many of his projects, notably Professor Gerald Bubis of

Hebrew Union College and Rabbi Uri Herscher of the Skirball Cultural Center.

This study is also based on an examination of records of Congregation Beth Abraham in Oakland and Valley Beth Shalom in Encino. Beth Abraham's congregational archive was destroyed in a flood during the 1970s. Only one volume of minutes of the congregation's board of directors survived the flood—fortuitously, those of 1952–53, the very year Schulweis was hired in Oakland and began his rabbinic career. Congregational yearbooks, newsletters, and personal correspondence provided by members, notably the Katzburg family in Oakland, provide a picture of Schulweis' time in that community. At Valley Beth Shalom, board of directors' minutes, congregational yearbooks, film, and photographic archives fill in details of his career.

This study suggests that Schulweis' rabbinate was expressed in three rabbinic voices: a theological voice, a prophetic voice, and the voice of the community builder. For each of these voices, Schulweis published a book. Schulweis' theology was first set out in his doctoral dissertation, "The Idea of Perfection and the Moral Failure of Traditional Theodicies: Towards a Predicate Theology" (1971), which was later published as *Evil and the Morality of God* (1984) and then developed into the popular volume *For Those Who Can't Believe* (1994). He published his prophetic reflections in *Conscience: The Duty to Obey and the Duty to Disobey*. His community-building work finds expression in a volume of collected essays and addresses, *In God's Mirror* (1990).

In 2016, while his office at Valley Beth Shalom was being cleaned out, a folder was discovered behind a bookcase containing an unpublished, unfinished manuscript of a book entitled "The Psychological Jew." This work, dated in the early 1980s, expressed his vision of Jewish identity and community life. Schulweis referenced this work in an interview article in 1982,[1] but it had never been seen until the discovery in 2016. The manuscript contains much of the material later anthologized as separate articles in *In God's Mirror* but synthesized into a coherent theory. The book was apparently left unfinished due to the heart attack Schulweis suffered in 1983. He never returned to the work but collected the articles on which it was based and published them as the anthology *In God's Mirror*.

ACKNOWLEDGMENTS

This work was originally prepared as part of a doctoral dissertation for the William Davidson Graduate School of Jewish Education at the Jewish Theological Seminary of America (JTS). I offer my deep gratitude to the faculty and administration of the seminary, and to my advisors and teachers, Professors Aryeh Davidson and Barry Holtz. It is presented with deep affection to my friend, neighbor, and colleague Dr. Ron Wolfson. I am grateful to the Davidson School for establishing the Executive Doctoral Program, allowing working professionals to engage in reflection, study, and research in the field of Jewish education. And to the foundations and funders who made this possible, I offer my warmest blessings.

The work is dedicated to the memory of my teacher Rabbi Harold Schulweis. It is dedicated as well, with deep love, to his loving wife and *hevrutah*, Malkah. Together, they showed me a way to a rabbinate that has sustained my soul.

My thanks to those who sat for interviews and provided personal perspectives on Rabbi Schulweis' life and career, and to all who shared their experiences, recollections, and memorabilia. Special gratitude is owed to the benefactors and leaders of the Harold M. Schulweis Institute, and its chair, Sylvia Bernstein Tregub, for all their work in preserving and disseminating the rabbi's writing, speaking, and teaching. Thank you to artist Hanna Drew for her splendid portrait of Rabbi Schulweis, which graces the cover.

Special thanks to Emily Wichland for her editorial genius, endless patience, and warm friendship. And warm thanks to Heather Howell and her team at Turner Publishing for supporting this project.

Rabbi Schulweis taught us that God lives in the "between" space, between I and Thou. What divinity I know I have certainly found in Nina, who has given me so much, including endless evenings surrendered to the project of research and writing, and in our children, Yonah and Rachel, Nessa and David, Raffi and Elana.

In my training to become a rabbi, I was taught never to expect congregants to become friends. We have found a different experience. We count among our closest friends those who have shared the task of building communities in Dallas and in Encino. They have been a singular blessing to our lives. I find myself often quoting a song lyric from my generation's music: "I thank the Lord for the people I have found."

NOTES

Introduction

1 Simon Rawidowicz, "Israel: The Ever-Dying People," in *State of Israel, Diaspora, and Jewish Continuity: Essays on the "Ever-Dying People"* (Waltham, MA: Brandeis University Press, 1986), 53.

Chapter 1   The American Rabbi, a Brief History

1 Arthur Hertzberg, "The Changing American Rabbinate," *Midstream* 12, no. 1 (January 1966): 16.

2 Jonathan D. Sarna, *American Judaism: A History* (New Haven, CT: Yale University Press, 2004), 79.

3 Sarna, *American Judaism*, 79.

4 Sarna, 91.

5 Sarna, 94.

6 Morris Schappes, ed., *A Documentary History of the Jews of the United States* (New York: Schocken, 1971), 554–55.

7 Marc Lee Raphael, *The Synagogue in America: A Short History* (New York: New York University Press, 2011), 134.

8 Israel Goldfarb, quoted in New York Board of Jewish Ministers, *Problems of the Jewish Ministry*, ed. Israel Goldstein (New York: New York Board of Jewish Ministers, 1927), 85ff.

9 Goldfarb, quoted in New York Board of Jewish Ministers, *Problems of the Jewish Ministry*, 91.

10 New York Board of Jewish Ministers, *Problems of the Jewish Ministry*, 1.

11 Abraham J. Feldman, *The American Reform Rabbi: A Profile of a Profession* (New York: Bloch Publishing, 1965), 105.

12 Deborah Dash Moore, "A Synagogue Center Grows in Brooklyn," in *The American Synagogue: A Sanctuary Transformed*, ed. Jack Wertheimer (Hanover, NH: Brandeis University Press, 1987), 312.

13 Moore, "Synagogue Center Grows in Brooklyn," 313.

14 New York Board of Jewish Ministers, *Problems of the Jewish Ministry*, 1.

15 Israel H. Levinthal, *Steering or Drifting—Which?* (New York: Funk & Wagnalls, 1928), 213.

16 Jacob Joseph Weinstein, *Solomon Goldman: A Rabbi's Rabbi* (New York: KTAV, 1973), 22.

17 Moore, "Synagogue Center Grows in Brooklyn."

18 Israel H. Levinthal, *A New World Is Born* (New York: Funk & Wagnalls, 1943), 210.

19 Levinthal, *New World Is Born*, 211.

20 Levinthal, 210.

21 Levinthal, 23.

22 Simon Noveck, *Milton Steinberg: Portrait of a Rabbi* (New York: KTAV, 1978), 61.

23 Noveck, *Milton Steinberg*, 61.

24 Moore, "Synagogue Center Grows in Brooklyn," 315.

25 Weinstein, *Solomon Goldman*, 25–26.

26 New York Board of Jewish Ministers, *Problems of the Jewish Ministry*, 113.

27 Marc Lee Raphael, *Abba Hillel Silver: A Portrait in American Judaism* (New York: Holmes & Meier, 1989), 53.

28 Carl Voss, ed., *Stephen S. Wise, Servant of the People: Selected Letters* (Philadelphia: Jewish Publication Society, 1970), 124.

29 Melvin I. Urofsky, *A Voice That Spoke for Justice: The Life and Times of Stephen S. Wise* (Albany: State University of New York Press, 1982), 68.

30 Urofsky, *Voice That Spoke for Justice*, 60.

31 Weinstein, *Solomon Goldman*, 91–92.

32 Urofsky, *Voice That Spoke for Justice*, 23.

33 Urofsky, 23.

34 Urofsky, 23.

35 Urofsky, 213.

36 Voss, *Stephen S. Wise, Servant of the People*, 72.

37 Urofsky, *Voice That Spoke for Justice*, 125.

38 Raphael, *Abba Hillel Silver*, 5.

39 Raphael, 28.

40 Raphael, 164–65.

41 Raphael, 214.

42 Raphael, 214.

43 Stephen S. Wise, *Challenging Years: The Autobiography of Stephen Wise* (New York: Putnam, 1949), 84–85.

44 Urofsky, *Voice That Spoke for Justice*, 53.

45 Wise, *Challenging Years*, 89.

46 Wise, 91.

47 Urofsky, *Voice That Spoke for Justice*, 57.

48 Urofsky, 45.

49 Urofsky, 84.

50 Wise, *Challenging Years*, 63.

51 Wise, 67.

52 Wise, 67.

53 Raphael, *Abba Hillel Silver*, 37.

54 Raphael, 59.

55 Raphael, 60.

56 Raphael, 61–62.

57 Simon Greenberg, personal communication, 1992.

Chapter 2   Three Languages, Three Voices

1 Harold Schulweis, "Chapter 1—The Family—Growing Up," interview by Edward Feinstein, September 9, 2008, video, 0:28, Harold M. Schulweis Institute, http://hmsi.info/the-rabbi-harold-m-schulweis-interviews-with-rabbi-ed-feinstein-chapter-1-the-family-growing-up.

2 American Jewish Committee, *The American Jewish Yearbook 5706: 1945–46*, vol. 47 (Philadelphia: Jewish Publication Society, 1945), http://www.ajcarchives.org/main.php?GroupingId=10080.

3   Seymour J. Perlin, "Remembrance of Synagogues Past: The Lost Civilization of the Jewish South Bronx," Bronx Synagogues, www .bronxsynagogues.org. undated.

4   Chaim Zhitlovsky, 1930, quoted in Max Rosenfeld, "Zhitlovsky: Philosopher of Jewish Secularism," *Jewish Currents* (June 1965): 84.

5   Rosenfeld, "Zhitlovsky."

6   Chaim Zhitlovsky, "The National Poetic Rebirth of the Jewish People" (1911), trans. Max Rosenfeld, JBooks.com, para. 2, http:// www.jbooks.com/secularculture/Zhitlovsky.htm.

7   Chaim Zhitlovsky, in Rosenfeld, "Zhitlovsky," 82.

8   Schulweis, "Chapter 1—The Family—Growing Up."

9   Schulweis, "Chapter 1—The Family—Growing Up."

10   Malkah Schulweis, personal communication, 2016.

11   Harold Schulweis to Menachem Butler, personal communication, 2015.

12   Yeshiva College Student Organization, *Masmid* (New York: Yeshiva University, 1956), 7, https://archive.org/details/masmid1956.

13   Harold Schulweis to Menachem Butler, personal communication, 2015.

14   Harold Schulweis, "Freedom and the Religion of the State," in Yeshiva College Student Organization, *Masmid 1945, Yeshiva College Yearbook* (New York: Yeshiva University, 1945), 102–5, http://www .archive.org/details/masmid1945.

15   Schulweis, "Freedom and the Religion of the State," 105.

16   Schulweis, 104.

17   Schulweis, 105.

18   Mordecai M. Kaplan, Kaplan diary, 16 June 1945, volume 13, 1944–1946, Ira and Judith Kaplan Eisenstein Archives, Reconstructionist Rabbinical College, Philadelphia.

19   "Orthodox Rabbis Excommunicate Author of Prayer Book Though He Is Not a Member," *New York Times,* June 15, 1945.

20   "Orthodox Rabbis Excommunicate Author."

21   Harold Schulweis, "Celebrating Mordecai Kaplan," *Moment Magazine* 6, no. 7 (July–August 1981): 13–23.

22   Mordecai M. Kaplan, *Judaism as a Civilization* (New York: Schocken, 1934), 3.

23 Harold Schulweis, "Mordecai Kaplan: Prayer and the Chosen People" (lecture), December 17, 1980, Temple Valley Beth Shalom, Encino, California, transcription of audio recording, Harold M. Schulweis Institute, http://hmsi.info/wp-content/uploads/2017/01/mordecai-kaplan-prayer-and-the-chosen-people.pdf.

24 Harold Schulweis, "A Reenactment" (lecture), as part of Spiritual Leaders Series: Mordecai M. Kaplan, January 19, 2001, Temple Valley Beth Shalom, Encino, California, https://www.vbs.org/worship/meet-our-clergy/rabbi-harold-schulweis/sermons/jewish-spiritual-leaders-series-mordechai-m.

25 Sidney Hook, *Out of Step: An Unquiet Life in the 20th Century* (New York: Harper & Row, 1987), 5.

26 Hook, *Out of Step*, 351–52.

27 Harold Schulweis, "Martin Buber: An Interview," *Reconstructionist* 18, no. 3 (March 21, 1952): 7.

28 Harold Schulweis, "Chapter 6—My Rabbinic Education—Meeting Malkah," interview by Edward Feinstein, September 9, 2008, video, 9:53, Harold M. Schulweis Institute, http://hmsi.info/the-rabbi-harold-m-schulweis-interviews-with-rabbi-ed-feinstein-chapter-6-my-rabbinic-education-meeting-malkah.

29 Frederick Isaac, *Jews of Oakland and Berkeley*. Mt. Pleasant, SC: Arcadia Publishing, 2009.

30 Temple Beth Abraham, ed., *L'Dor v'Dor: Temple Beth Abraham Celebrates One Hundred Years* (Oakland, CA: Temple Beth Abraham, 2007).

31 Temple Beth Abraham, Board of Directors minutes, Oakland, CA, January–March, 1952.

32 Temple Beth Abraham, Board of Directors minutes.

33 Pinky Pencovic, Agnes Pencovic, and Samuel Shafer, personal communication, February 21, 2012.

34 Mordecai M. Kaplan, *The Meaning of God in Modern Jewish Religion* (New York: Behrman House, 1937), 1.

35 Harold Schulweis, *For Those Who Can't Believe: Overcoming the Obstacles to Faith* (New York: Harper Perennial, 1994), 93.

36 Harold Schulweis, "The Problem of Evil and the Pastoral Situation," *Reconstructionist* 23, no. 13 (November 1, 1957): 18.

37 Harold Schulweis, personal communication, 2008.

38   Kaplan, *The Meaning of God in Modern Jewish Religion*, 68–87.

39   Schulweis, *For Those Who Can't Believe*, 141.

40   Abraham Joshua Heschel, *God in Search of Man* (New York: Farrar, Straus and Giroux, 1964), 1.

41   See Harold Schulweis, "Suffering and Evil," in *Great Jewish Ideas*, ed. Abraham Ezra Milgram (New York: B'nai B'rith Department of Adult Jewish Education, 1964), 198–220.

42   Schulweis, "Chapter 1—The Family—Growing Up."

43   Pinky Pencovic, Agnes Pencovic, and Samuel Shafer, personal communication, February 21, 2012.

44   Uri Herscher, eulogy, "Funeral Services for Rabbi Harold M. Schulweis," December 21, 2014, video, 2:52:56, https://vimeo.com/115137224.

45   Temple Beth Abraham, *L'Dor v'Dor*.

46   Harold Schulweis, "Letter," in *L'dor v'dor: Temple Beth Abraham Celebrates One Hundred Years*, ed. Temple Beth Abraham (Oakland, CA: Temple Beth Abraham, 2007), 13.

47   Harold Schulweis, "Chapter 10—First Pulpit—Prejudice," interview by Edward Feinstein, September 9, 2008, video, 13:06, Harold M. Schulweis Institute, http://hmsi.info/the-rabbi-harold-m-schulweis-interviews-with-rabbi-ed-feinstein-chapter-10-first-pulpit-prejudice.

48   Harold Schulweis, "The Voice of Esau," *Reconstructionist* 31, no. 16 (December 10, 1965): 9, http://hmsi.info/wp-content/uploads/2017/01/the-voice-of-esau.pdf.

49   Schulweis, "Voice of Esau," 10, 12.

50   Schulweis, 12, 13.

51   Harold Schulweis, "Chapter 3—Influencers," interview by Edward Feinstein, September 9, 2008, video, 25:37, Harold M. Schulweis Institute, http://hmsi.info/the-rabbi-harold-m-schulweis-interviews-with-rabbi-ed-feinstein-chapter-3-influencers.

52   Agnes Pencovic and Pinky Pencovic, personal communication, February 21, 2012.

53   Samuel Shafer, Agnes Pencovic, and Pinky Pencovic, personal communication, February 21, 2012; Rabbi Mark S. Bloom, personal communication, February 21, 2012.

Chapter 3   Encino, 1970

1   Sylvia Bernstein Tregub, personal communication, January 30, 2012.

2   Robert Gottlieb and Irene Wolt, *Thinking Big: The Story of the Los Angeles Times, Its Publishers, and Their Influence on Southern California* (New York: Putnam, 1977), 308–13.

3   Max Vorspan and Lloyd P. Gartner, *History of the Jews of Los Angeles* (Philadelphia: Jewish Publication Society, 1970).

4   Norton B. Stern, "Isaias W. Hellman: Pioneer Merchant and Banker of California 1842–1920," *Western States Jewish Historical Quarterly* 2, no. 1 (1969): 27–30.

5   Deborah Dash Moore, *To the Golden Cities: Pursuing the American Jewish Dream in Miami and L.A.* (New York: Free Press, 1994), 113–14.

6   Stefan Kanfer, *Groucho: The Life and Times of Julius Henry Marx* (New York: Knopf, 2000), para. 9, http://www.nytimes.com/books/first/k/kanfer-groucho.html.

7   Neal Gabler, *An Empire of Their Own: How the Jews Invented Hollywood* (New York: Crown, 1988), 5–6.

8   Gabler, *Empire of Their Own*, 57–60.

9   Mike Davis, *City of Quartz* (New York: Vintage, 1990), 116–28.

10 Moore, *To the Golden Cities*, 44.

11 Albert Isaac Gordon, *Jews in Suburbia* (Westport, CT: Greenwood Press, 1959), 1.

12 Bruce A. Phillips, "Los Angeles Jewry: A Demographic Portrait," in *American Jewish Yearbook*, vol. 86 (New York: American Jewish Committee, 1986), 141.

13 Vorspan and Gartner, *History of the Jews of Los Angeles*, 287.

14 Phillips, "Los Angeles Jewry."

15 Joel Kotkin and Erika Ozuna, *The Changing Face of the San Fernando Valley* (Malibu, CA: Pepperdine University, 2015), 8.

16 Phillips, "Los Angeles Jewry," 117.

17 Moore, *To the Golden Cities*.

18 Nathan Glazer, "Notes on Southern California: 'A Reasonable Suggestion as to How Things Can Be'?" *Commentary* 28 (August 1, 1959): para. 22, https://www.commentarymagazine.com/articles/notes-on-southern-californiaa-reasonable-suggestion-as-to-how-things-can-be.

19 Moore, *To the Golden Cities*, 30.

20 Moore, 30.

21 Marshall Sklare and Joseph Greenbaum, *Jewish Identity on the Suburban Frontier: A Study of Group Survival in the Open Society*, 2nd ed. (Chicago: University of Chicago Press, 1967), 102–4.

22 Moore, *To the Golden Cities*, 50.

23 Samuel C. Heilman, *Portrait of American Jews: The Last Half of the Twentieth Century* (Seattle: University of Washington Press, 1995), 10.

24 Douglas Miller and Marion Nowak, *The Fifties: The Way We Really Were* (New York: Doubleday, 1977), 133.

25 Robert D. Grove and Alice M. Hetzel, *Vital Statistic Rates in the United States 1940–1960*, National Center for Health Statistics (Washington, DC: US Department of Health, Education, and Welfare, 1968), 61, https://www.cdc.gov/nchs/data/vsus/vsrates1940_60.pdf.

26 Heilman, *Portrait of American Jews*, 11.

27 Nora Johnson, "The Captivity of Marriage," *Atlantic* 207, no. 6 (June 1961): https://www.theatlantic.com/magazine/archive/1961/06/the-captivity-of-marriage/308284.

28 Elizabeth Waldman, "Labor Force Statistics from a Family Perspective," *Monthly Labor Review* 106, no. 12 (1983): 16–20.

29 Alexander A. Plateris, *Divorce and Divorce Rates in the United States* (PHS 78-1907), (Hyattsville, MD: US Department of Health, Education, and Welfare, Public Health Sevice National Center for Health Statistics, 1978).

30 Phillips, "Los Angeles Jewry," 145.

31 David Frum, *How We Got Here—the 70s: The Decade That Brought You Modern Life—for Better or Worse* (New York: Basic Books, 2000), 5.

32 Frum, *How We Got Here—the 70s*, 5.

33 Cited in Frum, *How We Got Here—the 70s*, 5.

34 Daniel Yankelovich, *New Rules: Searching for Self-Fulfillment in a World Turned Upside Down* (New York: Random House, 1981), xix.

35 Frum, *How We Got Here—the 70s*, 148.

36 Frum, 153.

37 Frum, 153ff.

38 Frum, 155.

39 J. Gordon Melton and Robert L. Moore, *The Cult Experience: Responding to the New Religious Pluralism* (New York: Pilgrim Press, 1984), 8.

40 Peggy Lee, vocalist, "Is That All There Is?" by Jerry Leiber and Mike Stoller, track 1 on *Is That All There Is?* Capitol Records, 1969.

41 P. Weeks, "Reagan, Murphy, Yorty Hit Russia's Role in Mideast War," *Los Angeles Times*, June 12, 1967.

42 Neil C. Sandberg, *Jewish Life in Los Angeles* (Lanham, MD: University Press of America, 1986), 133–34.

43 Jonathan D. Sarna, *American Judaism: A History* (New Haven, CT: Yale University Press, 2004), 316–20.

44 Charles S. Liebman, *The Ambivalent American Jew: Politics, Religion and Family in American Jewish Life* (Philadelphia: Jewish Publication Society, 1973), vi.

45 Heilman, *Portrait of American Jews*, 19.

46 Phillips, "Los Angeles Jewry," 149ff.

47 Heilman, *Portrait of American Jews*, 22.

48 Jack Wertheimer, "The American Synagogue: Recent Issues and Trends," in *American Jewish Yearbook 2005: The Annual Record of Jewish Civilization*, ed. American Jewish Committee (New York: American Jewish Committee, 2005), 7.

49 Wertheimer, "American Synagogue," 11–12.

50 Gordon, *Jews in Suburbia*, 99.

51 Sklare and Greenbaum, *Jewish Identity on the Suburban Frontier*, 117.

52 Sklare and Greenbaum, 58–59.

53 Herbert J. Gans, "Park Forest: Birth of a Jewish Community," in *Making Sense of America: Sociological Analyses and Essays*, ed. Herbert J. Gans (Lanham, MD: Rowman & Littlefield, 1999), 142.

54 United Synagogue Youth, *The Last American Jew* (New York: United Synagogue Youth, n.d.).

Chaper 4   The Theological Voice

1 Mordecai M. Kaplan, Kaplan diary, 16 November 1954, Mordecai M. Kaplan Center for Jewish Peoplehood, Evanston, IL, https://kaplancenter.org/erics-forum-archive-1.

2 Harold Schulweis, *For Those Who Can't Believe: Overcoming the Obstacles to Faith* (New York: Harper Perennial, 1994), 2.

3   Schulweis, *For Those Who Can't Believe*, 17–18.

4   "A Portrait of Jewish Americans," Pew Research Center—Religion and Public Life, October 1, 2013, http://www.pewforum.org /2013/10/01/jewish-american-beliefs-attitudes-culture-survey.

5   Schulweis, *For Those Who Can't Believe*, 6.

6   Harold Schulweis, "Adonai-Elohim: The Two Faces of God," *Reconstructionism Today* 8, no. 1 (Autumn 2000): 4–5.

7   Schulweis, "Adonai-Elohim," 6.

8   Harold Schulweis, "Martin Buber: An Interview," *Reconstructionist* 18, no. 3 (March 21, 1952): 7–10.

9   Harold Schulweis, "Suffering and Evil," in *Great Jewish Ideas*, ed. Abraham Ezra Milgram (New York: B'nai B'rith Department of Adult Jewish Education, 1964), 198–220.

10   Harold Schulweis, *Evil and the Morality of God* (Cincinnati: UAHC Press, 1984), 1–2. Republished as *Evil and the Morality of God*. Jersey City, NJ: KTAV, 2010.

11   Schulweis, *Evil and the Morality of God*, 4.

12   Richard L. Rubenstein, *After Auschwitz: History, Theology, and Contemporary Judaism*, 2nd ed. (Baltimore: John Hopkins University Press, 1992), 153. First edition published as *After Auschwitz*. New York: Macmillan, 1966.

13   Harold Schulweis, "Freedom and the Religion of the State," in *Masmid 1945, Yeshiva College Yearbook* (New York: Yeshiva University, 1945), 105, http://www.archive.org/details/masmid1945.

14   Immanuel Kant, quoted in Schulweis, *Evil and the Morality of God*, 115.

15   Schulweis, *Evil and the Morality of God*, 48.

16   Schulweis, 48.

17   Charles Hartshorne, *The Logic of Perfection* (Chicago: Open Court, 1962), quoted in Schulweis, *Evil and the Morality of God*, 54.

18   Schulweis, *Evil and the Morality of God*, 60–61.

19   Maurice Friedman, *Martin Buber's Life and Work* (Detroit: Wayne State University Press, 1988), 186.

20   Martin Buber, "The Dialogue Between Heaven and Earth," in *Four Existentialist Theologians*, ed. Will Herberg, (New York: Doubleday, 1958), 269, quoted in Schulweis, *Evil and the Morality of God*, 100.

21 Buber, quoted in Schulweis, *Evil and the Morality of God*, 100.

22 Schulweis, "Martin Buber."

23 Martin Buber, "The Two Foci of the Jewish Soul" (1932), quoted in Schulweis, *Evil and the Morality of God*, 101.

24 Schulweis, *Evil and the Morality of God*, 100–101.

25 Schulweis, 84–85.

26 Schulweis, 85.

27 Karl Barth, *Church Dogmatics*, vol. 4 (Edinburgh: T. & T. Clark, 1961), pt. 3, sec. 70, quoted in Schulweis, *Evil and the Morality of God*, 86.

28 Schulweis, *Evil and the Morality of God*, 94.

29 John Stuart Mill, *An Examination of Sir William Hamilton's Philosophy* (New York: Library of Little Arts, 1867), 119–29, quoted in Schulweis, *Evil and the Morality of God*, 95.

30 Elie Wiesel, *The Accident* (New York: Bantam, 1990), quoted in Schulweis, *Evil and the Morality of God*, 145.

31 Schulweis, *Evil and the Morality of God*, 145.

32 Harold Schulweis, "From God to Godliness: Proposal for a Predicate Theology," *Reconstructionist* 41, no. 1 (February 1975): 17.

33 Schulweis, *For Those Who Can't Believe*, 133.

34 Schulweis, 135.

35 Schulweis, *For Those Who Can't Believe*, 11; Harold Schulweis, *Conscience: The Duty to Obey and the Duty to Disobey* (Woodstock, VT: Jewish Lights, 2008), 68ff.

36 Harold Schulweis, "Chapter 9—The God within God," interview by Edward Feinstein, September 9, 2008, video, 12:59, Harold M. Schulweis Institute, http://hmsi.info/the-rabbi-harold-m-schulweis -interviews-with-rabbi-ed-feinstein-chapter-9-the-god-within-god.

37 Harold Schulweis, "Chapter 12—Predicate Theology," interview by Edward Feinstein, September 9, 2008, video, 6:55, Harold M. Schulweis Institute, http://hmsi.info/the-rabbi-harold-m-schulweis -interviews-with-rabbi-ed-feinstein-chapter-12-predicate-theology.

38 Moses Maimonides, *The Guide of the Perplexed*, trans. Shlomo Pines (Chicago: University of Chicago Press, 1974), 3:54.

39 Maimonides, *Guide of the Perplexed*, 3:54.

40 Maimonides, 3:54.

41 Ludwig Andreas von Feuerbach, *The Essence of Christianity*, trans. George Eliot (New York: Harper Torchbooks, 1957), xv; originally published as *The Essence of Christianity*. Leipzig, Germany: Otto Wigand, 1841; quoted in Schulweis, *Evil and the Morality of God*, 115.

42 Feuerbach, *Essence of Christianity*, xv.

43 Feuerbach, 12, 19.

44 Feuerbach, xvi.

45 Feuerbach, xvi.

46 Karl Barth, introduction to *The Essence of Christianity*, by Ludwig Feuerbach, trans. George Eliot (New York: Harper Torchbooks, 1957), xvi.

47 Schulweis, *Evil and the Morality of God*, 138.

48 Schulweis, "From God to Godliness," 22.

49 Harold Schulweis, in *The Condition of Jewish Belief: A Symposium*, ed. the editors of *Commentary* (New York: Macmillan, 1966), 216.

50 Feuerbach, *Essence of Christianity*, xv.

51 Schulweis, *Evil and the Morality of God*, 128–29.

52 Harold Schulweis, "I Believe . . .," *Sh'ma* 24, no. 456 (September 3, 1993): 6–7.

53 William G. Braude and Israel J. Kapstein, eds. and trans., *Pesikta De-Rab Kahana* (Philadelphia: Jewish Publication Society, 1975), 249.

54 Schulweis, "I Believe . . .," 6–7.

55 Schulweis, "From God to Godliness," 22–23.

56 Feuerbach, *Essence of Christianity*, 18; translation modified.

57 Schulweis, *Evil and the Morality of God*, 142.

58 Schulweis, 132.

59 Schulweis, "Adonai-Elohim," 4–5.

60 Schulweis, *Evil and the Morality of God*, 139.

61 Harold Schulweis, *Living Our Legacy: From Prose to Poetry* (Encino, CA: Harold M. Schulweis Institute, 2015), 92.

62 Schulweis, *Evil and the Morality of God*, 141.

63 Harold Schulweis, "How Do You Pray, Rabbi?" (sermon), Temple Valley Beth Shalom, Encino, CA, September 9, 2010, para. 11, Harold M. Schulweis Institute, http://hmsi.info/wp-content/uploads/2017/02/how-do-you-pray-rabbi.pdf.

64 Schulweis, *Evil and the Morality of God*, 142.

65 Schulweis, "From God to Godliness," 22.

66 Schulweis, *Evil and the Morality of God*, 132.

67 Schulweis, 142.

68 Schulweis, "Chapter 12—Predicate Theology."

69 Malkah Schulweis, personal communication, 2016.

70 Schulweis, *For Those Who Can't Believe*, 160.

71 Harold Schulweis, "Chapter 3—Influencers," interview by Edward Feinstein, September 9, 2008, video, 25:37, Harold M. Schulweis Institute, http://hmsi.info/the-rabbi-harold-m-schulweis-interviews -with-rabbi-ed-feinstein-chapter-3-influencers.

72 Schulweis, *For Those Who Can't Believe*, 160.

73 Harold Schulweis, "Mordecai M. Kaplan's Theory of Soterics," in *Mordecai M. Kaplan: An Evaluation*, ed. Ira Eisenstein and Eugene Kohn (New York: Jewish Reconstructionist Foundation, 1952), 266.

74 Mordecai M. Kaplan, *Questions Jews Ask* (New York: Reconstructionist Press, 1956), 85.

75 Barth, introduction to *The Essence of Christianity*, xxviii.

76 Schulweis, *For Those Who Can't Believe*, 118ff.

77 Harold Schulweis, "Elohim-Adonai," Harold M. Schulweis Institute, June 2015, http://hmsi.info/wp-content/uploads/2015/06 /Elohim-Adonai1.pdf.

78 Schulweis, *For Those Who Can't Believe*, 116–17.

79 Schulweis, 113.

80 Schulweis, 113.

81 Schulweis, 143.

82 Schulweis, 144.

83 Schulweis, *Conscience*, 75.

84 Harold Schulweis, "Chapter 11—Righteous Christians," interview by Edward Feinstein, September 9, 2008, video, 12:42, Harold M. Schulweis Institute, http://hmsi.info/the-rabbi-harold-m-schulweis -interviews-with-rabbi-ed-feinstein-chapter-11-righteous-christians.

Chapter 5   The Prophetic Voice

1   Harold Schulweis, "Walk to End Genocide" (remarks at Jewish World Watch Walk to End Genocide), Jewish World Watch, April 27, 2014, www.jww.org/wp-content/uploads/2014/06/HMS-Speech-LA -Walk-2014.pdf.

2   Susan Freudenheim, "Rabbi Harold Schulweis: What Do We Owe the Stranger?" *Jewish Journal,* April 9, 2014, http://jewishjournal.com /culture/religion/passover/128275.

3   Colum Lynch, "Sudan Rejects Request to Allow U.N. Troops," *Washington Post,* September 20, 2006, http://www.washingtonpost.com /wp-dyn/content/article/2006/09/19/AR2006091901427.html.

4   Harold Schulweis, "An I for an I," *Moment Magazine* 6, no. 1 (December 1980): 22.

5   Harold Schulweis, "Freedom and the Religion of the State," in *Masmid 1945, Yeshiva College Yearbook* (New York: Yeshiva University, 1945), 105, http://www.archive.org/details/masmid1945.

6   Schulweis, "An I for an I," 23.

7   Schulweis, 23.

8   Harold Schulweis, "Yom Kippur with Morrie," *Tikkun* 16, no. 2 (March/April 2001): 76.

9   Schulweis, "Yom Kippur with Morrie," 78.

10   Harold Schulweis, *Conscience: The Duty to Obey and the Duty to Disobey* (Woodstock, VT: Jewish Lights, 2008), 5.

11   Harold Schulweis, "Chapter 9—The God within God," interview by Edward Feinstein, September 9, 2008, video, 12:59, Harold M. Schulweis Institute, http://hmsi.info/the-rabbi-harold-m-schulweis -interviews-with-rabbi-ed-feinstein-chapter-9-the-god-within-god.

12   Harold Schulweis, "The Individual in the Jew" (transcribed sermon), Temple Valley Beth Shalom, September 6, 1994, Valley Beth Shalom, https://www.vbs.org/worship/meet-our-clergy/rabbi-harold -schulweis/sermons/individual-jew.

13   Harold Schulweis, "The Bias against Man," *Jewish Education* 34, no. 1 (Fall 1963): 6–14.

14   Schulweis, "Bias against Man," 6.

15   Harold Schulweis, "The Dangers of Jewish Paranoia," *Baltimore Jewish Times,* 1976.

16   Harold Schulweis, "The Holocaust Dybbuk Debate: Cynthia Ozick vs. Harold Schulweis," *Moment Magazine* 1, no. 10 (May 1976): 77.

17   Samuel and Pearl Oliner, *The Altruistic Personality: Rescuers of Jews in Nazi Europe* (New York: Touchstone, 1992).

18   Cynthia Ozick, quoted in Schulweis, "Holocaust Dybbuk Debate," 77.

19   Harold Schulweis, "Globalism and the Jewish Conscience," in *Jews and Judaism in the 21st Century: Human Responsibility, the Presence of God and the Future of the Covenant*, ed. Edward Feinstein (Woodstock, VT: Jewish Lights, 2008), 14–15.

20   Jonathan D. Sarna, *American Judaism: A History* (New Haven, CT: Yale University Press, 2004), 307.

21   Harold Schulweis, "The Garden of Eden and the Garden of Encino" (sermon), Temple Valley Beth Shalom, Encino, CA, July 7, 1977, audio, 2:26:26, Harold M. Schulweis Institute, http://hmsi.info /garden-of-eden-and-garden-of-encino-a-sermon-by-rabbi-harold -m-schulweis.

22   Harold Schulweis, *In God's Mirror: Reflections and Essays* (Jersey City, NJ: KTAV, 1990), 276.

23   Harold Schulweis, "Loyalty to Jews or to Humanity? There Is No 'Either/Or,'" *Jewish Journal*, October 26, 2006, para. 3, http:// jewishjournal.com/opinion/13899.

24   Schulweis, "Loyalty to Jews or to Humanity?" para. 13.

25   Harold Schulweis, "Jonah in the Whale and in Us" (transcribed sermon), Temple Valley Beth Shalom, Encino, CA, September 15, 1994, para. 13, Valley Beth Shalom, https://www.vbs.org/worship /meet-our-clergy/rabbi-harold-schulweis/sermons/jonah-and -whale-and-us.

26   Schulweis, "Globalism and the Jewish Conscience," 11.

27   Harold Schulweis, "Globalism and Judaism" (transcribed ser- mon), Temple Valley Beth Shalom, Encino, CA, September 16, 2004, para. 31, Valley Beth Shalom, https://www.vbs.org/worship /meet-our-clergy/rabbi-harold-schulweis/sermons/globalism -and-judaism.

28   Harold Schulweis, "Get Out of the Cave" (transcribed sermon), Temple Valley Beth Shalom, Encino, CA, September 18, 2001, para. 19, Valley Beth Shalom, https://www.vbs.org/worship/meet-our -clergy/rabbi-harold-schulweis/sermons/get-out-cave.

29 Jerry Danzig, personal communication, June 5, 2012.

30 Harold Schulweis, "Morality, Legality and Homosexuality" (transcribed sermon), Temple Valley Beth Shalom, Encino, CA, September 27, 1992, p. 8, Harold M. Schulweis Institute, http://hmsi.info/wp -content/uploads/2014/10/Morality-Legality-and-Homosexuality —A-Rosh-Hashanah-Sermon-by-Rabbi-Harold-M.-Schulweis.pdf.

31 Harold Schulweis, "A Second Look at Homosexuality" (transcribed sermon), Temple Valley Beth Shalom, Encino, CA, October 2, 1997, para. 29, Valley Beth Shalom, https://www.vbs.org/worship/meet -our-clergy/rabbi-harold-schulweis/sermons/second-look -homosexuality.

32 Harold Schulweis, "The Character of Halachah Entering the Twenty-First Century" (transcribed keynote address), Rabbinical Assembly Convention, Los Angeles, CA, March 22, 1993, para. 25, Valley Beth Shalom, https://www.vbs.org/worship/meet -our-clergy/rabbi-harold-schulweis/sermons/character-halachah -entering-twenty-first.

33 Schulweis, "Character of Halachah Entering the Twenty-First Century," para. 27.

34 Schulweis, para. 40.

35 Schulweis, para. 30.

36 Ismar Schorsch, "Marching to the Wrong Drummer," *Conservative Judaism* 45, no. 4 (Summer 1993): 17.

37 Schorsch, "Marching to the Wrong Drummer," 19.

38 Harold Schulweis, "Chapter 4—Considering Obedience," interview by Edward Feinstein, September 9, 2008, video, 15:41, Harold M. Schulweis Institute, http://hmsi.info/the-rabbi-harold-m-schulweis -interviews-with-rabbi-ed-feinstein-chapter-4-considering -obedience; see also Schulweis, *Conscience*, 40.

39 David Hartman, *From Defender to Critic: The Search for a New Jewish Self* (Woodstock, VT: Jewish Lights, 2012).

40 Schulweis, *Conscience*, 48–52.

41 Harold Schulweis, "Obedience and Conscience" (transcribed sermon), Temple Valley Beth Shalom, Encino, CA, September 11, 1999, para. 27, Valley Beth Shalom, https://www.vbs.org/worship /meet-our-clergy/rabbi-harold-schulweis/sermons/obedience -and-conscience.

42 Harold Schulweis, *For Those Who Can't Believe: Overcoming the Obstacles to Faith* (New York: Harper Perennial, 1994), 87.

43 Deuteronomy 24:16, quoted in Schulweis, *Conscience*, 11.

44 Schulweis, *For Those Who Can't Believe*, 87–88.

45 Schulweis, *Conscience*, 2.

46 Schulweis, 2.

47 Schulweis, 126.

48 Harold Schulweis, personal communication, 2008.

Chapter 6   The Voice of Community

1   Jonathan Woocher, *Sacred Survival: The Civil Religion of American Jews* (Bloomington: Indiana University Press, 1986), 64.

2   Abraham Joshua Heschel, *Moral Grandeur and Spiritual Audacity*, ed. Susannah Heschel (New York: Farrar, Straus and Giroux, 1996), 29.

3   Harold Schulweis, "The Challenge of the New Secular Religions," *Conservative Judaism* 32, no. 4 (1979): 3–15.

4   Harold Schulweis, quoted in Neil Reisner, "Encino and Rabbi Schulweis," *Present Tense* 9, no. 3 (Spring 1982): 38.

5   Philip Rieff, *Freud: The Mind of the Moralist* (Chicago: University of Chicago Press, 1959), 356.

6   Rieff, *Freud*, 330.

7   Philip Rieff, *The Triumph of the Therapeutic: Uses of Faith After Freud*, 40th ann. ed. (Wilmington, DE: Intercollegiate Studies Institute, 2006), 207–8.

8   Rieff, *Triumph of the Therapeutic*, 18.

9   Harold Schulweis, "Restructuring the Synagogue," *Conservative Judaism* 27, no. 4 (1973): 13.

10 Schulweis, "Restructuring the Synagogue," 14.

11 Abraham J. Karp, "The Conservative Rabbi—'Dissatisfied but Not Unhappy,'" in *The American Rabbinate*, ed. Jacob R. Marcus and Abraham Peck (Hoboken, NJ: KTAV, 1985), 154.

12 Schulweis, "Restructuring the Synagogue," 14.

13 Schulweis, 16.

14 Harold Schulweis, *In God's Mirror: Reflections and Essays* (Jersey City, NJ: KTAV, 1990), 102.

15 Harold Schulweis, "The Psychological Jew" (unpublished manuscript, 1982), ch. 2, 31.

16 Schulweis, *In God's Mirror*, 105.

17 Jack Yellin and Lew Pollack, "My Yiddishe Momme" 1925, http://
lyricsplayground.com/alpha/songs/m/myyiddishemomme.shtml.

18 Schulweis, "Psychological Jew," ch. 1, 40.

19 Schulweis, *In God's Mirror*, 109.

20 Schulweis, "Psychological Jew," ch. 1, 25.

21 Schulweis, ch. 1, 50.

22 Schulweis, ch. 1, 50.

23 Robert N. Bellah et al., *Habits of the Heart: Individualism and Commitment in American Life* (New York: Harper & Row, 1985), vii.

24 Steven M. Cohen and Arnold M. Eisen, *The Jew Within: Self, Family,
and Community in America* (Bloomington: Indiana University Press,
2000), 7.

25 Harold Schulweis, "Changing Models of Synagogue and Rabbi's
Role," in *Central Conference of American Rabbis Yearbook*, vol. 85 (Cincinnati: Central Conference of American Rabbis, 1975), 140.

26 Max J. Routtenberg, quoted in Karp, "The Conservative Rabbi,"
151.

27 Schulweis, "Restructuring the Synagogue," 18.

28 Peter L. Berger and Hansfried Kellner, "Arnold Gehlen and the
Theory of Institutions," *Social Research* 32, no. 1 (1965), 110–15.

29 Peter L. Berger, *The Sacred Canopy: Elements of a Sociological Theory of
Religion* (New York: Doubleday, 1967), 45–48; Peter L. Berger and
Richard John Neuhaus, *To Empower People: From State to Civil Society*
(Washington, DC: American Enterprise Institute, 1976).

30 Schulweis, "Restructuring the Synagogue," 19.

31 Harold Schulweis, "Chapter 13—The Birth and Importance of the
Havurah," interview by Edward Feinstein, September 9, 2008, video,
49:42, Harold M. Schulweis Institute, http://hmsi.info/the-rabbi
-harold-m-schulweis-interviews-with-rabbi-ed-feinstein-chapter-13
-coming-to-vbs-and-the-birth-and-importance-of-the-havurah.

32 Jonathan D. Sarna, *American Judaism: A History* (New Haven, CT:
Yale University Press, 2004), 318–22.

33 Sylvia Bernstein Tregub, personal communication, January 30,
2012.

34 Schulweis, "Restructuring the Synagogue."

35 E. Anderman, quoted in Harry Wasserman, Gerald Bubis, and Alan Lert, "The Concept of Havurah: An Analysis," *Journal of Reform Judaism* 25–26 (Winter 1979): 41.

36 Wasserman, Bubis, and Lert, "Concept of Havurah," 44.

37 Sylvia Bernstein Tregub, personal communication, January 30, 2012.

38 Elaine and David Gill, personal communication, January 30, 2012.

39 Harry Wasserman, "The Havurah Experience," *Journal of Psychology and Judaism* 3, no. 3 (Spring 1979): 171.

40 Harold Schulweis, "What Hurts the Jews," *Moment Magazine* 4, no. 10 (1979): 12.

41 Schulweis, "Psychological Jew," ch. 2, 7.

42 Harold Schulweis, "The Individual in the Jew" (transcribed sermon), Temple Valley Beth Shalom, Encino, CA, September 6, 1994 , Valley Beth Shalom, https://www.vbs.org/worship/meet-our-clergy/rabbi-harold-schulweis/sermons/individual-jew.

43 Joseph B. Soloveitchik, *The Lonely Man of Faith* (New York: Penguin, 2006), 1. Reprinted from "The Lonely Man of Faith," *Tradition* 7, no. 2 (1965): 1–67. Page numbers refer to the Penguin edition.

44 Soloveitchik, *Lonely Man of Faith*, 1.

45 Schulweis, "What Hurts the Jews," 15.

46 Abraham Joshua Heschel, *The Insecurity of Freedom* (New York: Farrar, Straus and Giroux, 1966), 195.

47 Schulweis, "Psychological Jew," ch. 2, 16.

48 Schulweis, 16.

49 Sylvia Bernstein Tregub, and Elaine and David Gill, personal communication, January 30, 2012.

50 Schulweis, "Individual in the Jew," para. 28–30.

51 Schulweis, "Psychological Jew," ch. 2, 30.

52 Harold Schulweis, *Living Our Legacy: From Prose to Poetry* (Encino, CA: Harold M. Schulweis Institute, 2015), i.

53 Schulweis, *Living Our Legacy*, i.

54 Schulweis, 10.

55 Schulweis, 126.

56 Harold Schulweis, "Emotional Intelligence" (transcribed sermon), Temple Valley Beth Shalom, Encino, CA, September 29, 2011, para. 25, Valley Beth Shalom, https://www.vbs.org/worship/meet-our-clergy/rabbi-harold-schulweis/sermons/emotional-intelligence-rosh-hashanah-2011.

57 Schulweis, "Emotional Intelligence," para. 48.

58 Harold Schulweis, "The Rabbi as a Sacred Goat" (transcribed sermon), Temple Valley Beth Shalom, Encino, CA, September 20, 2003, para. 2, Valley Beth Shalom, https://www.vbs.org/worship/meet-our-clergy/rabbi-harold-schulweis/sermons/rabbi-sacred-goat.

59 Abraham J. Karp, "The Conservative Rabbi—'Dissatisfied but Not Unhappy,'" in *The American Rabbinate*, ed. Jacob R. Marcus and Abraham Peck (Hoboken, NJ: KTAV, 1985), 132–33.

60 Milton Himmelfarb, quoted in Karp, "The Conservative Rabbi," 141.

61 Karp, "Conservative Rabbi," 155.

62 Arthur Hertzberg, "The Changing Rabbinate," in *Being Jewish in America: The Modern Experience*, by Arthur Hertzberg (New York: Schocken, 1979), 124.

63 Findings of the Blue Ribbon Committee, quoted in Karp, "Conservative Rabbi," 162.

64 Daniel J. Elazar and Rela Mintz Geffen, *The Conservative Movement in Judaism: Dilemmas and Opportunities* (Albany: State University of New York Press, 2000), 120–21.

65 Edgar H. Schein, *Organizational Culture and Leadership*, 4th ed. (San Francisco: Jossey-Bass, 2010), 57.

66 Karp, "Conservative Rabbi," 140.

67 Isa Aron, "Collaborative Leadership: When Leaders Learn to Follow and Followers Learn to Lead," in *The Self-Renewing Congregation: Organizational Strategies for Revitalizing Congregational Life*, by Isa Aron (Woodstock, VT: Jewish Lights, 2002), 82.

68 Marshall Sklare, *Conservative Judaism: An American Religious Movement* (Glencoe, IL: Free Press, 1955), 177.

69 Sylvia Bernstein Tregub, personal communication, January 30, 2012.

70 Harold Schulweis, "Changing Models of Synagogue and Rabbi's Role," in *Central Conference of American Rabbis Yearbook*, vol. 85 (Cincinnati, OH: Central Conference of American Rabbis, 1975), 3.

71 Schulweis, "What Hurts the Jews," 16.

72 Schulweis, 17.

73 William Drath and Charles Palus, quoted in Aron, "Collaborative Leadership," 87.

74 Ronald A. Heifetz, *Leadership without Easy Answers* (Cambridge, MA: Belknap Press, 1994).

75 See Isa Aron et al., *Sacred Strategies: Transforming Synagogues from Function to Visionary* (Herndon, VA: Alban Institute, 2010).

76 Aron, "Collaborative Leadership"; Jack Wertheimer, "The American Synagogue: Recent Issues and Trends," in *American Jewish Yearbook 2005: The Annual Record of Jewish Civilization*, ed. American Jewish Committee (New York: American Jewish Committee, 2005).

77 Ronald A. Heifetz, "Adaptive Leadership," *Creelman Research* 2, no. 5 (2009): 2, http://www.creelmanresearch.com/files/Creelman-2009vol2_5.pdf.

78 Schein, *Organizational Culture and Leadership*, 305.

79 Harold Schulweis, "Confessions of a Rabbi" (transcribed sermon), Temple Valley Beth Shalom, Encino, CA, October 20, 1978, para. 20–21, Harold M. Schulweis Institute, http://hmsi.info/wp-content/uploads/2017/04/confessions-of-a-rabbi-schilweis_10-20-1978-ft4_.pdf.

80 Schulweis, "Confessions of a Rabbi," para. 5.

Epilogue

1 Sidney Hook, *The Hero in History* (New York: John Day Company, 1943), 116.

Notes on Sources

1 Neil Reisner, "Encino and Rabbi Schulweis," *Present Tense* 9, no. 3 (Spring 1982): 37–39.

BIBLIOGRAPHY

Books by Harold M. Schulweis

Schulweis, Harold, with Daniel J. Bronstein. *Approaches to the Philosophy of Religion: A Book of Readings*. Upper Saddle River, NJ: Prentice Hall, 1954.

Schulweis, Harold. "The Idea of Perfection and the Moral Failure of Traditional Theodicies: Toward a Predicate Theology." PhD diss., Pacific School of Religion, 1971. University Microfilms.

Schulweis, Harold. "The Psychological Jew." Unpublished manuscript, 1982.

Schulweis, Harold. *Evil and the Morality of God*. Cincinnati: UAHC Press, 1984. Republished as *Evil and the Morality of God*. Jersey City, NJ: KTAV, 2010.

Schulweis, Harold. *In God's mirror: Reflections and Essays*. Jersey City, NJ: KTAV, 1990.

Schulweis, Harold. "When You're Older You'll Understand: Rekindling the Religious Questions of Our Youth." Unpublished manuscript, 1992.

Schulweis, Harold. *For Those Who Can't Believe: Overcoming the Obstacles to Faith*. New York: Harper Perennial, 1994.

Schulweis, Harold. *From Birth to Immortality: Meditations on the Rites of Passage*. Encino, CA: Valley Beth Shalom, 1998.

Schulweis, Harold. *When You Lie Down and When You Rise Up: Nightstand Meditation*. Encino, CA: Valley Beth Shalom, 2001.

Schulweis, Harold. *Finding Each Other in Judaism: Meditations on the Rites of Passage from Birth to Immortality*. New York: URJ Press, 2001.

Schulweis, Harold. *Conscience: The Duty to Obey and the Duty to Disobey.* Woodstock, VT: Jewish Lights, 2008.

Schulweis, Harold. *Embracing the Seeker.* Edited by Michael Halperin. Jersey City, NJ: KTAV, 2010.

Schulweis, Harold. *Living Our Legacy: From Prose to Poetry.* Encino, CA: Harold M. Schulweis Institute, 2015.

Articles and Addresses by Harold M. Schulweis

Schulweis, Harold. "Freedom and the Religion of the State." In *Masmid 1945, Yeshiva College Yearbook,* edited by Yeshiva College Student Organization, 102–5. New York: Yeshiva University, 1945. http://www.archive.org/details/masmid1945.

Schulweis, Harold. "Martin Buber: An Interview." *Reconstructionist* 18, no. 3 (March 21, 1952): 7–10.

Schulweis, Harold. "Mordecai M. Kaplan's Theory of Soterics." In *Mordecai M. Kaplan: An Evaluation,* edited by Ira Eisenstein and Eugene Kohn, 263–67. New York: Jewish Reconstructionist Foundation, 1952.

Schulweis, Harold. "The Temper of Reconstructionism." *Judaism* 3, no. 4 (1954): 321–32. Reprinted in Theodore Friedman and Robert Gordis, eds., *Jewish Life in America.* New York: Horizon Press, 1955.

Schulweis, Harold. "The Problem of Evil and the Pastoral Situation." *Reconstructionist* 23, no. 13 (November 1, 1957): 18–21.

Schulweis, Harold. "The Bias against Man." *Jewish Education* 34, no. 1 (Fall 1963): 6–14.

Schulweis, Harold. "Suffering and Evil." In *Great Jewish Ideas,* edited by Abraham E. Milgram, 198–220. New York: B'nai B'rith Department of Adult Jewish Education, 1964.

Schulweis, Harold. "The Voice of Esau." *Reconstructionist* 31, no. 16 (December 10, 1965): 7–14. http://hmsi.info/wp-content/uploads/2017/01/the-voice-of-esau.pdf.

Schulweis, Harold. In *The Condition of Jewish Belief: A Symposium,* edited by the Editors of *Commentary,* 216–21. New York: Macmillan, 1966.

Schulweis, Harold. "Restructuring the Synagogue." *Conservative Judaism* 27, no. 4 (1973): 13–23.

Schulweis, Harold. "Changing Models of Synagogue and Rabbi's Role." In *Central Conference of American Rabbis Yearbook*. Vol. 85, 136–43. Cincinnati, OH: Central Conference of American Rabbis, 1975.

Schulweis, Harold. "From God to Godliness: Proposal for a Predicate Theology." *Reconstructionist* 41, no. 1 (February 1975): 16–26.

Schulweis, Harold. "The Dangers of Jewish Paranoia." *Baltimore Jewish Times*, 1976.

Schulweis, Harold. "The Holocaust Dybbuk Debate: Cynthia Ozick vs. Harold Schulweis." *Moment Magazine* 1, no. 10 (May 1976): 77–80.

Schulweis, Harold. "The Garden of Eden and the Garden of Encino." Sermon presented July 7, 1977, Temple Valley Beth Shalom, Encino, CA. Audio, 2:26:26. http://hmsi.info/garden-of-eden-and-garden-of -encino-a-sermon-by-rabbi-harold-m-schulweis.

Schulweis, Harold. "Confessions of a Rabbi." The Harold M. Schulweis Institute (1978): http://hmsi.info/wp-content/uploads/2017/04/confessions-of-a-rabbi-schilweis_10-20-1978-ft4_.pdf.

Schulweis, Harold. "The Challenge of the New Secular Religions." *Conservative Judaism* 32, no. 4 (1979): 3–15.

Schulweis, Harold. "What Hurts the Jews." *Moment Magazine* 4, no. 10 (1979): 12–18.

Schulweis, Harold. "An I for an I." *Moment Magazine* 6, no. 1 (December 1980): 20–24.

Schulweis, Harold. "Mordecai Kaplan: Prayer and the Chosen People." Lecture, Temple Valley Beth Shalom, Encino, CA, December 17, 1980. http://hmsi.info/wp-content/uploads/2017/01/mordecai-kaplan -prayer-and-the-chosen-people.pdf.

Schulweis, Harold. "Reconstructionism and the Philosophy of Mordecai Kaplan." Unpublished lectures. November/December 1980. Retrieved from Harold M. Schulweis professional files.

Schulweis, Harold. "Celebrating Mordecai Kaplan." *Moment Magazine*, 6, no. 7 (July–August 1981): 13–23.

Schulweis, Harold. "Helping Rabbis Be Shul-Wise." *Moment Magazine* 9, no. 2 (January 1984): 38–41.

Schulweis, Harold. "Morality, Legality and Homosexuality." Sermon, Temple Valley Beth Shalom, Encino, CA, September 27, 1992. http://hmsi.info/wp-content/uploads/2014/10/Morality-Legality -and-Homosexuality-—-A-Rosh-Hashanah-Sermon-by-Rabbi -Harold-M.-Schulweis.pdf.

Schulweis, Harold. "The Character of Halachah Entering the Twen-ty-First Century." Keynote address, Rabbinical Assembly Conven-tion, Los Angeles, March 22, 1993. https://www.vbs.org/worship /meet-our-clergy/rabbi-harold-schulweis/sermons/character -halachah-entering-twenty-first.

Schulweis, Harold. "I Believe . . ." *Sh'ma* 24, no. 456 (September 3, 1993): 6–7.

Schulweis, Harold. "The Individual in the Jew." Sermon, Temple Valley Beth Shalom, Encino, CA, September 6, 1994. https://www.vbs.org /worship/meet-our-clergy/rabbi-harold-schulweis/sermons /individual-jew.

Schulweis, Harold. "Jonah in the Whale and in Us." Sermon, Temple Valley Beth Shalom, Encino, CA, September 15, 1994. https://www.vbs.org /worship/meet-our-clergy/rabbi-harold-schulweis/sermons /jonah-and-whale-and-us.

Schulweis, Harold. "A Second Look at Homosexuality." Sermon, Temple Valley Beth Shalom, Encino, CA, October 2, 1997. https://www.vbs.org /worship/meet-our-clergy/rabbi-harold-schulweis/sermons/second -look-homosexuality.

Schulweis, Harold. "Restructuring the Synagogue: The Creation of Havurot within the Synagogue." Sermon, Temple Valley Beth Sha-lom, Encino, CA, September 10, 1998. http://hmsi.info/wp-content /uploads/2017/01/restructuring-the-synagogue-the-creation-of -havurot-within-the-synagogue.pdf.

Schulweis, Harold. "Obedience and Conscience." Sermon, Temple Valley Beth Shalom, Encino, CA, September 20, 1999. https://www.vbs.org /worship/meet-our-clergy/rabbi-harold-schulweis/sermons /obedience-and-conscience.

Schulweis, Harold. "Adonai-Elohim: The Two Faces of God." *Reconstruc-tionism Today* 8, no. 1 (Autumn 2000): 4–6.

Schulweis, Harold. "Get Out of the Cave." Sermon, Temple Valley Beth Shalom, Encino, CA, September 18, 2001. https://www.vbs.org /worship/meet-our-clergy/rabbi-harold-schulweis/sermons/get -out-cave.

Schulweis, Harold. "Spiritual Leaders Series: Mordecai M. Kaplan," Sermon, Temple Valley Beth Shalom , Encino, CA, January 19, 2001. https://www.vbs.org/worship/meet-our-clergy/rabbi-harold -schulweis/sermons/jewish-spiritual-leaders-series-mordechai-m.

Schulweis, Harold. "Yom Kippur with Morrie." *Tikkun* 16, no. 2 (March/ April 2001): 75–78.

Schulweis, Harold. "The Rabbi as a Sacred Goat." Sermon, Temple Valley Beth Shalom, Encino, CA, September 20, 2003. https://www.vbs.org /worship/meet-our-clergy/rabbi-harold-schulweis/sermons/rabbi -sacred-goat.

Schulweis, Harold. "Globalism and Judaism." Sermon, Temple Valley Beth Shalom, Encino, CA, September 16, 2004. https://www.vbs.org /worship/meet-our-clergy/rabbi-harold-schulweis/sermons /globalism-and-judaism.

Schulweis, Harold. "Loyalty to Jews or to Humanity? There Is No 'Either/ Or.'" *Jewish Journal,* October 26, 2006. http://jewishjournal.com /opinion/13899.

Schulweis, Harold. Letter. In *L'dor v'dor: Temple Beth Abraham Celebrates One Hundred Years,* edited by Temple Beth Abraham, 12–14. Oakland, CA: Temple Beth Abraham, 2007.

Schulweis, Harold. "Globalism and the Jewish Conscience." In *Jews and Judaism in the 21st century: Human Responsibility, the Presence of God and the Future of the Covenant,* edited by Edward Feinstein, 7–19. Woodstock, VT: Jewish Lights, 2008.

Schulweis, Harold. "How Do You Pray, Rabbi?" Sermon, Temple Valley Beth Shalom, Encino, CA, September 9, 2010. http://hmsi.info /wp-content/uploads/2017/02/how-do-you-pray-rabbi.pdf.

Schulweis, Harold. "Emotional Intelligence." Sermon, Temple Valley Beth Shalom, Encino, CA, September 29, 2011. https://www.vbs.org /worship/meet-our-clergy/rabbi-harold-schulweis/sermons /emotional-intelligence-rosh-hashanah-2011.

Schulweis, Harold. "Walk to End Genocide." Remarks at Jewish World Watch Walk to End Genocide. Jewish World Watch. April 27, 2014. www.jww.org/wp-content/uploads/2014/06/HMS-Speech-LA -Walk-2014.pdf.

Schulweis, Harold. "Elohim-Adonai." Harold M. Schulweis Institute. 2015. http://hmsi.info/wp-content/uploads/2015/06/Elohim -Adonai1.pdf.

Interviews with Harold M. Schulweis

Schulweis, Harold. "Chapter 1—The Family—Growing Up." Interview by Edward Feinstein. Setpember 9, 2008. Video, 28:00. http://hmsi.info /the-rabbi-harold-m-schulweis-interviews-with-rabbi-ed-feinstein -chapter-1-the-family-growing-up.

Schulweis, Harold. "Chapter 2—Boxing." Interview by Edward Feinstein. Setpember 9, 2008. Video, 5:50. http://hmsi.info/the-rabbi-harold -m-schulweis-interviews-with-rabbi-ed-feinstein-chapter-2-boxing.

Schulweis, Harold. "Chapter 3—Influencers." Interview by Edward Feinstein. Setpember 9, 2008. Video, 25:37. http://hmsi.info/the-rabbi -harold-m-schulweis-interviews-with-rabbi-ed-feinstein-chapter-3 -influencers.

Schulweis, Harold. "Chapter 4—Considering Obedience." Interview by Edward Feinstein. Setpember 9, 2008. Video, 15:41. http://hmsi.info /the-rabbi-harold-m-schulweis-interviews-with-rabbi-ed-feinstein -chapter-4-considering-obedience.

Schulweis, Harold. "Chapter 5—Challenging Religious Authority." Interview by Edward Feinstein. Setpember 9, 2008. Video, 19:55. http://hmsi.info/the-rabbi-harold-m-schulweis-interviews-with-rabbi -ed-feinstein-chapter-5-challenging-religious-authority.

Schulweis, Harold. "Chapter 6—My Rabbinic Education—Meeting Malkah." Interview by Edward Feinstein. Setpember 9, 2008. Video, 9:53. http://hmsi.info/the-rabbi-harold-m-schulweis-interviews-with -rabbi-ed-feinstein-chapter-6-my-rabbinic-education-meeting-malkah.

Schulweis, Harold. "Chapter 7—Conscience (Part 1)." Interview by Edward Feinstein. Setpember 9, 2008. Video, 4:48. http://hmsi.info /the-rabbi-harold-m-schulweis-interviews-with-rabbi-ed-feinstein -chapter-7-conscience-2.

Schulweis, Harold. "Chapter 8—Conscience (Part 2)." Interview by Edward Feinstein. Setpember 9, 2008. Video, 15:02. http://hmsi.info /the-rabbi-harold-m-schulweis-interviews-with-rabbi-ed-feinstein -chapter-8-conscience-contd.

Schulweis, Harold. "Chapter 9—The God within God." Interview by Edward Feinstein. Setpember 9, 2008. Video, 12:59. http://hmsi.info /the-rabbi-harold-m-schulweis-interviews-with-rabbi-ed-feinstein -chapter-9-the-god-within-god.

Schulweis, Harold. "Chapter 10—First Pulpit—Prejudice." Interview by Edward Feinstein. Setpember 9, 2008. Video, 13:06. http://hmsi.info /the-rabbi-harold-m-schulweis-interviews-with-rabbi-ed-feinstein -chapter-10-first-pulpit-prejudice.

Schulweis, Harold. "Chapter 11—Righteous Christians." Interview by Edward Feinstein. Setpember 9, 2008. Video, 12:42. http://hmsi.info /the-rabbi-harold-m-schulweis-interviews-with-rabbi-ed-feinstein -chapter-11-righteous-christians.

Schulweis, Harold. "Chapter 12—Predicate Theology." Interview by Edward Feinstein. Setpember 9, 2008. Video, 6:55. http://hmsi.info /the-rabbi-harold-m-schulweis-interviews-with-rabbi-ed-feinstein -chapter-12-predicate-theology.

Schulweis, Harold. "Chapter 13—The Birth and Importance of the *Havurah*." Interview by Edward Feinstein. September 9, 2008. Video, 49:42. http://hmsi.info/the-rabbi-harold-m-schulweis-interviews-with -rabbi-ed-feinstein-chapter-13-coming-to-vbs-and-the-birth-and -importance-of-the-havurah.

Other Sources

Albom, Mitch. *Tuesdays with Morrie: An Old Man, a Young Man, and Life's Greatest Lesson.* New York: Doubleday, 1997.

American Jewish Committee. *The American Jewish Yearbook 5706: 1945–46.* Vol. 47. Philadelphia, PA: Jewish Publication Society, 1945. Retrieved from http://www.ajcarchives.org/main.php?GroupingId=10080.

Aron, Isa. "Collaborative Leadership: When Leaders Learn to Follow and Followers Learn to Lead." In *The Self-Renewing Congregation: Organizational Strategies for Revitalizing Congregational Life*, 81–100. Woodstock, VT: Jewish Lights, 2002.

Aron, Isa, Steven M. Cohen, Lawrence A. Hoffman, and Ari Y. Kelman. *Sacred Strategies: Transforming Synagogues from Function to Visionary.* Herndon, VA: Alban Institute, 2010.

Aron, Isa, Sara Lee, and Seymour Rossel, eds. *A Congregation of Learners: Transforming the Synagogue Into a Learning Community.* New York: UAHC Press, 1995.

Bellah, Robert N., Richard Madsen, William M. Sullivan, Ann Swidler, and Steven M. Tipton. *Habits of the Heart: Individualism and Commitment in American Life.* New York: Harper & Row, 1985.

Berger, Peter L. *The Sacred Canopy: Elements of a Sociological Theory of Religion.* New York: Doubleday, 1967.

Berger, Peter L., and Handfried Kellner. "Arnold Gehlen and the Theory of Institutions." *Social Research* 32, no. 1 (1965): 110–15.

Berger, Peter L., and Richard J. Neuhaus. *To Empower People: From State to Civil Society.* Washington, DC: American Enterprise Institute, 1976.

Berrin, Susan, ed. "What Should We Expect from Rabbis? Reflections of Rabbinic Training." Special double issue. *Sh'ma: A Journal of Jewish Responsibility* 33, nos. 597/598 (January–February 2003).

Borowitz, Eugene, ed. "How Are You Training Your Rabbis for the Challenges of the 21st Century?" Entire issue. *Sh'ma: A Journal of Jewish Responsibility* 27, no. 527 (February 7, 1997).

Braude, William G., and Israel J. Kapstein, eds. and trans. *Pesikta De-Rab Kahana.* Philadelphia: Jewish Publication Society, 1975.

Buber, Martin. *Eclipse of God.* New York: Harper and Brothers, 1952.

Cohen, Steven M., and Arnold M. Eisen. *The Jew Within: Self, Family, and Community in America.* Bloomington: Indiana University Press, 2000.

Cohen, Steven M., Jeffrey Kress, and Aryeh Davidson. "Rating Rabbinic Roles: A Survey of Conservative Congregational Rabbis and Lay Leaders." *Conservative Judaism* 56, no. 1 (September 2003): 71–89.

Davis, Mike. *City of Quartz.* New York: Vintage, 1990.

Elazar, Daniel J., and Rela Mintz Geffen. *The Conservative Movement in Judaism: Dilemmas and Opportunities.* Albany: State University of New York Press, 2000.

Feldman, Abraham Jehiel. *The American Reform Rabbi: A Profile of a Profession.* New York: Bloch Publishing, 1965.

Feuerbach, Ludwig. *The Essence of Christianity.* Translated by George Eliot. New York: Harper Torchbooks, 1957. Originally published as *The Essence of Christianity.* Leipzig, Germany: Otto Wigand, 1841.

Freudenheim, Susan. "Rabbi Harold Schulweis: What Do We Owe the Stranger?" *Jewish Journal,* April 9, 2014, http://jewishjournal.com/culture/religion/passover/128275.

Friedman, Maurice. *Martin Buber's Life and Work.* Detroit: Wayne State University Press, 1988.

Frum, David. *How We Got Here—The 70's: The Decade That Brought You Modern Life—for Better or Worse.* New York: Basic Books, 2000.

Gabler, Neal. *An Empire of Their Own: How the Jews Invented Hollywood.* New York: Crown, 1988.

Gans, Herbert J. "Park Forest: Birth of a Jewish Community." In *Making Sense of America: Sociological Analyses and Essays,* edited by Herbert J. Gans, 136–67. Lanham, MD: Rowman & Littlefield, 1999.

Glazer, Nathan. "Notes on Southern California: 'A Reasonable Suggestion as to How Things Can Be'?" *Commentary,* August 1, 1959, https://www.commentarymagazine.com/articles/notes-on-southern-californiaa-reasonable-suggestion-as-to-how-things-can-be.

Goldman, Solomon. *A Rabbi Takes Stock.* New York: Harper & Brothers, 1931.

Goldstein, Israel. *Toward a Solution.* New York: Putnam, 1940.

Gordon, Albert Isaac. *Jews in Suburbia.* Westport, CT: Greenwood Press, 1959.

Gottlieb, Robert, and Irene Wolt. *Thinking Big: The Story of the Los Angeles Times, Its Publishers, and Their Influence on Southern California.* New York: Putnam, 1977.

Grove, Robert D., and Alice M. Hetzel. *Vital Statistic Rates in the United States 1940–1960.* Washington, DC: US Department of Health, Education, and Welfare, 1968. https://www.cdc.gov/nchs/data/vsus/vsrates1940_60.pdf.

Gurock, Jeffrey S. "American Judaism between the Two World Wars." In *The Columbia History of Jews and Judaism in America,* edited by Marc L. Raphael, 93–113. New York: Columbia University, 2008.

Hartman, David. *From Defender to Critic: The Search for a New Jewish Self.* Woodstock, VT: Jewish Lights, 2012.

Heifetz, Ronald A. "Adaptive Leadership." *Creelman Research* 2, no. 5 (2009): http://www.creelmanresearch.com/files/Creelman2009vol2_5.pdf.

Heifetz, Ronald A. *Leadership Without Easy Answers*. Cambridge, MA: Belknap Press, 1994.

Heifetz, Ronald A., and Marty Linsky. *Leadership on the Line: Staying Alive through the Dangers of Change*. Cambridge, MA: Harvard Business Review Press, 2002.

Heilman, Samuel C. *Portrait of American Jews: The Last Half of the Twentieth Century*. Seattle: University of Washington Press, 1995.

Heilman, Samuel C. *Synagogue Life: A Study in Symbolic Action*. New Brunswick, NJ: Transaction Publishers, 1998.

Herscher, Uri. "Eulogy for Rabbi Harold Schulweis." *Funeral Services for Rabbi Harold M. Schulweis*. Filmed December 21, 2014, Valley Beth Shalom, Encino, CA. Video, 1:47:10. https://vimeo.com/115137224.

Hertzberg, Arthur. "The Changing American Rabbinate." *Midstream* 12, no. 1 (January 1966): 16–29.

Hertzberg, Arthur. "The Changing Rabbinate." In *Being Jewish in America: The Modern Experience*, 116–24. New York: Schocken, 1979.

Heschel, Abraham Joshua. *God in Search of Man*. New York: Farrar, Straus and Giroux, 1964.

Heschel, Abraham Joshua. *The Insecurity of Freedom*. New York: Farrar, Straus and Giroux, 1966.

Heschel, Abraham Joshua. *Moral Grandeur and Spiritual Audacity*. Edited by Susannah Heschel. New York: Farrar, Straus and Giroux, 1996.

Hirsch, Richard, ed. "The Role of the Rabbi." *Reconstuctionist* 64, no. 1 (Fall 1999): 7–65.

Hook, Sidney. *The Hero in History*. New York: John Day Company, 1943.

Hook, Sidney. *Out of Step: An Unquiet Life in the 20th Century*. New York: Harper & Row, 1987.

Isaac, Frederick. *Jews of Oakland and Berkeley*. Mt. Pleasant, SC: Arcadia Publishing, 2009.

Johnson, Nora. "The Captivity of Marriage." *Atlantic*, June 1961. https://www.theatlantic.com/magazine/archive/1961/06/the-captivity-of-marriage/308284.

Joselit, Jenna Weissman. *The Wonders of America: Reinventing Jewish Culture 1880–1950*. New York: Henry Holt, 1994.

Kanfer, Stefan. *Groucho: The Life and Times of Julius Henry Marx*. New York: Knopf, 2000.

Kaplan, Mordecai M. *Judaism as a Civilization*. New York: Schocken, 1934.

Kaplan, Mordecai M. *The Meaning of God in Modern Jewish Religion*. New York: Behrman House, 1937.

Kaplan, Mordecai M. *Questions Jews Ask*. New York: Reconstructionist Press, 1956.

Karp, Abraham J. "The Conservative Rabbi—'Dissatisfied but Not Unhappy.'" In *The American Rabbinate*, edited by Jacob Rader Marcus and Abraham J. Peck, 98–172. Hoboken, NJ: KTAV, 1985.

Karp, Abraham J. *Jewish Continuity in America: Creative Survival in a Free Society*. Tuscaloosa: University of Alabama Press, 1988.

Kaufman, David. *Shul with a Pool: The "Synagogue-Center" in American Jewish History*. Waltham, MA: Brandeis University Press, 1999.

Kotkin, Joel, and Erika Ozuna. *The Changing Face of the San Fernando Valley*. Malibu, CA: Pepperdine University, 2015.

Leiber, Jerry, and Mike Stoller. "Is That All There Is?" Recorded by Peggy Lee, 1969. *Is That All There Is?* Los Angeles, CA: Capitol Records.

Levinthal, Israel H. *A New World Is Born*. New York: Funk & Wagnalls, 1943.

Levinthal, Israel H. *Steering or Drifting—Which?* New York: Funk & Wagnalls, 1928.

Liebman, Charles S. *The Ambivalent American Jew: Politics, Religion and Family in American Jewish Life*. Philadelphia: Jewish Publication Society, 1973.

Lynch, Colum. "Sudan Rejects Request to Allow U.N. Troops." *Washington Post*, September 20, 2006. http://www.washingtonpost.com/wp-dyn/content/article/2006/09/19/AR2006091901427.html.

Maimonides, Moses. *The Guide of the Perplexed*. Translated by Shlomo Pines. Chicago: University of Chicago Press, 1974.

Marcus, Jacob Rader, and Abraham J. Peck, eds. *The American Rabbinate: A Century of Continuity and Change, 1883–1983*. Hoboken, NJ: KTAV, 1985.

Melton, J. Gordon, and Robert L. Moore. *The Cult Experience: Responding to the New Religious Pluralism.* New York: Pilgrim Press, 1984.

Miller, Douglas T., and Marion Nowak. *The Fifties: The Way We Really Were.* New York: Doubleday, 1977.

Moore, Deborah Dash. "Jewish Migration in Postwar America: The Case of Miami and Los Angeles." In *A New Jewry? America Since the Second World War,* ed. Peter Y. Medding. 102–16. Vol. 8 of *Studies in Contemporary Jewry.* London: Oxford University Press, 1992.

Moore, Deborah Dash. "A Synagogue Center Grows in Brooklyn." In *The American Synagogue: A Sanctuary Transformed,* edited by Jack Wertheimer, 297–326. Hanover, NH: Brandeis University Press, 1987.

Moore, Deborah Dash. *To the Golden Cities: Pursuing the American Jewish Dream in Miami and L.A.* New York: Free Press, 1994.

New York Board of Jewish Ministers. *Problems of the Jewish Ministry.* Edited by Israel Goldstein. New York: New York Board of Jewish Ministers, 1927.

Noveck, Simon. *Milton Steinberg: Portrait of a Rabbi.* New York: KTAV, 1978.

Oliner, Samuel P., and Pearl Oliner. *The Altruistic Personality: Rescuers of Jews in Nazi Europe.* New York: Touchstone, 1992.

"Orthodox Rabbis Excommunicate Author of Prayer Book Though He Is Not A Member." *New York Times,* June 15, 1945.

Perlin, Seymour J. "Remembrance of Synagogues Past: The Lost Civilization of the Jewish South Bronx." www.bronxsynagogues.org. Undated.

Pew Research Center. "A Portrait of Jewish Americans." Pew Research Center—Religion and Public Life. October 1, 2013. http://www.pewforum.org/2013/10/01/jewish-american-beliefs-attitudes-culture-survey.

Phillips, Bruce. "Los Angeles Jewry: A Demographic Portrait." In *American Jewish Yearbook,* edited by American Jewish Committee, 126–95. New York: American Jewish Committee, 1986.

Plateris, Alexander A. *Divorce and Divorce Rates in the United States* (PHS 78-1907). Hyattsville, MD: U.S. Department of Health, Education, and Welfare, Public Health Sevice National Center for Health Statistics, 1978.

Prell, Riv-Ellen. "Triumph, Accommodation, and Resistance: American Jewish Life from the End of World War II to the Six-Day War." In *The Columbia History of Jews and Judaism in America*, edited by Marc L. Raphael, 114–41. New York: Columbia University Press, 2008.

Prinz, Joachim. *Joachim Prinz, Rebellious Rabbi: An Autobiography—The German and Early American Years*. Edited by Michael Meyer. Bloomington: Indiana University Press, 2008.

Raphael, Marc L. *Abba Hillel Silver: A Portrait in American Judaism*. New York: Holmes & Meier, 1989.

Raphael, Marc L. *The Synagogue in America: A Short History*. New York: New York University Press, 2011.

Rawidowicz, Simon. "Israel: The Ever-Dying People." In *State of Israel, Diaspora, and Jewish Continuity: Essays on the "Ever-Dying People,"* 53–63. Waltham, MA: Brandeis University Press, 1986.

Reisner. Neil. "Encino and Rabbi Schulweis." *Present Tense* 9, no. 3 (spring 1982): 37–39.

Rieff, Philip. *Freud: The Mind of the Moralist*. Chicago: University of Chicago Press, 1959.

Rieff, Philip. *The Triumph of the Therapeutic: Uses of Faith after Freud*. 40th ann. ed. Wilmington, DE: Intercollegiate Studies Institute, 2006.

Rosenfeld, Max. "Zhitlovsky: Philosopher of Jewish Secularism." *Jewish Currents* (June 1965): 78–89.

Rubenstein, Richard L. *After Auschwitz: History, Theology, and Contemporary Judaism*. 2nd ed. Baltimore, MD: John Hopkins University Press, 1992. Originally published as *After Auschwitz*. New York: Macmillan, 1966.

Sandberg, Neil C. *Jewish Life in Los Angeles*. Lanham, MD: University Press of America, 1986.

Sarna, Jonathan D. *American Judaism: A History*. New Haven, CT: Yale University Press, 2004.

Schappes, Morris, ed. *A Documentary History of the Jews of the United States*. New York: Schocken, 1971.

Schein, Edgar H. *Organizational Culture and Leadership*, 4th ed. San Francisco: Jossey-Bass, 2010.

Schorsch, Ismar. "Marching to the Wrong Drummer." *Conservative Judaism* 45, no. 4 (Summer 1993): 14–19.

Schwartz, Shuly Rubin. *The Rabbi's Wife: The Rebbetzin in American Jewish Life*. New York: New York University Press, 2006.

Schwarz, Sid. *Finding a Spiritual Home: How a New Generation of Jews Can Transform the American Synagogue*. Woodstock, VT: Jewish Lights, 2003.

Shapiro, Edward S. *A Time for Healing: American Jewry Since World War II*. Baltimore, MD: Johns Hopkins University Press, 1992.

Shepard, Richard F. "Museum Exhibition Shows Bronx Jews in Halcyon Decades Between Wars." *New York Times*, December 22, 1985. http://www.nytimes.com/1985/12/22/arts/museum-exhibition-shows-bronx-jews-in-halcy-on-decades-between-wars.html.

Silver, Zachary. "The Excommunication of Mordecai Kaplan." *American Jewish Archives Journal* 62, no. 1 (2010): 21–48. http://americanjewisharchives.org/publications/journal/PDF/2010_62_01_00_silver.pdf.

Sklare, Marshall. *Conservative Judaism: An American Religious Movement*. Glencoe, IL: Free Press, 1995.

Sklare, Marshall, and Joseph Greenbaum. *Jewish Identity on the Suburban Frontier: A Study of Group Survival in the Open Society*. 2nd ed. Chicago: University of Chicago Press, 1967.

Soloveitchik, Joseph B. *The Lonely Man of Faith*. New York: Penguin, 2006. Reprinted from "The Lonely Man of Faith." *Tradition* 7, no. 2 (1965): 1–67.

Steinberg, Jonathan. "Milton Steinberg: American Rabbi—Thoughts on His Centenary." *Jewish Quarterly Review* 95, no. 3 (2005): 579–600.

Stern, Norton B. "Isaias W. Hellman: Pioneer Merchant and Banker of California 1842–1920." *Western States Jewish Historical Quarterly* 2, no. 1 (1969): 27–43.

Temple Beth Abraham. Board of Directors minutes. 1952. Oakland, CA.

Temple Beth Abraham, eds. *L'Dor v'Dor: Temple Beth Abraham Celebrates One Hundred Years*. Oakland, CA: Temple Beth Abraham, 2007.

United Synagogue Youth. *The Last American Jew*. New York: United Synagogue Youth, n.d.

Urofsky, Melvin I. *A Voice That Spoke for Justice: The Life and Times of Stephen S. Wise*. Albany: State University of New York Press, 1982.

Vorspan, Max, and Lloyd P. Gartner. *History of the Jews of Los Angeles*. Philadelphia: Jewish Publication Society, 1970.

Voss, Carl, ed. *Stephen S. Wise, Servant of the People: Selected Letters*. Philadelphia: Jewish Publication Society, 1970.

Waldman, Elizabeth. "Labor Force Statistics from a Family Perspective." *Monthly Labor Review* 106, no. 12 (1983): 16–20.

Warren, Rick. *The Purpose Driven Church: Every Church Is Big in God's Eyes*. Grand Rapids, MI: Zondervan, 1995.

Wasserman, Harry. "The Havurah Experience." *Journal of Psychology and Judaism* 3, no. 3 (Spring 1979): 168–83.

Wasserman, Harry, Gerald Bubis, and Alan Lert. "The Concept of Havurah: An Analysis." *Journal of Reform Judaism* 25–26 (Winter 1979): 35–49.

Weeks, P. "Reagan, Murphy, Yorty Hit Russia's Role in Mideast War." *Los Angeles Times,* June 12, 1967.

Weinstein, Jacob Joseph. *Solomon Goldman: A Rabbi's Rabbi*. New York: KTAV, 1973.

Wertheimer, Jack. "The American Synagogue: Recent Issues and Trends." In *American Jewish Yearbook 2005: The Annual Record of Jewish Civilization,* edited by American Jewish Committee, 3–86. New York: American Jewish Committee, 2005.

Wertheimer, Jack, ed. *The American Synagogue: A Sanctuary Transformed*. Waltham, MA: Brandeis University Press, 1995.

Wertheimer, Jack, ed. *Imagining the American Jewish Community*. Waltham, MA: Brandeis University Press, 2007.

Wertheimer, Jack, ed. *Jewish Religious Leadership: Image and Reality*. Vols. 1–2. New York: Jewish Theological Seminary Press, 2004.

Wertheimer, Jack, ed. *Jews in the Center: Conservative Synagogues and Their Members*. New Brunswick, NJ: Rutgers University Press, 2000.

Wise, Stephen S. *Challenging Years: The Autobiography of Stephen Wise*. New York: Putnam, 1949.

Wolf, Arnold Jacob, ed. *Unfinished Rabbi: Selected Writings of Arnold Jacob Wolf*. Chicago: Ivan R. Dee, 1998.

Wolfson, Ron. *Relational Judaism: Using the Power of Relationships to Transform the Jewish Community*. Woodstock, VT: Jewish Lights, 2013.

Wolfson, Ron. *The Spirituality of Welcoming: How to Transform Your Congregation Into a Sacred Community*. Woodstock, VT: Jewish Lights, 2011.

Woocher, Jonathan. *Sacred Survival: The Civil Religion of American Jews.* Bloomington: Indiana University Press, 1986.

Wuthnow, Robert. *After Heaven: Spirituality in America Since the 1950s.* Berkeley: University of California Press, 1998.

Yankelovich, Daniel. *New Rules: Searching for Self-Fulfillment in a World Turned Upside Down.* New York: Random House, 1981.

Zhitlovsky, Chaim. *The National Poetic Rebirth of the Jewish People.* Translated by Max Rosenfeld. 1911. Retrieved from http://www.jbooks.com/secularculture/Zhitlovsky.htm.

INDEX